MABERLY'S
MAMMALS
OF SOUTHERN AFRICA

MABERLY'S
MAMMALS
OF SOUTHERN AFRICA

A revision by
RICHARD GOSS
of Charles Astley Maberly's
'The Game Animals of
Southern Africa'

JONATHAN BALL AND AD. DONKER PUBLISHERS

All rights reserved. No part of this publication
may be reproduced, stored in a retrieval system,
or transmitted in any form or by any means,
electronic, mechanical, photocopying, recording
or otherwise, without the prior permission
of the publisher.

©line drawings, A. Maberly 1986
©revised text, Richard Goss 1986
©The copyright of the colour photographs
   remains with the photographers (see page 348).

First published in 1986 by Delta Books (Pty) Limited

This edition published in 1990 by
Jonathan Ball and Ad. Donker Publishers
Subsidiaries of Book Marketing and Distribution (Pty) Limited
P O Box 2105
Parklands 2121
(011) 880-3116

ISBN 0 947464 29 8

Text typeset by Triangle Typesetters (Pty) Ltd, Johannesburg
Colour reproduction by Cline Colour
Printed and bound by Creda Press (Pty) Ltd, Cape Town
Cover design by Michael Barnett

Contents

Colour section showing 95 species is between pages 176 and 177

Detailed photographic acknowledgements are on page 348

Preface 7
Hedgehog 11
Lesser bushbaby 13
Thick-tailed bushbaby 17
Chacma baboon 20
Vervet monkey 24
Samango monkey 28
Pangolin 31
Scrub hare 33
Cape hare 35
Smith's red rock rabbit 37
Natal red rock rabbit 37
Jameson's red rock rabbit 38
Riverine rabbit 39
Porcupine 40
Springhare 44
Ground squirrel 46
Sun squirrel 49
Striped tree squirrel 50
Red squirrel 51
Tree squirrel 52
Greater canerat 55
Dassie rat 57
Aardwolf 58
Spotted hyaena 60
Brown hyaena 68
Cheetah 73
Leopard 79
Lion 86
Caracal 99
Small spotted cat 102
African wild cat 105
Serval 106
Bat-eared fox 108
Wild dog 110
Cape fox 117
Black-backed jackal 119
Side-striped jackal 123
Cape clawless otter 125
Spotted-necked otter 128
Honey badger 130
Striped weasel 133
Striped polecat 135
Tree civet 138
African civet 140
Small-spotted genet 143
Large-spotted genet 147
Suricate 149
Selous' mongoose 154
Bushy-tailed mongoose 155
Yellow mongoose 156
Large grey mongoose 158
Slender mongoose 160
Small grey mongoose 162
Meller's mongoose 164
White-tailed mongoose 165
Water mongoose 167
Banded mongoose 170
Dwarf mongoose 174
Antbear 177
Elephant 180
Rock dassie 188
Tree dassie 192

White rhinoceros 193
Black rhinoceros 198
Cape mountain zebra 204
Hartmann's mountain zebra 206
Burchell's zebra 207
Bushpig 211
Warthog 215
Hippopotamus 219
Giraffe 225
Black wildebeest 230
Blue wildebeest 233
Lichtenstein's hartebeest 238
Red hartebeest 240
Bontebok 244
Blesbok 247
Tsessebe 249
Blue duiker 254
Red duiker 254
Grey duiker 256
Springbok 259
Klipspringer 264
Damara dik-dik 267
Oribi 269
Steenbok 272
Grysbok 275
Sharpe's grysbok 277
Suni 279
Impala 281
Grey rhebok 285
Roan 288
Sable 292
Gemsbok 296
Buffalo 301
Kudu 305
Sitatunga 309
Nyala 311
Bushbuck 316
Eland 320
Reedbuck 325
Mountain reedbuck 328
Waterbuck 330
Red lechwe 333
Puku 335
Glossary 337
Select Bibliography 339
Index of English Names 340
Index of Scientific Names 343
Index of Afrikaans Names 345
Photographic Acknowledgements 348

Preface

The late Charles Astley Maberly's book *The Game Animals of Southern Africa* is almost as much a part of our wildlife as are the animals themselves. Over the last twenty years or so it has been an invaluable source of information to anyone with an interest in the wildlife of our country and, in recent times, the lament has often been heard from people clutching well-worn or dilapidated copies, that they would give virtually anything to have the book back in print. As a result of this, and because there is no field guide to the more commonly seen mammals of southern Africa, it was decided to update and republish the book.

Since the original book was first published, an enormous amount of wildlife research has been undertaken, public awareness of our wild mammals and natural heritage has increased dramatically and there has been a subsequent advance in our knowledge of the biology of the mammals of southern Africa. This has meant that a major revision of Maberly's book was an essential part of its republication. *The Game Animals of Southern Africa* was characterised by its immaculate line drawings that capture the various species in a way which indicates the empathy that Maberly had with them. These drawings are an integral part of this new, updated book which has been written with one thought foremost in my mind: to try to keep the original text as intact as possible so that the wonderful style and charm of the writing might be preserved. As far as possible I have also endeavoured to write in a way which is compatible with it.

It is a great credit to Maberly's talents as a naturalist that by far the majority of changes which had to be made to his writing were in the form of additions; the deletions required and any inaccuracies were conspicuous by their absence. In trying to keep the appealing 'flavour' of the original writing, I have taken some licence, and have left certain passages intact which, in the strictest scientific sense, might have needed editing. This book is a *popular* field guide aimed at the amateur naturalist rather than the scientist, although the bulk of the data emanates from the labours of the latter. To ensure that the text did not become dry and difficult to read it was necessary to adopt a more flexible approach than would be entirely acceptable if one were writing in a scientific journal for a readership of scientists. Having said that, I must stress that all the facts stated in the book are, to the best of my knowledge, correct. I hope that the text is reasonably comprehensive; obviously everything known about each species could not be included and I have therefore tried to give preference to the material which I felt would be of the most interest to the readers at whom this book is aimed.

The original book covered only the Republic of South Africa. In this book the area under consideration has been enlarged to include the whole of the southern African subregion (the boundaries of this region are shown on the map below). The text and drawings on the additional species

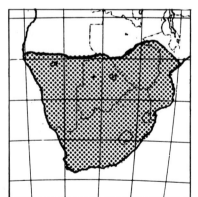
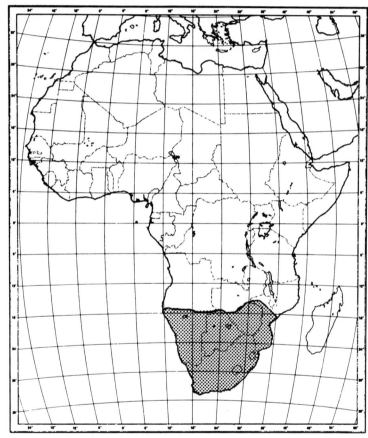

included as a result of this change are based on the relevant sections in Maberly's book *Animals of Rhodesia*.

In order to make this field guide as informative as possible and to keep its length down to manageable proportions, the marine mammals of our area have had to be excluded. It has also not been possible to include the bats, the smaller rodents and the insectivores (shrews, moles and elephant shrews). An exception to the last group is the hedgehog which was included because it is so frequently found or caught and is such a well known animal. Species which have been introduced to southern Africa have been excluded.

Where a species has two or more acceptable and widely-used common names, the preferred name is given in large type, with the alternative(s) given in brackets in smaller print. The order in which the species are dealt with is the conventional scientific order. Under the heading **Descriptive notes**, emphasis has been placed on features such as colour, which are not apparent on the line drawings, and it is recommended that this section be used in conjunction with the drawings and colour photographs (where applicable) when identifying an animal. The same applies to the distribution maps and the notes on each animal's distribution: these two should be used in conjunction since the map indicates the animal's southern African distribution whereas the text supplements this data by giving a general description of its global distribution.

With reference to the facts and figures in the margins: where no sex is indicated, the figure is for an adult male; *length:* refers to the animal's total length from nose to tip of tail; the figures for horns are measured along the outer edge of the curve. It should be remembered that all these statistics are presented to give the reader a general idea of the magnitude of the various parameters and that they are broad averages; there may be a substantial range in nature which, in the interests of simplicity, has not been given.

Many books, articles and scientific papers were consulted in the preparation of the text. A few of the main sources of information are listed in the bibliography, but one particular book was extensively used and deserves special mention: Reay Smithers's mammoth work *The Mammals of the Southern African Subregion* proved to be an invaluable reference in every respect. I have kept to its taxonomic conventions and have also largely followed the common names used in it. This outstanding book, by one of South Africa's great zoologists, is undoubtedly the authoritative work in its field. The permission of the University of Pretoria to reproduce the distribution maps from this book is gratefully acknowledged. I would like to thank Pete le Roux for photographs of thick-tailed bushbaby, large-spotted genet and waterbuck; and John Trathen for photographs of rock dassie, elephant, white rhino and zebra.

Thanks are also due to Mrs Astley Maberly for her enthusiasm and support for the project. I sincerely hope that the book will help keep alive the name and work of one of our most talented naturalists and artists whose contribution to wildlife and its conservation was cut short as a result of his tragic and untimely death.

Richard Goss
1986

South African Hedgehog

Erinaceus frontalis

Suid-Afrikaanse Krimpvarkie

Descriptive notes

The hedgehog of southern Africa greatly resembles the well-known European species, except that it is slightly smaller and has a most pronounced white or whitish frontal band (across the forehead) extending downwards on either side of the head below the ears. The upper part of the body is covered with short brown and white spines which project at all angles. It curls up into a prickly ball when alarmed.

Distribution and habits

The South African hedgehog is found only in southern Africa and the south-west corner of Angola.

As a general rule, hedgehogs are nocturnal but they may also be seen about on damp or rainy days. During the day they normally curl up under bushes, in thick grass or holes, or burrow into the leaf litter. They are solitary and although they move about slowly when undisturbed, they can move surprisingly quickly when under stress. They hibernate during the colder months in the same sorts of places in which they may rest during the day.

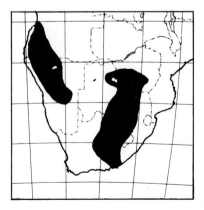

Hedgehogs have a well-developed sense of smell but cannot see well. Most of their prey is probably located by scent and they can quite clearly be heard snuffling about as they forage. Their diet consists mainly of insects, millipedes and earthworms, but they also eat fairly large amounts of small rodents, eggs, chicks, frogs and vegetable matter. They are not dependent on drinking water in the arid regions.

weight: 350 g
length: 20 cm
gestation: 1 month
number of young: 1 – 9
birth weight: 10 g

Order: *Insectivora*
Family: *Erinaceidae*

These little animals are preyed upon by almost any carnivore clever enough to side-track their defensive curling up process and they are hunted in large numbers by the local people. They utter a blood-curdling screaming cry when alarmed and when two hedgehogs meet they snuffle, snort and butt heads. Unfortunately they are disappearing from many parts of their range as a result of the increasing use of effective insecticides.

Breeding

Hedgehogs are born in summer in the summer rainfall areas. There are normally about four young to a litter but this varies greatly. They are born in a nest in the grass, in holes in the ground or under logs and are initially blind and almost naked. The short, soft white spines with which they are born harden after a week and are replaced by darker adult spines at about a month to six weeks of age. At this age, the young hedgehogs leave the seclusion of their nest and move about with their mother.

Lesser Bushbaby
(Lesser Galago)

Galago senegalensis

Nagapie

Descriptive notes

This is the smaller of the two species of bushbabies or galagos occurring in southern Africa and is a most delightful squirrel-like creature with enormous hazel-coloured eyes and delicate membranous ears. The rather fine but woolly hair is mousy-grey, darker along the back and more rufous-tinged along the haunches and flanks. There are dark markings around the eyes and a whitish streak down the nose and around the lips. The tail is long and slender, becoming more fluffed out at the tip and the muzzle is pointed but very short. The pupils of the reddish-hazel eyes contract to mere specks in strong daylight. It is strictly arboreal and nocturnal, and a most wonderful leaper.

Distribution and habits

The lesser bushbaby is distributed over most of sub-Saharan Africa, being absent from the very wet and very dry areas such as the Central African forests and the semi-arid parts of southern Africa.

This charming sprite-like creature is usually found in savanna bushveld, particularly where there are plenty of acacia thorn trees, and it tends to avoid dense forests. They are very strictly nocturnal, sleeping soundly in family groups of two to seven during the day, curled up in a tree hollow, in a tangle of creepers or on a platform-like nest, and usually only venturing forth alone at dusk to forage (though they may occasionally be seen about during dull or misty weather). The bushbaby proceeds in a series of most remarkable hops or jumps from twig to twig or tree to tree, clinging temporarily to the most delicate swaying vines. During such leaps its long and rather slender tail is used as a balancer, as with the vervet monkey. Very often one may observe a party of three or four so disporting together at dusk.

This species is much more arboreal than the next one and seldom ventures onto the ground although when it does, it hops on its back legs. Some of its jumps will cover the most astonishing distances, and in captivity it becomes a real menace to pictures or ornaments. Normally it is a very quiet little creature; very often the first intimation of

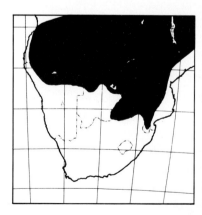

weight: about 160 g
length: about 37 cm
gestation: 4 months
number of young: 1 or 2 (rarely 3)
birth weight: 9 g

Order: *Primates*
Family: *Lorisidae*

its presence may be the ghost-like arrival of this elfin being on a twig close to the watcher. As it clings to the perch its enormous round eyes eagerly study its surroundings for prey; its eyes are unable to move in their sockets and the bushbaby is thus continually turning its head around as it looks about. The large, delicate ears are also constantly turning this way and that and are capable of being folded downwards to protect the ear orifices from moisture or heavy dew. These extremely acute senses also enable the animal to detect the approach of owls, probably its major enemy, in time to take evasive action. Before starting its foraging for the night it will usually conscientiously groom itself with its teeth and claws. They are usually most active in the early evening and morning, with an inactive period around midnight — this is a pattern frequently observed in nocturnal mammals; some of the smaller ones do not observe the second period of activity in the early morning.

During the mating season and at other times (notably when intrigued or annoyed by a light) this galago utters a very distinctive cry which at once proclaims its presence in an area. This is a rather rapidly uttered, high-pitched chirp or croak, which sounds rather like '*Hyip! Hyip! Hyip! Hyip*' — sometimes faster, sometimes slower, and often varied with chattering sounds. A number of animals may sometimes call together. They seem to be particularly prone to call on bright moonlight nights.

Another call is a very plaintive, rather musical, '*Chweee-ooo! Chwee-OOOOOOOooo!*' running down the scale at the end. It is a rather pathetic sobbing note as if the little creature were feeling very sad!

Lesser bushbabies exhibit a number of behaviour patterns which are related to dominance, territoriality and various sexual aspects. These include urine-washing (i.e. wiping urine on the soles of the feet with the hands in order to spread the animal's odour more effectively), the male rubbing his chest glands (and scent) against the female, scentmarking with urine and touching noses in greeting. The males sometimes fight viciously, grappling with and biting each other with such intensity that death may result.

Although these animals tend to remain largely in well-defined home ranges, these may change in shape and size over time. Dominant males have territories which encompass those of one or more females, and as the young males mature, they may contest a territory or move into a vacant area with a female or two in order to establish a new area in which to live. They live mainly on the gum which is exuded by many species of trees; this is either licked or chewed. Insects are also caught, in the hands, and the bushbaby closes its eyes and folds back its ears as it does so, in order to protect them. The prey is then bitten in the head and killed, at which time the eyes are opened and ears held upright again. Bushbabies are independent of drinking water; they obtain necessary moisture from their food.

One can spend many moments watching these active small creatures by means of a torch at night, as their huge eyes reflect the light like brilliant red jewels gleaming out from the foliage — so revealing them. Torchlight seems to fascinate them, and they will advance to scold angrily.

Their principal enemies are probably genets and the larger owls.

Breeding

When males are in the company of oestrus females, they frequently urine-wash. The female may also do the same. The dominant male (and sometimes the female too) will chase any other males which approach the female and she will move away from the dominant male for a period before allowing him to mount. The male calls loudly when copulating and should he attempt to mount a pregnant female she will slap his face! When males fight, they use the forepaws a great deal, appearing much like miniature boxers.

One or two young are usually born at the beginning or end of summer in the nest or hole. They are grey and are quite active shortly after birth. The mother will 'park' the young on a branch away from the nest while she is out foraging and then return them to it at dawn. This is presumably to prevent them being eaten by a predator coming across the nest, which would be more noticeable than the small animals in a tree.

After about ten days the young begin to venture away from the nest but the mother frequently retrieves them, carrying them by the scruff of their necks. The young frequently play and wrestle, being agile and fairly confident in the trees from a relatively early age. From about four weeks they begin to catch their own prey and start to become independent of the nest.

Thick-tailed Bushbaby
(Greater Galago)

Galago crassicaudatus

Bosnagaap

Descriptive notes

The thick-tailed bushbaby, also referred to as the greater galago, superficially resembles the last species, but is very much larger (about the size of a small monkey) with a coarser, woollier coat, more pointed (fox-like) face and a long, woolly-furred tail. The eyes are large, but proportionately not as enormous as in the last species and there are no dark patches round them and no white streak down the muzzle. The fur is generally greyish-brown, scattered with long projecting black hairs. The cheeks, under-surface of the body and insides of limbs are lighter, darkest above; sometimes the underparts are washed with yellowish-brown. The long shaggy tail is dull buff-reddish-brown, sometimes darker and sometimes lighter, but is not fluffed out at the tip.

Distribution and habits

To the north of our area these animals are found more or less across the continent as far as the equator. On the western side they are only found in northern Angola but are much more widely distributed in the east.

Thick-tailed bushbabies sleep together in holes in trees or in high, dense foliage in groups of two to about six animals. The males have territories which may contain the territories of one or more females. Like the previous species, they urine-wash, chest-rub and scentmark with various parts of the body, particularly the chest. These marks indicate to others of its kind the animal's movements in its area. This species also grooms itself prior to becoming active for the night and is busiest from sunset to midnight. They move about the home range on well-defined pathways through the trees, and although communal resters, the family group splits up at night and its members forage individually.

One quickly becomes aware of the presence of this bushbaby in a neighbourhood because its strident, raucous screams are frequently audible at night. This squalling cry may be likened to *'Peeyah! Peeyah! Peeyah! Pya-Pya-wa-wa!'* and is probably used to advertise the animal's presence in its territory. It is varied with sundry odd chuckl-

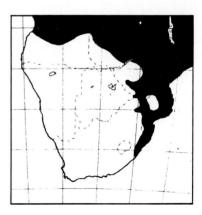

weight: 1,2 kg
length: 73 cm
gestation: 4,5 months
number of young: 1 or 2
weaning: 3 months

Order: *Primates*
Family: *Lorisidae*

ing and chattering notes and can sound most sinister to the uninformed. The tone of the full cry certainly has some resemblance to the squalls of a rather bad-tempered infant — hence the popular name of bushbaby. When angered or defiant (as when enveloped by torchlight at night) it growls rather harshly and forbiddingly.

This bushbaby, though of course mainly arboreal like its smaller relative, quite often descends from the trees to prowl about on the ground at night, and at such times it often carries its long tail erect, like a cat. It is clumsy and awkward on the ground, however, and can very easily be caught by a dog or any other carnivore, in which case frenzied, monkey-like screams rend the night air. It is a more sluggish animal in every way than the spritely lesser bushbaby and it prowls steadily along the branches, not jumping from place to place like the former. None the less it is an excellent jumper when the occasion arises, and the hind limbs are enormously powerful and well developed for this purpose — imparting a clumsy effect to its form, and it has a somewhat 'bow-legged' gait.

The face is very rounded with bluntly-pointed muzzle, and the large, rather oval-shaped ears can be folded back at the side of the head. The light brown eyes, encircled by rather bilious-looking pale yellow lids, though large are not so relatively huge as in the lesser species,. and are also unable to move in their sockets; the animal has to turn its head in order to redirect its gaze. The teeth are surprisingly powerful, particularly the canines, indicating that it is certainly more carnivorous than the smaller species. It undoubtedly robs birds' nests of eggs or young, eats insects of all kinds and probably geckos, although wild fruits and seeds and the gum from acacia trees, of which it is very fond, make up the bulk of its diet. In fact it may be said to be fairly omnivorous.

Like the primates generally, these bushbabies are very partial to 'spirituous liquors', and numbers are found intoxicated and helpless after lapping the 'palm wine' collected in containers by Africans after tapping the stems of certain wild palms. A tame one knocked over several bottles of stout on Maberly's sideboard one night, lapped up all the contents and slept for several days and nights afterwards! After that he became a real nuisance, as any bottle, no matter how small, encountered during his nocturnal rambles about the house was promptly knocked down and thus smashed so that the contents could be investigated.

At certain seasons these creatures become very noisy at night, calling and replying to one another throughout the bush. Africans are often very superstitious about the cries — particularly the laughing, chattering sounds — attributing them to a mysterious giant snake with feathers on its head and arrayed in rainbow colours, which is said to kill any intruder into its haunts by 'pecking' a neat hole in the top of the head.

These bushbabies suffer terribly in the devastating bush fires that sweep the countryside at the end of the dry season, as they are usually engulfed while still sound asleep (during the daytime of course). Those that manage to escape the flames are frequently badly burnt and often doomed to die a lingering, painful death, tortured by the pursuing hosts of blowflies and their resulting maggots.

Owls are probably the major predator of these animals, together with the leopard. They are, however, well equipped to deal with these threats: their massive ears pick up the slightest sound and even an owl gliding silently through the night air will be heard. With its tremendous agility and powerful leap the bushbaby can then escape to safety.

Breeding

Two light grey young are usually born in nests, high in the trees in spring or midsummer. They are able to see at birth and are fairly active shortly thereafter. From about one to six weeks of age they move about with the mother, clinging to her back or chest.

to show claw on second toe

Chacma Baboon

Papio ursinus

Kaapse Bobbejaan

Descriptive notes

The chacma baboon is a large, powerful, mainly terrestrial monkey with a long, prominent 'dog-like' muzzle and massive jaw, and small, closely-set yellowish-brown eyes under a beetling brow. Male baboons are larger and much heavier than females. Generally speaking, it is dark yellowish-brown in colour; darkest on the crown and along the spine where the hairs are long, forming a mantle or crest. It is pale greyish-white below, especially on the chin, lower cheeks and throat. The chacma of the south-western Cape districts is rather darker generally, with a slightly shorter jaw than that of the northern Transvaal.

In the far north-east of the southern African subregion the yellow baboon *Papio cynocephalus* occurs marginally. It is yellower, more slimly built and has different facial features to the chacma.

Distribution and habits

Apart from its occurrence in southern Africa, this species is found in the south of Angola and in Zambia.

Chacma baboons live in troops ranging in size from less than 10 to over 100 animals. Several large dominant males usually accompany a troop and within the troop there is a strict and clear-cut order of dominance. Vicious fighting, which can result in death, may take place over leadership of the group but such fights do not occur often since gestures and displays usually defuse aggressive situations and sort out who is boss before they get out of hand.

The younger baboons are strictly disciplined by their elders. Maberly often saw the elders begin their early morning foraging, after descending from the trees, by chasing every youngster in sight, grunting ferociously until, screaming with fear, the youngsters scrambled to the topmost branches of the nearest tree. After this, the youngsters were permitted to come down and daily foraging began.

Mutual grooming, often initiated by the dominant males, plays an important part in cementing the very strong bonds which exist between the members of a troop. Adult males may move between troops to some extent.

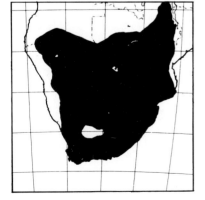

The large males lead the troop and are most involved in the defence of its members; they also act as sentinels, do the mating and lead the troop in conflicts with other groups. Such conflicts are uncommon and usually involve a great deal of shouting and screaming but rather less direct aggression. Within the troop there may be intense aggression between the males and other members of the group but although they may bite each other, injuries are rarely severe. Most of the fights are settled through ritual displays and vocalisations.

These baboons are diurnal and mainly terrestrial in habit, though in the more wooded areas they resort to trees for roosting at night and when the fruits are ripe. But whereas the truly arboreal monkeys will take refuge in trees when danger threatens, baboons will usually jump down from any trees in which they may be temporarily perched, to scamper away over the ground. In mountainous areas they haunt the most inaccessible cliffs and krantzes, and so have survived in many areas where otherwise they would probably have been exterminated by settlers. It is wonderful to watch a troop of baboons quietly travelling along the narrowest edges of the steepest rock faces. They also haunt the boulder-clad hillocks in the bushveld areas.

They usually begin to move about well before sunrise and may move up to 15 km in a day, usually resting when it is warmer and arriving at their resting site (usually tall trees or rocky krantzes) well before sunset. When sleeping

weight ♂: 32 kg
♀: 15 kg
length ♂: 150 cm
♀: 120 cm
sexual maturity: 4 – 6 years
gestation: 6 months
number of young: 1 infant (rarely twins)
longevity: 45 years

Order: *Primates*
Suborder: *Anthropoidea*
Family: *Cercopithecidae*
Subfamily: *Cercopithecinae*

the whole troop is usually quite widely dispersed with small groups of animals forming more concentrated clumps.

When foraging, baboons wander through the veld in a sort of irregular 'extended order' formation, with the younger animals in the middle and the large males on the flanks. They eat roots, grass, leaves and shoots of various kinds, tubers, grubs, insects, scorpions, wild fruits, beetles and a variety of fare including rodents' and birds' eggs. In settled sheep-farming areas they attack young lambs and even half-grown sheep. They are known to attack and kill small antelopes as well as the hiding young of many larger species, if they come across them. This is not a general procedure, and other animals most often betray no alarm at the presence of baboons, with whom they often associate quite closely. Baboons have to drink water regularly in order to survive and do not eat carrion.

Though lions kill and occasionally eat baboons, the chief enemy of the baboon is the leopard, and the former views this great cat with the utmost dread and hatred. The mere sight of a leopard is sufficient to cause the wildest and most sustained outcry of grunts, barks and screams, audible for considerable distances. The baboons will endeavour to keep their hated enemy in sight, uttering the most threatening clamour as they quickly retreat to secure positions. Such outbursts may often be heard during the night or early mornings. During the day, however, the tables are frequently turned, and many a leopard has had to dash to safety with a group of infuriated adult male baboons, vicious canines and sharp claws at the ready, hot on its heels.

The usual cry is a raucous, screaming grunt or bark, which sounds like *'waa-hoo!'* repeated several times or just singly. Soft chattering sounds denote pleasure, and they may 'converse' in abrupt grunting notes; in fear the most hysterical screams and yells are uttered. When going to roost in the evening, the old males of a troop utter a sing-song series of grunting notes — somewhat sinister in the dusk.

The chacma baboon possesses intelligence of a very high order, in fact he is probably our most intelligent wild animal. All other animals appear to respect the keen-sightedness and intelligence of baboons, and when the latter are present, complete confidence is placed in their watchfulness. Their eyesight is remarkably sharp, hearing good, but smell not much better developed than that of human beings. Like all other monkeys and apes, however, they possess (like us) 'stereoscopic sight', which enables them to discern quite motionless objects which (if the wind is not in their favour) may completely baffle other animals.

Baboons, more readily than other wild animals, learn to associate tourists with titbits in national parks, and they very soon learn to line the roads, lolling about all day in the hopes of being fed, and not infrequently climbing onto passing cars to look for food. The old males are immensely powerful, with canines even larger than those of a leopard. They are of uncertain temper and can quickly become aggressive if in any way thwarted or suddenly frightened. They may also become a serious problem in agricultural areas on account of their crop raiding practices.

Breeding

When a female chacma comes into season, the bare pinkish patches on either side of her tail become immensely swollen and bright pink in colour. During this time she is accompanied by one or more dominant males which may mate with her frequently and in close succession. In some cases she may pair up with a single male which will aggressively keep any other males attempting to approach her at bay.

There is no fixed breeding season and tiny infants can be seen at any time. When very young the face is flesh-coloured and the newly-borns are carried clinging to their mothers' breasts and underparts, as with vervet monkeys. Later they adopt a jockey-like attitude on their mothers' backs. Like vervet monkeys, chacma baboons are extremely devoted to their young and will behave very bravely in their defence. The infants are carried, protected, groomed and played with by all the members of the troop, except the dominant males. Other males may avoid being bullied by a dominant male by quickly grabbing an infant if it appears that they may be in for a bruising. The young become sexually mature at about four to six years of age and are full grown at about eight.

fore

hind

Vervet Monkey

Cercopithecus pygerythrus

Blouaap

Descriptive notes

This is the most common and widely-spread of our monkeys and is well known. Generally speaking, the vervet is of a grizzled-grey above, often washed with a yellowish tinge, or even rufous, according to locality, but always with a black face (in adults and large juveniles), hands and feet and tip of the long graceful tail. The speckled effect of the coat is because the long hairs are greyish at the roots, then banded alternately black and pale yellow. The arms and legs are greyer than the sides. The vervet has white side-whiskers, and the narrow band above the eyes, the throat and the underparts are white (more rufous-tinted in the western forms). The scrotum of the male is a brilliant greenish-blue and the penis is scarlet. There is a brilliant rufous, almost scarlet, bare patch at the base of the tail. The newly-born young have very short and sparse blackish-grey coats, and their faces are a sallow flesh colour at first. Albino individuals are not uncommon. The males are generally a little bigger than the females.

Distribution and habits

Vervets are found in the savanna woodland and riverine areas south of the forests of Central Africa, also occurring up the east side of the continent as far as southern Ethiopia.

Vervets are diurnal, sociable and gregarious, associating in troops of up to eighty or more in favoured localities where undisturbed, but more generally in smaller bands of about fifteen to thirty. Such a group will consist, say, of a large senior male who acts as leader, several less powerful males, females and juveniles. There is a well-defined dominance hierarchy or 'pecking order' which is enforced by threat displays or by aggression: usually the lower-ranking animals are bitten at the base of the tail. The males normally do the sentry work and defend the members of the troop where possible; the job of teaching, disciplining and generally caring for the young animals is left largely to the females. Males stay with the troop until they are about four years old when they are chased off by the leader of the troop to live alone. Females may remain with the troop for life.

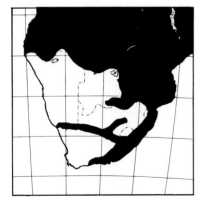

On the whole, members of a particular troop live very amicably together, and one seldom sees serious fights — even between the males — though there may often be brief quarrels over food, and the outraged screams of some of the younger members as they argue over superiority can sometimes be heard. Social bonds and cohesion between members of a group are very strong indeed. These are cemented by frequent mutual grooming sessions and by sleeping together: the more senior members of the group sleep in trees or rocky areas in close proximity to each other, whilst the lower-ranking animals form another, separate group close by.

weight ♂: 5,5 kg
♀: 4,0 kg
length ♂: 115 cm
♀: 100 cm
gestation: 7 months
number of young: 1 infant (rarely twins)
birth weight: 350 g
longevity: 24 years

Order: *Primates*
Suborder: *Anthropoidea*
Family: *Cercopithecidae*
Subfamily: *Cercopithecinae*

A full-grown male vervet in good condition is an extremely handsome creature, and he strolls about with a quiet dignity of manner quite in keeping with his appearance. Such big males have extremely powerful canine teeth, and can give a good account of themselves if caught by a dog or other carnivore. The juveniles wander in distinct 'age-groups', and they are always active, noisy and full of boundless energy and fun, constantly playing, wrestling and waylaying one another, and always most entertaining to watch. The mothers are utterly devoted to their young, attending to them as carefully and thoroughly as women. All female monkeys seem equally devoted to

the youngsters and constantly fondle one another's offspring; even very young females show extremely strong maternal instincts. Maberly recounts a case where a female vervet of his local wild troop promptly adopted and took away with her a newly-born monkey which Maberly had taken from a piccanin in a village 16 km away. In another case, after a newly-born youngster had died, its bereaved mother was observed to carry the body about with her for at least four days until, as a result of the constant handling and the close, humid and rainy weather, it was practically putrid. She sat huddled dejectedly over it, patting and warding off the swarming flies, and desperately trying to urge it to suckle. She carried it about by grasping the neck with one hand.

Vervets are primarily vegetarian, eating a great variety of fruits, seeds, pods, flowers, leaves and shoots. They even devour the terrible fiery stinging beans of the wild velvet bean (*brandboontjies*) in times of scarcity, apparently feeling only a slight irritation, to judge by the careless patting of paws against a branch, and apparently no discomfort to their mouths!

In addition to this vegetarian fare, vervets eat eggs, nestling birds, locusts, spiders, yellow garden slugs, grubs of various kinds as well as other insects, and the glue-like gum exuding from acacia trees. They will continually raid poultry runs for eggs unless prevented, their method being to squeeze the eggs between the hands, lapping up the liquid contents. Their depredations among all forms of growing crops and fruit can become a serious problem in some areas.

Vervets are equally at home in the trees or on the ground and are active agents in the forest seed dispersal. As they sit in the branches eating fruits, a constant patter of fruits, seeds and droppings falls to the ground below, the droppings being filled with seeds or pips. Vervets will also sometimes follow a sounder of bushpigs, snatching titbits uprooted by the vigorous snouts; and the pigs in turn devour fruits dropped by the monkeys. The monkeys' principal call is a loud, raucous, chattering cough: '*Yokko-yorgo-yorgo-yorgo!*' This is varied with grunts, subdued chattering cries and whistling sounds; frenzied screams betray extreme fear; gentle chattering sounds denote pleasure.

Although they become extremely shy and cautious where persecuted, vervets quickly become very tame and bold where their presence is tolerated. It is never wise to feed them near a dwelling, as once they realise food is available they will soon attempt to enter the house itself, and then can become a great nuisance. They are very intelligent and soon learn where they receive protection; in such cases mothers will even allow one to approach quite close when they have small infants.

They are, however, exceedingly nervous, highly strung and excitable by nature and though generally of a gentle disposition in the wild state, and capable of great affection when in captivity, they cannot endure teasing of any kind. When attacked by dogs, vervets invariably seek refuge in trees, where they will cackle and cough at their pursuers; but Maberly reports seeing large males attempt to grab small terriers and pull them up into the trees. The leopard and the great crowned eagle of the forests are their worst natural enemies. They will follow a prowling leopard, barking and coughing at it incessantly from the trees — so betraying its movements, as do baboons. When a large crowned eagle appears in the sky — no matter how high — its arrival is raucously signalled from troop to troop, the monkeys all sitting in the crowns of the trees to watch its movements. The leopard, no doubt, occasionally catches monkeys as they roost together in the crowns of large trees at night.

Breeding

Copulation between vervet monkeys is rarely seen since they are nervous at this time and will discontinue any such attempts at the slightest disturbance.

Young are born throughout the year and all females in the group show great interest in, and protective instincts towards, infants; the males, however, show little interest. Normally the infants cling to their mothers' breasts and underparts, their heads just below the closely-set, pointed nipples — both of which they will often draw into their mouths simultaneously when they require nourishment as they are carried along. Often the infant's tail is coiled lightly round the base of that of its mother, as an additional anchor.

Samango Monkey

Cercopithecus albogularis

Samango-aap

Descriptive notes

This entirely forest-dwelling monkey of the evergreen, montane forest is much the same size though slightly heavier than the vervet, and has a coat of beautifully dark, long and fine hair. The males are larger and much heavier than the females. This monkey is usually black, but ticked or sprinkled with white or yellow — imparting an attractively soft and speckled appearance. The samango may briefly be described as being black above, the hairs ticked with yellow; darker on the head and shoulders. The hair of the cheeks is long, forming side-whiskers, but only slightly paler than the face — not white (as in the vervet). There is no white band across the forehead. The face is dark brown, whitish on the upper lips and on the rather hairy throat. The underparts are buffy-white. The ears are dark brown with tufts of buffy-white hairs on the upper rim. From the shoulders backwards the general colour becomes paler progressively until it becomes speckled buffy-white above the root of the tail and along the top of the tail, darkening to brownish about the first third to middle of the tail; the rest is black.

Distribution and habits

Samango monkeys are found along the eastern margin of the continent as far as northern Kenya. The presence of the samango in evergreen forests is usually revealed first of all by the characteristic abrupt single 'bark' which it utters as an alarm signal — which might be likened to *'Jack!'* Although it is a much quieter species than the vervet, such sounds are not infrequently heard in its habitat and are certain indicators of its presence. After the call, the crash of foliage as the monkeys leap from tree to tree helps to guide you to the locality; and then, if you are very patient and quiet, you may be lucky enough to glimpse a very handsome creature; its long, soft mantle-like coat of dark, light-specked fur being set off by the long black tail.

Samangos are diurnal but are not often seen on account of the impenetrable nature of the forest which they usually inhabit. They move about through the trees in troops, varying in number from four to over thirty, which are composed of females, young males, infants and from one to about five adult males, depending on the size of the troop. The adult males are responsible for keeping a lookout for danger and leading the troop while the females attend to the young.

Unlike vervets, there is virtually no mutual grooming between adult samango monkeys.

In order to communicate effectively in the thick forest areas they have a number of calls including 'jacks', pants, booms, chuckles, bird-like calls, squeals, chatters and screams. Fighting over females may take place between adult males, but this is rare.

weight ♂: 9 kg
♀: 5 kg
length ♂: 140 cm
♀: 120 cm
number of young: 1 infant (sometimes 2)

Order: *Primates*
Suborder: *Anthropoidea*
Family: *Cercopithecidae*
Subfamily: *Cercopithecinae*

Samango monkeys subsist principally upon fruits, flowers, leaves, seeds and insects. The samango is shy and unobtrusive, and because of this, and its strict adherence to true forest, is far less destructive to farm or garden produce than the vervet. Its beautiful skin was formerly in great demand among the Zulu and kindred tribes and its natural enemies are the leopard and the crowned eagle of

the forests. FitzSimons describes a captive one as being 'calm, self-possessed and deliberate in its movements, contrasting strangely with the excitable, nervous, fidgety manner of the vervet.'

Breeding

Infants appear to be born in the warm, wet summer months when food is plentiful. They are dark grey or black at birth and become independent at about two months.

Pangolin

Manis temminckii

Ietermagog

Descriptive notes

This unmistakable quaint 'armadillo-like' (almost reptilian) mammal is covered with light brown horny scales or plates which are fibrous, considerably indented or serrated, and overlap above and below. Stongly-curved digging claws furnish the feet and, like the antbear, the pangolin has a long narrow and sticky tongue which it inserts into broken anthills. There is no external ear and the eyes are small and beady. The tongue, when fully stretched, extends 30 cm beyond the mouth. The scaly plating on the back of the mature pangolin is so strong and streamlined that it will ward off a .303 bullet fired head on from a distance of 100 metres. As a protective measure, this animal can exude a most repulsive odour from certain glands.

Distribution and habits

This pangolin is found in southern Africa, parts of Angola and up the eastern side of the continent in a narrow belt running as far as the Sudan.

These animals are solitary and almost exclusively nocturnal. They live largely on ants but will eat termites if these are not available. The long, sticky tongue is kept in a pouch in the throat when not being used to lick up ants. The animal has no teeth at all and relies on its strong stomach muscles to grind up the insects with soil which it eats. Their curved claws are used to dig for food, but they do not dig nearly as well as the antbear. The abandoned holes of this and other animals are used by the pangolin to lie up in during the day. They may also curl up in the undergrowth, under a log, or bury themselves in a pile of debris.

The pangolin has a curious means of locomotion, usually shuffling along almost erect on its hind limbs with its body looped over forwards, holding the short fore limbs turned inwards. Less often it progresses normally on all fours. When caught in the open it instantly curls up into a tight ball, head tucked beneath the broad tail, when it at once becomes impregnable to ordinary attack. Under these circumstances, if interfered with, it maintains a constant slapping and grinding motion of the tail against the body,

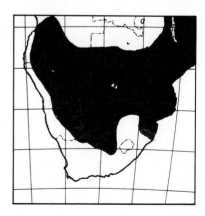

weight: 8 kg (up to 15 kg)
length: 80 cm
number of young: 1
longevity: 12 years

Order: *Pholidota*
Family: *Manidae*

in the hope of catching some convenient part of its adversary. Should this occur, the pangolin begins to saw backwards and forwards with its tail and it can cause severe injury in this way; one has even been known to almost sever a dog's foreleg.

According to Maberly the Lobedu tribe (whose hereditary chief is the famous Modjadjie — Rain Queen of the north-eastern Transvaal) had always to bring a pangolin straight to the royal kraal, where it was held to be most potent medicine. As the bearer of the wrapped-up beast proceeded on his way to the kraal he would hand it to the first inquisitive person who asked him what he was carrying; and this hapless individual had, forthwith, to abandon whatever he was engaged on and bear 'the burden' onwards until or unless he or she was lucky enough to be similarly questioned by somebody else while on the way — when it would silently be handed to the latter, and so on.

Breeding

A single young is apparently normally born during winter. Its scales do not harden until the second day. The youngster usually travels on its mother's back, clinging tightly to her scales with its long claws, and with its tail across the base of hers. If threatened, the mother will curl up around her offspring in order to protect it, but if necessary the youngster will curl up on its own. The young appear to remain with their mothers for a considerable time.

Descriptive notes

The scrub hare is very like a smaller version of the European hare. Its general colour is drab-brown above, pencilled with black and the flanks are lighter. The underside of the tail is white with a broad black stripe above; there is usually a white spot on the forehead and there are white rings around the eyes. The back of the neck is rufous and the insides of the limbs and the feet are pure white. The eyes are tawny-straw-coloured. The females are slightly larger and heavier than the males. It may be confused with the next species. (*see* Cape hare: descriptive notes.)

Distribution and habits

The scrub hare is absent from the forests of Central and West Africa and from the entire dry northern and north-eastern portions of the continent but is widely distributed over the rest of Africa.

This is the hare so often noticed darting along a road at night in front of your car, varying its forward gallop with many violent zigzag jerking leaps to right or left from time to time (a device to confuse and elude any pursuer). It is mainly nocturnal, lying up by day under a bush or in a tuft of grass in a 'form' to which it regularly returns. When resting it always lies dead still until you are very close, dashing away suddenly only when you are almost about to tread on it.

The scrub hare usually begins to feed, on grass, at dusk, and it often enters gardens on the fringes of the bush. It is destructive to many young plants. A pair inhabiting the outskirts of Maberly's garden used frequently to chase each other about and play vigorously on the lawn on moonlight nights. Quite often he encountered one or other of them feeding among the vegetation in his aloe rockery at dusk or shortly thereafter. On such occasions the hare would remain perfectly still – even at very close quarters – if it thought it could escape observation.

They normally occur singly, although one or more males may be seen with a female when she is in oestrus. At these times the males may fight viciously, lashing out with their clawed front paws and kicking with their powerful hind

Scrub Hare

Lepus saxatilis

Kolhaas

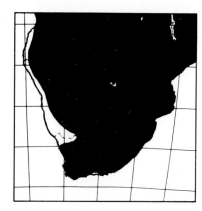

weight ♂: 2,5 kg
♀: 3 kg
length ♂: 55 cm
♀: 56 cm
gestation: 6 weeks
number of young: 1 – 3 leverets
longevity: 5 years

Order: *Lagomorpha*
Family: *Leporidae*

legs. The scrub hare is a very fast runner when hunted, and it can swim well as an additional method of escape. It has numerous enemies, as almost every type of carnivorous mammal, bird or reptile preys upon it, and the Africans incessantly hunt and snare it for food. In spite of this, it remains a fairly plentiful species in most types of country (except pure forest) though it seems to prefer rocky surroundings. Like the porcupine, this animal has been helped to some extent by the agricultural development of much of its range. They are normally silent, but bite, kick and squeal when caught.

Like all hares and rabbits, this species probably has the habit of eating its faecal pellets, a behaviour known as coprophagy. Coprophagy enables the animal to extract more nutrients from its food which passes through the digestive system twice. It also helps to replenish the microfauna in the gut which are essential for the digestion of plant matter.

Breeding

One to three young (known as leverets) are born in cover under bushes at any time of the year, with a peak in the rainy season. The young are well developed at birth and are very active within a few minutes of being born.

Like all the rabbits and hares, females of this species can breed a number of times each year and the young are able to reproduce about six months after birth.

Cape Hare

Lepus capensis

Vlakhaas

Descriptive notes

The Cape hare is smaller than the previous species and has a buffy-grey rather than pale rufous back to the neck. Its ears are also relatively shorter and it prefers more arid areas and open grassland whereas the scrub hare tends to keep to scrub and savanna woodland. The white spot which is usually present on the forehead of the scrub hare is not present in this species.

The general colour is yellowish grey-brown, mottled with darker colouring. The sides are ruddier, the underside is whitish and the ring around the eyes is almost entirely white with a dark brown spot above the eye. The limbs and feet are yellowish and the females are slightly larger and heavier than the males.

Distribution and habits

Cape hares are found widely in East Africa and along the northern and north-western margins of the continent. They also occur in western Asia.

Like the previous species, this hare lies up under small bushes with its ears folded back during the day, relying on its camouflage to prevent its discovery and only running off when one is very close to it. It may return to its resting spot day after day, and the imprint of the animal

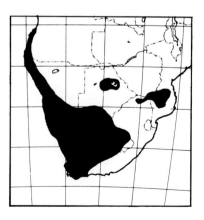

weight ♂: 1,5 kg
      ♀: 2 kg
length ♂: 49 cm
       ♀: 51 cm
gestation: 6 weeks
number of young: 1 – 3 leverets
weaning: 1 month
longevity: 5 years

Order: *Lagomorpha*
Family: *Leporidae*

can be clearly seen in the ground, since it tends to lie in exactly the same place and with the same orientation every time. These spots are known as 'forms'.

This species runs much closer to the ground, more like a rabbit, than the scrub hare, with its irregular bounding and leaping motion. This is facilitated by the more open country which the Cape hare inhabits. The Cape hare also occasionally takes refuge in the underground burrows of other species, something which the scrub hare never does.

In all other respects this species appears seems be similar in habits to the scrub hare; for more details see p. 33.

Breeding

Up to four litters may be produced by a female in a year. There are usually one or two young (leverets) in the litter and they are able to move about shortly after birth. They grow fast and are independent at about a month old.

Smith's Red Rock Rabbit
Pronolagus rupestris

Smith se Rooiklipkonyn

Natal Red Rock Rabbit
Pronolagus crassicaudatus

Natalse Rooiklipkonyn

Descriptive notes

These three species are shorter-legged, shorter-eared and more rabbit-like than the previous two species. They are easily distinguished as their short and very broad tails are a bright rich reddish-brown, like their legs and feet, with no contrasting black and white as in the hares. Their fur is thicker and softer, speckled yellowish-brown and black – imparting a warm, brownish hue to the upper parts – and reddish-white below.

The individual species are very difficult to tell apart in the field. The Natal red rock rabbit is larger than Jameson's (about 2,5 kg in weight and 46 cm long) which in turn is larger than Smith's red rock rabbit. The last two species have very bushy tails with black tips whereas the Natal species has a thin uniformly coloured tail. For our purpose it is probably best to identify the species apart on the basis of their distribution patterns which are indicated on the accompanying maps.

Distribution and habits

Of the three species, only Smith's red rock rabbit is not exclusively southern African, being found in a relatively small area in central East Africa as well.

Red rock rabbits inhabit rocky ravines, steep boulder-strewn hillsides and krantzes. They require grass as cover and are strictly grazers, preferring short grass, particularly that which has been burnt. They lie up during the day in 'forms' (*see* Cape hare) in clumps of grass or amongst boulders, and may become active around sunset, but are predominantly nocturnal. Although they are probably not as fast as the hares, they are capable of moving at breakneck speed through the steep rocky terrain which they usually inhabit. These rabbits are usually seen alone when out foraging but live together in colonies amongst the rocks. They sometimes use latrines when defecating.

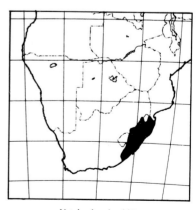

Natal red rock rabbit

Jameson's Red Rock Rabbit

Pronolagus randensis

Jameson se Rooiklipkonyn

Order: *Lagomorpha*
Family: *Leporidae*

Breeding

There is little information on when these animals breed, but it appears that they may give birth throughout the year or during the warm wet season. One or two young are born, after a gestation period of about one month, in a secluded spot and the female may pluck her own fur to line the nest. The young are blind and poorly developed at birth and remain in the nest for some time.

Red rock rabbit

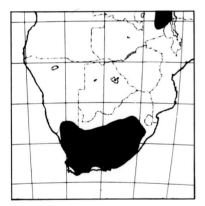

Smith's red rock rabbit

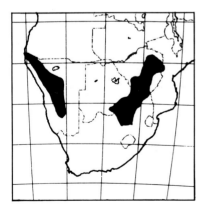

Jameson's red rock rabbit

Riverine Rabbit

Bunolagus monticularis

Rivierkonyn

weight: about 1,0 – 1,5 kg
length: 430 cm

Order: *Lagomorpha*
Family: *Leporidae*

Descriptive notes

This is a very rare species (among the rarest in southern Africa).

It is only slightly larger than the red rock rabbits but can be distinguished from these species by the distinct dark brown line running along the lower jaw towards the ear. The eyes are encircled with white rings. They are grizzled drab-grey on the upper parts but darker on the flanks and lighter underneath; the texture of the fur is similar to that of the red rock rabbits. The fluffy tail is uniform pale brown in colour.

Distribution and habits

This species is confined to the dense riverine bush in the area shown on the distribution map. It is found only in southern Africa and large periods of time tend to elapse between confirmed sightings.

Virtually nothing is known of this rare and endangered rabbit except that it is said to run slowly and rather clumsily and is easily caught.

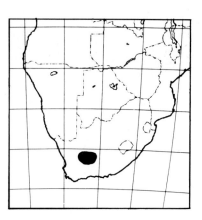

Porcupine

Hystrix africaeaustralis

Ystervark

Descriptive notes

This animal is easily recognised by the long black and white quills which cover its back and tail, and the crest of long wiry bristles on top of the head. These quills are modified hairs and are very stout and sharp. They detach easily and when lodged in the flesh can cause suppurating wounds, which may ultimately prove fatal, in the jaws and feet of lions, dogs and other predators which rashly attack porcupines. The feet are equipped with stout digging claws, and the footprint is not unlike that of a small bear. The newly-born young have quite soft quills, only about 2 cm long. There are specially adapted hollow quills on the tail which are open-ended; when the animal shakes its tail they rattle against each other and make a surprisingly loud noise. Females are a little heavier than males — the largest rodents in southern Africa.

Distribution and habits

Porcupines are found across the African continent, from the Cape in the south, as far north as the equator on the eastern side and up to about 6° south on the western side. As with the canerat, agriculture has improved the porcupine's lot. In some areas, however, they may be a serious problem to the farmers. Although so widely distributed, and in places still very common, porcupines are so nocturnal that they are comparatively rarely seen, and then mainly when they are encountered along roads or tracks at night. Their presence, however, is often indicated by the dropped quills which lie about after they have passed; and also by the sight of deep grooves and cuts often gnawed in the trunks of trees near the ground. The droppings are easily recognisable, being shaped rather like large date-stones, fibrous and 'woody' in texture.

Porcupines usually remain in their deep burrows (often formerly inhabited and excavated by antbears) or in clefts or caves among rocks until dusk, or later, when they begin their nightly prowls. They may sometimes be seen sunbathing at their burrow entrances, but usually rush underground at the slightest disturbance. They gnaw old bones to sharpen their teeth and to obtain minerals and these

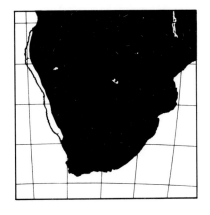

may often be seen lying around burrow entrances together with the quills and, in soft or moist soil, the footprints. Sometimes, too, muffled grunting sounds can be heard emanating from the depths.

These rodents usually live in groups of three to four but split up at night to forage alone. A mother and her offspring may also sometimes be seen together as they move along in a lumbering sort of way. They normally stand still when disturbed, in the hope of being overlooked, but are also able to run quite quickly at times.

weight: 17 kg
length: 84 cm
gestation: 7 weeks
number of young: 1 – 4
birth weight: 315 g
weaning: 7 weeks
longevity: 8 years

Order: *Rodentia*
Family: *Hystricidae*

Porcupines are very destructive to all root crops, bulbs, tubers, the bark of certain trees, and they devour fallen fruits of all kinds and vegetable matter generally. They often travel great distances at night in search of particularly tempting food, and they may then be encountered ambling along a road. They will speed up at a shambling gallop ahead of a car, their quills raised in alarm, causing them to appear as giant, animated pincushions bouncing along in the glare of the headlights! They have been said to travel up to 20 km to a special feeding place. They are exceedingly cautious animals, intelligent and difficult to trap, but the flesh tastes very good when carefully cooked and is a delicacy amongst the indigenous people.

aspect when running ahead of a car at night

As they wander along, their presence is often betrayed by the rattling sound of the quills, and they often utter grunting noises. It has been suggested that the constant quill-rattling is a warning to predaceous creatures (sabre-rattling in the true sense of the word!) that they attack at their peril. When threatened they stamp their back feet hard. Certainly it takes a skilled and experienced predator to attack a porcupine unscathed. Its method when attacked or angered is suddenly to jerk backwards, with all its quills raised and swished from side to side, and the quilled tail lashing vigorously sideways. As the quills are loosely attached in the skin, a certain number of them become lodged in any part of the anatomy of the attacker which they happen to pierce. Even if the greater part is broken off, the tips usually become deeply lodged, and gradually work their way deeper into the flesh, causing most fearful suppurating wounds, which are severely painful. If lodged in the throat of a dog or lion, or within the lips or jaws, the whole area will ultimately swell up and death from eventual starvation may result.

claw

Like many other large rodents, (and also, incidentally, the ratel) the porcupine may be killed by a heavy blow across the muzzle, and no doubt a lion or other large carnivore can easily dispatch one with a blow of the paw if it can surprise it suddenly from the front. Cheetahs are said to be peculiarly efficient at dealing with porcupines. In the Kalahari, lions take large numbers of these rodents which feature very prominently in their diet and leopards also kill them, usually by knocking the animal over from the side and then pouncing to deliver a killing bite to the throat or neck. The rather persistent belief that the porcupine can 'shoot' its quills at an antagonist is of course nonsense, and is no doubt due to the rapid backward jerk of the animal, and the ease and rapidity with which its quills become detached in the victim.

Breeding

In courtship the female porcupine solicits the male by backing up to him with her spiny tail raised vertically in order to allow him to stand on his hind legs and mount her, with his under-surface pressed against her now 'disarmed' rear.

Usually one or two young are born in a burrow or cave during the summer months in summer rainfall areas. They are born with their eyes open and the quills are initially white and soft. They remain in the burrow until the quills are hard and may then accompany the mother on her foraging expeditions. The young are independent by two months of age.

Springhare

Pedetes capensis

Springhaas

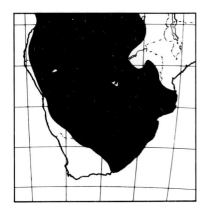

Descriptive notes

This is a rather extraordinary African mammal which has the action, and to a certain extent the appearance, of a small kangaroo. In general appearance it resembles a hare, with fairly short forepaws and extremely long and powerful hind ones; and a long hairy tail which becomes blackish and bushy at the tip. The eyes are large and dark. Its colour is pale rufous-brown above, paler on the flanks and white below. The fore limbs are armed with short, curved claws for digging and are very much shorter than the hind ones.

Distribution and habits

To the north of southern Africa the distribution of this species extends over most of Angola and Zambia and into southern Zaire. In East Africa it also occurs in large parts of Kenya and Tanzania.

The name springhare is something of a misnomer as this animal is a rodent and not a hare at all. It is, however, well entrenched and very descriptive of the animal's characteristic locomotive style.

Springhares are found in more open terrain where there is sandy soil in which they can dig the burrows in which they rest during the day. They do not live in colonies and their burrows are clearly recognisable, as they are usually characterised by an open tunnel sloping inwards, with the loose earth thrown out in front. These burrows provide refuge for many species of smaller mammals which may modify them to suit their particular needs in some cases. Springhares are strictly nocturnal and only emerge from these underground refuges well after dark.

They are grazers and eat almost only grass, the actual part of the plant varying from one season to another. They may scratch up roots and rhizomes or eat the upper parts of the plants by nipping them off and then holding them to the mouth with their forepaws. They are a serious problem in many areas where they destroy large amounts of agricultural produce.

Although the springhare is strictly nocturnal, it is easily observed at night in the light of an electric torch or a spotlight (or in the glare of car lights), because the enormous eye reflects the light brilliantly like an orange-red globe. This globe appears to bounce along in the most fascinating manner through the surrounding darkness, as the creature moves in powerful jumps covering up to two metres at a time. Springhares are frequently fascinated by the light and remain to stare at it, thereby offering an easy mark for the shotgun of the farmer whose crops they have been devouring.

Springhares are caught and eaten by many predators and man is no exception. In Botswana they represent a fairly major supply of meat for the local people and the Bushmen in particular make good use of their meat and pelts.

weight: 3 kg
length: 90 cm
gestation: 3 months
number of young: 1 (very rarely 2)
longevity: 6 years
birthweight: 290 g

Order: *Rodentia*
Family: *Pedetidae*

Breeding

Female springhares give birth in their burrows to a single young at any time of the year. They may have three or four litters a year and the young, born with its eyes closed, is able to see after about three days. It only leaves the burrow after about seven weeks and is weaned at about the same time.

Ground Squirrel

Xerus inauris

Waaierstert-grondeekhoring
(Erdmannetjie)

Descriptive notes

This ground-dwelling, burrowing squirrel is larger and more robust than the other tree-living squirrels of our area. They are unmistakable with their pronounced white stripe along the flanks and large, flattened but bushy, black and white tails. It is sandy brown or cinnamon above and whitish below.

Distribution and habits

Ground squirrels are found only in southern Africa. In the rocky areas of Namibia and southern Angola the mountain ground squirrel *(Xerus princeps)* occurs. This species looks identical to the ground squirrel but lives under rocks as opposed to living in burrows as the ground squirrel does.

Ground squirrels are quaint little animals which are most often found in open areas with short grass and a firm substrate in which they can dig their burrow systems or warrens. Their colonies may number up to thirty and they may share burrow systems with suricates or yellow mongooses. These two species are dominant over the squirrels and the yellow mongoose may kill and eat old squirrels. The warrens usually have many entrances and the chambers are lined with vegetation. They may often be seen at the burrow entrances, either sitting or standing upright with their paws hanging down, whisking their conspicuous tails up and down from time to time when nervous.

They are exclusively diurnal animals, not emerging from their underground refuges until it is quite warm, and going down again before sunset. They love to sunbathe, and also dustbathe lying spreadeagled on their stomachs ('hearthrugging') and throwing sand and dust backwards over themselves with their forepaws.

The colonies appear to consist of females and their young which are joined by adult males when a female is in oestrus. The females are arranged in a 'pecking order' or dominance hierarchy which is maintained by threats and displays, and members of the group greet each other by touching noses. They will defend the immediate vicinity of the warren very aggressively against intruders. Members of the group frequently groom themselves or others when sitting around near the warren but when out foraging (usually within a few hundred metres of the burrow) they are usually too busy scratching about for their food of grass, bulbs, roots and seeds, that there is little time for such activities. They may also eat fruits and insects at times. When food is scarce they will eat almost any vegetation provided, including dry twigs, and on one occasion my carefully constructed cardboard replica of a film camera, which had been placed near a warren to overcome the animals' camera-shyness, was completely demolished and devoured by two squirrels in the space of a morning!

weight ♂: 650 g
   ♀: 600 g
length: 45 cm (both sexes)
gestation: 6 weeks
number of young: 1 – 3
birth weight: 20 g
weaning: 7 weeks

Order: *Rodentia*
Family: *Sciuridae*

Ground squirrels usually walk about with their noses close to the ground and appear to smell out much of their underground food which is then efficiently dug up with their strong foreclaws. When alarmed they will head for the nearest burrow (usually but not always their main warren) with an unusual, bouncing type of gait. When chased or really scared they run extremely fast, their bodies pressed close to the ground, jinking from side to side and throwing their bushy tails about in order to confuse their pursuer. Their alarm call is a weird whining shriek or whistle.

Ground squirrels are well adapted to the hot, semi-arid areas in which they live, and are able to withstand great heat and do without water. Their extremely efficient kidneys enable them to concentrate their urine to conserve moisture, and although they make use of shade when this is available, on very hot days they use their wide tails as 'umbrellas' by curving them over their backs and spreading them out, thereby keeping out of the fierce African sun.

Birds of prey, jackals and various other carnivores prey on these squirrels but they are not easily caught on account of their very alert nature and great speed.

Breeding

One to three young are born underground in the warren at any time of the year. They are born blind and naked. Their hair has grown by about two weeks and their eyes open after about five weeks. They begin to leave the burrow from six weeks of age and start being weaned at about seven weeks. Young ground squirrels may be very playful, often wrestling and tumbling about in the vicinity of the warren.

Sun Squirrel

Heliosciurus rufobrachium

Soneekhoring

weight: 400 g
length: 50 cm

Order: *Rodentia*
Family: *Sciuridae*

Descriptive notes

This is a relatively large squirrel which is unmistakable due to its rather bushy but shortish-haired tail which has about twelve to fifteen lighter and darker bands running around it. The body colour is very variable above but is generally a grizzled light brown; the underside is white or yellowish-white.

Distribution and habits

These squirrels are found in the forests of south-eastern, Central and West Africa.

As their name suggests, these squirrels love basking in the sun, particularly when it is cool. They are diurnal, usually being seen singly or in pairs and tend to take refuge high up in the tall trees in which they live. Under such conditions they flick their tails and chuck loudly. They may forage on the ground and are primarily vegetarian (eating flowers, leaves, buds, fruits, nuts etc.), but also eat insects. They rest in holes in trees, and give birth there in the winter months.

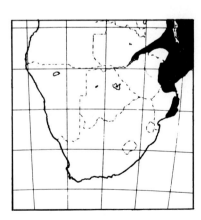

Striped Tree Squirrel

Funisciurus congicus

Gestreepte Boomeekhoring

weight: 110 g
length: 30 cm
number of young: 1 or 2

Order: *Rodentia*
Family: *Sciuridae*

Descriptive notes

This species is easily recognised by its very small size and by the distinct white stripe running down the sides of its body. The overall body colour is buffy yellow with rusty patches on the head, thighs and back. There are darker bands above and below the white body stripe and the pale-coloured tail is very bushy, as in all squirrels.

Distribution and habits

The striped tree squirrel is found in western Angola and the forests of Zaire, apart from its occurrence in the far north of Namibia.

These squirrels are active by day and are found in small family groups of up to four, whilst foraging on the ground or moving about in the trees. They dislike cold and spend much time, when out of their nests, sunbathing in holes in trees or dreys (nests made of vegetation in the forks of trees).

They may use their bushy tails as 'umbrellas' in order to keep the hot sun off their bodies and these tails are normally carried bent over their backs. They chirp and chatter and, although not as nervous as other squirrels, when disturbed they flick their tails and chatter in a high-pitched excited manner which sounds like the scolding of a bird.

They are in most respects similar in their general and breeding habits to the bush or tree squirrels but appear to breed mainly in October and March and to spend a comparatively high proportion of their foraging time on the ground.

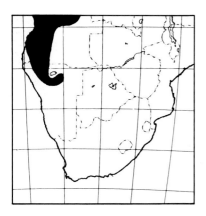

Descriptive notes

These squirrels are larger than their close relatives, the tree squirrels. They are also much more rufous in overall colouring, although they may be very yellow in some cases. The redder or yellower colour of the tail, flanks, limbs and underparts renders them unmistakable in the field.

Distribution and habits

They are found along the eastern margin of Africa, from Natal in the south to Kenya in the north.

Red squirrels are found in much more dense forest than are tree or bush squirrels and they often flick and fluff their tails, necessary behaviour if they are to communicate in their dense habitat.

They forage solitarily during the day and their diet is similar to that of the tree squirrel. They feed both on the forest floor and in the trees. When disturbed they make for dense cover or for their nest which may be high in a tree or in a fallen log. These squirrels live in family groups and a number of males may accompany a female in oestrus. Under such conditions the males may grunt, growl and hiss, and murmuring is also common. When alert they utter a *'chuck'* sound which may become a trill as they get more excited. When startled they give a deep bark. Apart from these sounds, they communicate with each other by scentmarking on various objects.

Breeding behaviour is very similar to that of the tree squirrel except that the female does not allow the male near the nest while the young are inside.

Red Squirrel

Paraxerus palliatus

Rooi Eekhoring

weight: 300 g
length: 40 cm
gestation: 2 months
number of young: 1 or 2
weaning: 40 days

Order: *Rodentia*
Family: *Sciuridae*

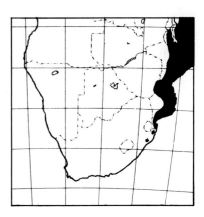

Tree Squirrel
(Yellow-footed Squirrel)
(Bush Squirrel)

Paraxerus cepapi

Boomeekhoring
(Geelpooteekhoring)

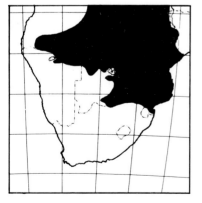

Descriptive notes

This small squirrel is common in the bushveld or savanna woodland and is also known as the bush or yellow-footed squirrel. Its general colour is buffy above, darkened on the head and back by blackish tips to the hairs, and the tail is darkened by three blackish bands on the hairs. The forearms and hind feet are uniform and often more richly coloured buffy-yellow. The backs of the ears are dark brown; the eyebrows, sides of the face, chin, throat, breast and inside of the forelegs are white — sometimes very slightly tinged with yellow — but the remaining underparts are always more or less yellowish and contrast with the breast and throat. The large eyes are dark brown and the males are a little bigger than the females.

The grey tree squirrel which is found in the vicinity of the Cape Peninsula is not indigenous but was introduced from Britain by Cecil John Rhodes around 1900.

Distribution and habits

To the north of the southern African subregion these squirrels are found in southern Angola, Zambia, southern Zaire and Tanzania.

Although tree squirrels spend a great deal of their time, and in fact make their nests, in trees, they do much of their foraging on the ground. They are seen singly or in pairs or small family groups and are strictly diurnal, usually only emerging from their holes when it is warmer, and then setting off immediately to forage. On cooler mornings, however, they will first sunbathe and groom.

The adult males in a group defend the territory in which they live. The members of the group (usually consisting of a couple of adult males and females and their offspring) are arranged in order of dominance, and group cohesion is strong on account of mutual grooming and their marking each other. The territory is also marked by all the members of the group and they share the same nest — usually a hole in a tree (possibly made by barbets or woodpeckers) which is lined with vegetation.

When it is very hot they may retire to the nest during the hottest part of the day. Like most squirrels, these delightful little creatures will often sit on a branch, jerking their feathery tails and scolding away an intruder (or a snake) in a perfect volley of high-pitched chattering whinnies varied with querulous croaking notes, often sounding more like birds than mammals. Their more normal call is an oft-repeated *'chuck'*. They will often dart across a road right in front of an oncoming car, and many of them are killed in this way.

They are very nervous on the ground, moving jerkily forward with their tails twitching and will dash quickly for a tree at the slightest sign of danger, often launching themselves at it while still a metre or two away. They are very agile and quick in the trees and will usually make for their nest when threatened, performing various acrobatic leaps along the way.

weight: 190 g
length: 35 cm
sexual maturity: 10 months
gestation: 2 months
number of young: 1 – 3
birth weight: 10 g
weaning: 5 weeks

Order: *Rodentia*
Family: *Sciuridae*

Tree squirrels eat a wide variety of bush fruits, seeds, berries, bark, leaves and flowers. Insects are also eaten to a small extent. Like other squirrels, the bush squirrel will store quantities of seeds, nuts, marula kernels etc., in underground places and rock crevices (much of this hidden treasure seems to be forgotten or stolen by others!) and they are remarkably adept at gnawing and chiselling away with their sharp incisors at the marula nuts in order to get at the sweet and tasty kernels. A squirrel sitting up, hold-

Grey tree squirrel (introduced by Rhodes)

a nut between its front paws, the sharp teeth boring through the extremely hard nut in a matter of seconds, is a fairly common sight.

They frequently mob tree snakes and other animals (including quite large mambas) by perching close to them and scolding incessantly, with whisking tails, though there is evidence that the mamba will catch and devour squirrels when the opportunity arises. Apart from snakes their principal enemies are hawks and owls, genets, wild cats and pythons. African children kill many with their dogs and sticks.

These little squirrels become very tame where they are unmolested, and Maberly remembers those haunting the garden of Colonel Stevenson-Hamilton's house at Skukuza when the latter was warden of the Kruger National Park. They would fearlessly approach and nibble peanuts from a tin box placed on his lap as he sat in the garden!

They may become cunning thieving little rascals when tasty food, such as fruit or nuts, is left by the uninitiated in an accessible place!

Breeding

An oestrus female attracts a number of males by chattering excitedly in a way which is similar to when she is alarmed, but more intense. This may continue incessantly for many hours while the males follow her around murmuring and flicking their tails. The male grooms the female before mounting and both animals groom themselves afterwards.

Normally two young are born in the nest at any time of the year. Their eyes only open after about a week and the female grooms them, remaining with them in the nest for the first few days after they are born, and may move them about and change the bedding in the nest. The male chases intruders away and may also groom the young.

The young leave the nest after about three weeks at which stage they are also weaned. They remain with the parents until they are about ten months old, but have to find all their own food during this time.

Greater Canerat

Thryonomys swinderianus

Groot Rietrot

Descriptive notes

This is an extremely large rodent (second only in size and weight in southern Africa to the porcupine) with enormous orange-yellow incisor teeth and a shortish rat-like tail which is covered with scales and short hairs. The rather spiny hairs of the coat (in texture not unlike those of the klipspringer) present a slightly speckled effect, as each brownish hair has a yellowish band near its tip.

The lesser canerat (*Thryonomys gregorianus*), which is found in parts of Zimbabwe, is very similar in most respects to the greater canerat, but is smaller and has a comparatively shorter tail.

Distribution and habits

Greater canerats are found in all the wetter areas of Africa but are absent from the forests of Zaire. They live exclusively in areas of tall, thick grass or reedbeds — the lesser canerat is more catholic in its choice of habitat and is sometimes found in drier or more rocky areas.

This animal is never found far from water and it may dwell alone, or in pairs, or in small parties of up to eight or ten, among the ranker undergrowth where little heaps of closely-cut bits of grass stems, with the oval, fibrous droppings and very obvious well-defined pathways and runs indicate its presence. It feeds voraciously, mainly on grasses and reeds, but also eats bulbs, roots and bark; it is a serious pest to agricultural cereal crops, sweet potatoes etc., and particularly injurious to sugar-cane plantations (where pythons are sometimes preserved as a useful check on its abundance). They are mainly active at night but may also be seen at dusk and dawn. During the day they lie up in flattened reedbeds. If there is insufficient cover they use holes in banks but are poor diggers and rarely excavate their own burrows.

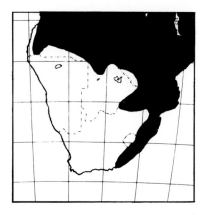

When alarmed in its haunts at night, it utters a curious booming grunt or whistle and stamps loudly with its hind feet. Dogs cannot resist chasing canerats, and the latter double most skilfully back and forth among the undergrowth, and do not hesitate to take to the water where they swim well. Africans make wedge-shaped, net-like traps into which their dogs chase them. They are prized

weight ♂: 4,5 kg
 (up to 7 kg)
 ♀: 3,6 kg
length: 70 cm
gestation: 5 months
number of young: 1 – 8
(av. 4)
birth weight: 80 g – 190 g

Order: *Rodentia*
Family: *Thryonomidae*

highly as excellent food; in fact it is surprising that these animals are not bred for food in Africa. Leopards are particularly fond of canerats and hunt them assiduously. Most of the reasonably large smaller carnivora prey on them; also eagles, hawks, pythons and baboons.

Breeding

Canerats give birth in their resting places in reedbeds or in holes which are lined with grass or shredded reeds. The young appear to be born mainly in the spring or early summer. They normally number about four in a litter and are able to follow their mother around about an hour after birth.

Dassie Rat

Petromus typicus

Dassierot

weight: 220 g
length: 30 cm

Order: *Rodentia*
Family: *Petromuridae*

Descriptive notes

Dassie rats are so called because they live in very rocky terrain much as dassies do. They are, however, more like squirrels in size and appearance but lack the very bushy tail of squirrels. Their overall colour varies from a grizzled pale grey through chocolate brown to almost black. The underparts vary from pure white to yellowish.

Distribution and habits

These animals are confined to southern Africa and live in rocky areas on the arid side of the subcontinent. They are seen singly or in pairs or small family groups, often sunning themselves near the entrance to a crevice in which they will have their nest. They eat flowers, grasses, leaves and fruit and may climb trees in search of food.

When disturbed they dash nimbly and quickly across the rocks to their shelters with their longish tails streaming out behind them.

The well-developed young are born in the nests during summer.

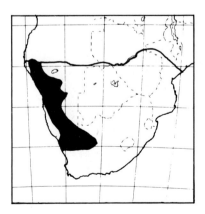

Aardwolf

Proteles cristatus

Aardwolf

Descriptive notes

The aardwolf is a nocturnal and rarely seen animal, about the size of a small jackal. It rather resembles a hyaena in overall shape, the forequarters being higher and stronger than the hindquarters. It is pale sandy-rufous in ground colour, marked with a few conspicuous vertical dark brown stripes on the sides, with horizontal bands on the upper parts of the limbs and conspicuous longitudinal bands across the chest. There is a heavy mane of long hairs (with black tips) along the back, and this can be steeply erected when the aardwolf is excited. The limbs towards the feet are black, as is the bushy tail along the terminal half. The face below the eyes is black and the ears are long, narrow and pointed. Males and females are alike in appearance and size.

Distribution and habits

Outside southern Africa, the aardwolf is found in southern Angola and East and north-east Africa. It is another of the more peculiar mammals of Africa; it is considered to bridge the gap between the civets and mongooses, and the hyaenas. Unlike the latter, it has four toes on the hind feet and five on the front (the hyaenas have only four toes on each foot), and its teeth are very small and reduced in number. Heavy teeth are unnecessary in dealing with its diet of insects, but it does have long canines which are used in defence, digging and fighting. It inhabits scrubby bush coun-

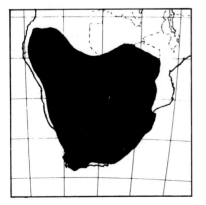

try or open sand plains and is not generally found in true forest areas. During the day the aardwolf usually lies up in an underground burrow and several individuals may occupy one earth, which they may dig themselves or take over from other animals and then enlarge or modify to suit their requirements.

The aardwolf is usually observed singly — occasionally in family parties of four or five. It is a secretive, shy creature, and as its diet is almost entirely an insectivorous one, it rarely provides much indication of its presence, so that its existence in a neighbourhood may continue to be unsuspected for years. When viewed indistinctly, the animal may first be mistaken for a jackal, until one notices the rougher coat and relatively small head, and of course a clear view will indicate the conspicuous darker stripes. Unfortunately its timid nature seldom permits it to grant one a reasonably steady view of it. It moves at a trot, its shaggy tail usually carried more or less straight out behind it, and when frightened, will run to a hole down which it will disappear. It is confused by bright lights, and unfortunately many are killed by cars.

These animals possess exceedingly small, weak and widely-separated teeth, and subsist almost exclusively on termites which are licked up with the aid of copious sticky saliva. They may dig with their canines, and locate their prey by sound or scent and then sight. Insects may also be eaten. When angered or excited, the aardwolf growls threateningly, barks and raises its long dorsal hairs into a striking crest or mantle and looks twice its size — a forbidding-looking object! If attacked, the aardwolf ejects a musky fluid from its anal glands but it is not as powerful or nauseating as that of the striped polecat. Leopards, in particular, prey on this species which is probably also killed by other large carnivores.

Breeding

Three young are usually born in a burrow during the summer months. It appears that only the female tends the cubs until they leave the burrow when they are joined by the male. If disturbed the mother may move the cubs, carrying them by the scruff of their necks, to a new den.

shoulder height: 50 cm
weight: 11 kg
length: 90 cm
gestation: 2 months
number of young: 2 – 4 cubs
longevity: 12 years

Order: *Carnivora*
Family: *Hyaenidae*
Subfamily: *Protelinae*

Spotted Hyaena

Crocuta crocuta

Gevlekte Hiëna

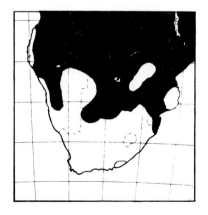

Descriptive notes

The spotted hyaena is about as big as a large, powerfully-built dog, but with a back that slopes fairly sharply from the exceptionally strong shoulders towards the more lightly-built hindquarters. It is greyish-drab to rufous in body colour and is covered with large, more or less oval, but irregularly distributed dark brown spots. The front of the face and the lower parts of the limbs are more or less black or dark brown. The nose is broad and moist, indicating keen scenting powers, the ears are large and rounded, and the rather wistful eyes are large and dark. The tail is fairly short, ending in a tufted bushy tip. The head is broad, massive and bluntly pointed, and there is a slight forward-directed mane of scruffy longer hairs along the back of the neck — from the very powerful shoulders. Very young cubs are at first almost black, the spots becoming more evident as the coat brightens in hue; at first it is fairly shaggy. Young adult hyaenas are more richly marked, with finer coats, than older individuals which frequently become very mangy and bloated in appearance.

The *Hyaenidae* are related to the civets and mongooses (the *Viverridae*) rather than to the *Canidae,* or true dogs, and might be said to form a sort of connecting link between the 'dogs' and the 'cats'. They possess extremely powerful jaws with tremendously strong facial muscles and exceedingly well-developed and robust teeth which enable them to crack the toughest and largest bones that no other large carnivore can tackle. The African spotted hyaena is the largest and most widely distributed of the three existing species (the brown, striped and spotted hyaenas) and it is confined to the African continent. It is at once recognisable by its irregular spotted markings over the wiry and coarse but comparatively short coat, and the large *rounded* ears (the brown hyaena has decidedly pointed and rather narrow ears and a long shaggy coat) which are shaped not unlike those of a lion.

Distribution and habits

Like many other large southern African mammals (and in particular the carnivores), the spotted hyaena has been driven out of large parts of its former range by human presence. In former times it was common from the Cape northwards, but today it is limited to the areas shown on the distribution map. The species is found almost throughout the rest of sub-Saharan Africa, with the exception of the forests of the Congo Basin and the West African coast, and even in the face of persecution it is probably the most numerous large African carnivore.

shoulder height: 80 cm
weight ♂: 60 kg
    ♀: 70 kg (up to about 80 kg)
length: 1,5 m
running speed: 60 km/h
sexual maturity ♂: 2 years
    ♀: 3 years
gestation: 3,5 months
number of young: 2 cubs (1 – 4)
birth weight: 1,5 kg
weaning: 1 year
longevity: 20 years

Order: *Carnivora*
Family: *Hyaenidae*
Subfamily: *Hyaeninae*

The spotted hyaenas do best in an open savanna habitat which favours their hunting habits. They are independent of water, but require an ample food supply. In East Africa hyaenas form clans which may number up to eighty animals and which defend a relatively small and clearly defined territory. In the wetter parts of southern Africa the clans only consist of up to about twelve animals and have similar-sized territories to those in East Africa, whereas in drier habitats with less food, the territories are larger and the clans are smaller, the extreme cases occurring in the Namib desert where clans consisting of several animals occupy areas which are several hundred square kilometres in size.

Territories are demarcated by scentmarking with anal glands, by using well-established latrines, and by patrolling and calling. These mechanisms are usually successful in avoiding conflict and bloodshed between clans, but aggression near the territorial boundaries does sometimes take place. The latrines which hyaenas use may be placed at strategic sites such as near landmarks or dens and these tend to be used for many years. Large numbers of droppings, with their characteristic white colour, a result of their high bone (and calcium) content, may be found at these latrines. Small temporary latrines may also be established near kill sites but whatever the case, any particular latrine will be used exclusively by the members of one clan only.

Within the clan, the females are clearly dominant and the society is undoubtedly matriarchal. Being larger than the males, the females are able to enforce their authority and are capable of defending their young cubs from the males which have been known to eat them when they are left unprotected. The members of the group are arranged in a hierarchy, or pecking order, with the larger females dominating the males which in turn dominate the younger animals. Spotted hyaenas have a ritualised greeting ceremony when meeting each other after a period of time. This involves the submissive animal squealing, a sign of fear, while the two animals sniff each other's head and genitals. The ears and tail of the hyaena clearly indicate the animal's state of mind; when excited or attacking, the ears are cocked and the tail is held high over the back, and when scared the ears are pressed flat and the tail held between the legs. The normal position of the tail is drooping straight down and the ears are normally held upright.

Spotted hyaenas are mainly nocturnal but may also be active during the day, particularly in the late afternoon or early morning, preferring to rest in a hole or in the shade during the hotter hours of the day.

To those who love the wilder places of Africa, the curious and rather eerie wailing howl of the spotted hyaena is a common nocturnal sound. It cannot be mistaken for anything else, as it begins low, often in rather a hoarse tone, rising sharply to a high-pitched scream which sometimes falls to a lower key again as it ends. It might be written: *'Auuur-eee-oooo! Oooo-wee! Oooo-wee! Oooo-wee!'* Hyaenas utter this series of 'whoops' as they move through the veld at night. Often, when one calls, another takes up the message, and gradually they gather from all points of the compass: on the outskirts of a hunting camp, where there is an abundance of meat hanging in the nearby trees, they may keep up this rather dismal serenade for hours at a time. The hyaenas eagerly (but at a discreet distance) follow the footsteps of hunting lions, and as soon as they or the lions make a kill they can be heard wailing and howling and chuckling in ghoulish excitement (together with the piercing cries of the jackals); and at such times, when they are especially excited or frustrated, you will hear the famous laughing sounds so popularly associated with spotted hyaenas. These are a series of chattering howls, extraordinarily human in tone, but resembling maniacal rather than good-humoured laughter. A really gruesome noise, worthy of the witches of *Macbeth*! Spotted hyaenas only utter this laughing noise when they are thoroughly excited. In addition, they utter many odd and frequently bewildering sounds on various occasions, such as chuckles, groans, moans, grunts, growls and yells.

To me, spotted hyaenas are one of the most fascinating and interesting animals of the African bush. Not only do they have a remarkable social system which is very interesting to the human observer, but they also have unbelievably well-developed senses of smell and hearing (apart from their excellent night vision). Their efficiency in all respects is remarkable. They may travel up to 80 km over the course of a single night, moving at a steady walk, or occasional easy canter.

To witness these predators in action on a clear moonlight night is a truly unforgettable experience. The whole clan does not always hunt together and they may move about singly on occasions. With their acute hearing they may hear their prey several kilometres away, long before you have any idea that the hunt is about to begin. They may also follow the spoor of their prey on the ground like bloodhounds and are apparently able to distinguish whether or not there are young, vulnerable animals in a herd. Once the chase is on they literally 'fly' along at a gallop of about 50 km/h which they can keep up for up to five kilometres or so. Eventually getting up to speeds of 60 km/h the ghostly shadows may manage to overtake their prey which, in the case of smaller or weaker animals, is then pulled down and torn apart, while larger or more dangerous animals such as eland or gemsbok may manage to keep them at bay for a while or even hold out until the hyaenas give up; this defence is often achieved by the animal backing into an impenetrable thorn thicket and then defending itself with its lethal horns and hooves. Although the hyaenas' method of killing by dismembering and tearing their quarry apart seems at first sight to be a vicious and particularly painful way of dispatching the prey, it is in many cases much quicker and possibly less traumatic than the slower method of strangulation used by many other carnivores. In any event, we must guard against transferring our human emotions and values to wild animals and the natural devices which they employ in order to survive.

In the case of large clans, the hyaenas may devour the carcass very quickly — a 100 kg wildebeest has been seen to be consumed in a mere ten minutes. Although there is much noise and activity at such a kill site, there is little or no real aggression; each animal simply eats as much as it can, as fast as it can. Small clans tend to take longer to eat and may spend several days eating off a large carcass. There have been cases in East Africa where spotted hyaenas have killed large numbers of prey when these have been handicapped by events such as torrential storms at night. Over 100 gazelles were killed or injured in one such case but such mass killing is not unique to hyaenas — in most predators the killing instinct is so strong that they will kill prey which can be easily or fortuitously caught even if it is more than they can cope with. Such occurrences are, however, very infrequent.

For a long time spotted hyaenas had the reputation of being almost exclusively scavengers, and though it is now known that they are extremely efficient predators in their own right, they do eat a great deal of carrion, playing an important role in the bush as nature's 'dustmen', a role for which they are extremely well adapted. The great strength of their shoulders can be appreciated when one watches them tearing the toughest carcasses to pieces or carrying massive chunks of the skeleton away with relative ease. Their jaws, and teeth in particular, are well adapted to splintering and crushing even the toughest bones, or shearing through sinew and hide. Their digestive system is able to break down bone and other tough parts of their prey, but they regurgitate most of the hair that is swallowed — hence the small percentage of this substance in their conspicuously white droppings. They also have the rather unusual habit of sometimes dragging their food into water

and leaving it there. This may be a way of storing it safely, since they have been seen to return and actually disappear underwater to retrieve it on occasions.

Apart from preying on larger herbivores and scavenging from the kills of other carnivores, spotted hyaenas eat a great variety of other food items such as birds, small mammals, insects, fish, reptiles and fruit. They also scavenge frequently from human settlements and in some places in North Africa they are fed in order to encourage this habit, which helps to keep the villages clean. They even used to scavenge refuse in Cape Town in the eighteenth century! All sorts of unusual man-made items may be swallowed, usually inadvertently, while devouring more palatable food. They will also attempt to dispossess other carnivores of their kills; this is most easily achieved with cheetah since leopards take their food up into trees in order to ensure its safety and wild dogs and lions are usually able to successfully defend their kills unless they are outnumbered by the hyaenas. When this is the case, the lions may be forced to flee to the safety of a tree in order to avoid the vicious jaws of the hyaena horde. The two species are certainly extremely antagonistic towards each other, as is the spotted towards the brown hyaena which can easily be overpowered if caught by the former.

Many a lion or lioness that reaches helpless and weakened old age is followed, worried constantly, and finally overwhelmed and torn to pieces by groups of hyaenas. It is a harsh, undignified end for so noble a beast as a lion, yet not unmerciful, as the lives of such surviving ancient beasts become increasingly wretched and miserable. The tables are frequently turned, however, and many a spotted hyaena has been killed or mutilated by lions.

Spotted hyaenas tend to become very tame when not persecuted by humans and sometimes show very little fear of man under such circumstances. Although they can become well habituated to humans when frequently exposed to them in the wild, and can then be readily approached to within very close distances on foot (particularly the younger animals), they can become man-eaters under certain circumstances. In Malawi there have been instances when spotted hyaenas have specialised in attacking humans, even during the day, and in one district in that country twenty-seven people were killed by these animals over a period of six years.

A hungry hyaena will display the utmost cunning and determination, and while camping in the bush in Tanzania, Maberly experienced one rushing up close enough almost to snatch a pan of frying eggs and bacon out of his hand. I have had very similar experiences on numerous occasions in northern Botswana. Hyaenas are probably more dangerous than the average lion if you are sleeping out in the open at night. A lion may often approach close to, and possibly walk all around sleeping humans, out of curiosity, but in most cases it will not attack, except perhaps the domestic animals which may be sharing the camp. A spotted hyaena, however, may well rush in and grab anything handy, ranging from boots and clothing, to portions out of a sleeping human being; many Africans have terribly mutilated faces, and have perhaps even had half the face bitten off, by a venturesome hyaena. Its method is to sneak up as close as possible, then rush and bite off a portion with which it at once retreats.

They are particularly prone to enter tents, or the open doors of houses, if tempting-smelling morsels are inside. Of course such venturesome behaviour only occurs at night; in daylight hyaenas are always very shy and furtive, and seldom move about except during the very early morning hours, or in the late afternoon or dusk.

The widespread belief that the spotted hyaena is a hermaphrodite is incorrect. This erroneous assumption arises from the fact that the external genitalia in the female are usually developed, and may easily be mistaken for the scrotum of the male.

In African superstition, the hyaena ranks high. It is closely connected with witches (of either sex), who are said to ride about on a hyaena at night and frequently to turn temporarily into one for the easier performance of their evil activities. The tail, ears and whiskers of hyaenas are highly valued by witchdoctors. In fact, to a great extent the hyaena takes the place in Africa of the werewolf in Europe. The uncanny sounds and legend-provoking habits (such as exhuming and devouring corpses) of the animal undoubtedly lend colour to the beliefs. In parts of Africa, hyaenas are regarded as natural undertakers — the dead or dying being purposely left out to be 'suitably' dealt with by them!

Breeding

Spotted hyaena cubs may be born throughout the year, but there tends to be a peak in births in late summer, when many of the hyaenas' prey species have their young. The female gives birth to about two cubs in a disused antbear, or other, hole. The cubs are well developed at birth with their eyes open and a covering of soft fur. They are very dark brown to black at birth, their heads going grey after two months and their spots starting to become apparent after about four months.

In the den the cubs excavate narrow passages into which only they can fit and this enables them to escape from any large predator which may enter the hole. A week or two after birth the mother moves the cubs to a communal den which is already being used by other cubs of the clan. These communal dens are regularly visited by all clan members and form the social hub of the group. Very little food is carried back to the den (unlike the brown hyaena) and cubs are only suckled by their mother (also unlike the brown hyaena). The cubs start to follow their mother on her movements around the territory after a few months and are particularly vulnerable to attacks from lions at this stage. They only begin to kill once they are almost fully mature. Females tend to remain with the clan for a great deal longer (usually for life) than the males, which tend to disperse some time after reaching maturity.

Brown Hyaena

Hyaena brunnea

Bruin Hiëna
(Strandwolf)

Descriptive notes

The brown hyaena is smaller and less robustly built than its spotted relative. It has a much longer shaggier coat of coarse dark umber or ashy-brown hair, forming a thick mantle or mane down the back. There is a paler (and less coarse) patch of creamy-brown coloured hair round the neck, forming a broad 'collar', and the limbs are irregularly horizontally banded or striped darker. The thickly bushed tail is of medium length, appearing somewhat truncated. The front of the massive-jawed face is blackish; the ears are much longer than those of the spotted hyaena and are extremely pointed at the top; the eyes are soft and gentle-looking. This animal has the typical 'hyaena' appearance, with its strong forequarters and poorly developed hindquarters. The female's genitals do not resemble those of the male, as is the case with the spotted hyaena. At a distance it resembles a very dark collie dog with an excessively sloping back and an unusual shuffling gait.

Distribution and habits

The brown hyaena is a purely southern African carnivore, whose distribution has shrunk rapidly in recent times. At one time they were reasonably plentiful along the coast and were found over almost the entire subcontinent. Persecution, disturbance and destruction of food supplies have resulted in their disappearance from the southern parts of their former range.

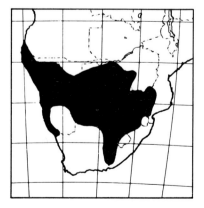

The brown hyaena is an opportunistic and highly flexible scavenger which will kill small prey if and when the opportunity arises. Although they forage alone, several hyaenas may congregate at large carcasses. Groups of related females, and young males together with nomadic breeding males defend territories which are between about ten and five hundred square kilometres depending on environmental conditions. These groups may number between three or four and about fifteen individuals.

With a special gland at the base of their tails, the hyaenas mark their entire territory with a scent which is composed of two specific substances (one white and one dark brown), which allows them to communicate with each other. They also frequently use well-established latrines which may become extremely large over time. Perhaps as a result of this behaviour and in keeping with their secretive nature, brown hyaenas are normally silent (unlike their extremely vocal spotted relatives) except when interacting with others of their kind. When fighting with intruding neighbours, or in order to establish dominance within the group, the hyaenas shake each other violently by the neck (which is protected by long coarse hair and thick skin) while growling, snarling and shrieking in a very eerie and distinctive manner. Although large neck wounds may result, the contestants never injure each other fatally or even seriously. They also have a specific greeting ceremony when two individuals from the same group meet; this involves crawling, whining and the sniffing of each other's head and genital regions.

shoulder height: 80 cm
weight: 50 kg
length: 150 cm
gestation: 3 months
number of young: 1 – 3 cubs
weaning: 15 months
longevity: 25 years

Order: *Carnivora*
Family: *Hyaenidae*
Subfamily: *Hyaeninae*

Although brown hyaenas are predominantly scavengers, their diet includes a wide range of small mammals, birds, reptiles, fruit, eggs and insects. On one occasion, near the town of Lüderitz, in Namibia, I saw a hyaena dash about 100 m across a shallow lagoon and snatch a flamingo out of the air as it was taking off. They can survive indefinitely without drinking water, but will drink regularly if water is available. Along the Namib coast the animals patrol the water's edge for marine mammals, birds and fish — hence their old name 'strandwolf'. I have seen them swimming out to islands through the waves but they do not spend long periods in the very cold water and cannot be said to be strong swimmers.

If a brown hyaena finds more food than it can manage at one time, it will break up the food and hide it under bushes or rocks over a wide area, in order to prevent it from being eaten by other scavengers; it then returns later to eat at its leisure. It is very well equipped with a powerful set of jaws and teeth which, although not as powerful as those of the spotted hyaena, have a wider gape and are capable of cracking most bones and utilising the parts of a carcass which other carnivores have to leave behind. Unlike the spotted hyaena, the brown hyaena eats a great deal of hair which it does not regurgitate; although its droppings are also very white as a result of the large amount of bone eaten, the smaller size and higher hair content of the brown's scats make them recognisable from those of the spotted species. Brown hyaenas have an extremely well-developed sense of smell and this is the primary sense used in locating food, other brown hyaenas, and potentially dangerous larger carnivores such as lions and spotted hyaenas.

The brown hyaena is almost exclusively nocturnal except in areas where it is not harassed by man when it will become active around sunset and lie up some time after sunrise, especially when the weather is reasonably cool. During the day they lie up in caves, holes or under rocky ledges or bushes where they are unlikely to be discovered. When it is threatened or aggressive, the hyaena raises the long hair on its back and neck, making it appear much larger and more formidable than it really is.

The animal normally avoids confrontations with other large carnivores such as lions or spotted hyaenas. In the Kalahari Gemsbok National Park I saw a brown hyaena which had been caught by a lion pride being severely mauled. The hyaena shammed death and curled up tight in order to protect its vulnerable belly; the strategy seemed to work, and when the lions lost interest the hyaena surprised one of the young lions, which was attempting to uncurl it, by leaping to its feet with a sudden shriek and limping off. Unfortunately the hyaena had already been severely injured and almost certainly did not survive — it was seen three days later, almost unable to walk. Spotted hyaenas also maul brown hyaenas when they encounter them and high densities of these animals limit the numbers of brown hyaenas in an area. Only in places where conditions are not favourable for large numbers of spotted hyaenas does one find reasonably high densities of the brown species since they are better adapted to harsher environmental conditions and a less reliable food supply. Such areas include the Namib and Kalahari deserts.

The brown hyaena is still persecuted in many agricultural areas as a result of its reputation as a stock-thief. This reputation certainly stems largely from the farmers' ignorance of the animal's behaviour, as a result of its shyness and secrecy. Although substantiated cases of stock-theft have occurred, these have been extremely rare and are limited to specific individuals which have learned that domestic stock are 'soft' targets.

As a result of their secrecy and ability to live off a wide range of food types, the brown hyaena is able to survive in populated areas. They frequently enter the town of Lüderitz to scavenge and have been reported in the vicinity of Pretoria and on one occasion even in the centre of Johannesburg. Certain individuals may become great wanderers, sometimes covering incredible distances; a radio-collared hyaena released near Rustenburg travelled some 800 km to be shot eventually near Trompsburg in the Orange Free State, and at the time of writing, a dominant male from the vicinity of Lüderitz was shot at the mouth of the Olifants River, well over 600 km further south down the Atlantic Coast!

Today the brown hyaena still survives in areas which offer it refuge, such as mountain ranges with productive areas nearby, but the persecution of this unusual (and often wrongly maligned) animal, which is found only in southern Africa, needs to be halted if the animal is not to be banished to our national parks.

Breeding

It appears that nomadic, rather than group-living, males mate with female brown hyaenas when they come into oestrus usually during the summer months. The females give birth to their cubs at the entrance to, or in, a disused antbear hole or cave into which they are able to flee if danger threatens. The hole entrance is usually too small for even the mother to enter and potentially dangerous large predators are thus prevented from reaching the helpless cubs whose eyes only open about two weeks after birth.

In the first two months of their lives the mother may move them to a communal den, in which a number of females may suckle the cubs, and where other cubs may also be being raised. Food is brought to this den by other members of the group to feed the mother and/or cubs. This food may be carried very long distances; Gus Mills (then biologist of the Kalahari Gemsbok National Park) saw a brown hyaena carry the remains of a domestic calf, weighing 7,5 kg, 15 km to a den. The den tends to become the focal point of the clan's social life and although it may be moved quite frequently, the area in which the dens are located is usually relatively small. The large numbers of bones and other relatively unpalatable pieces of food which litter the area surrounding a brown hyaena den make it immediately recognisable as such, and the status of the den can be gauged by the age of these remains. The cubs begin to leave the den frequently from about fifteen months of age.

Cheetah

Acinonyx jubatus

Jagluiperd

Descriptive notes

The cheetah must surely be the most elegant of the large cats. Its tall slender build and long tail, together with its aristocratic air give it a distinctly dignified and regal appearance. It is a lanky, hollow-backed animal about as long as a leopard, but higher on the legs, which are thin and muscular. It is not a true cat, inasmuch as it cannot fully sheathe its claws, which are blunt like those of a dog. The head is smaller and more rounded, with a weaker jaw than that of the leopard, and the forehead is more prominent (this is very noticeable if a cheetah's skull is compared with that of a leopard), and the whiskers are short and relatively insignificant. The canine teeth are smaller than those of a leopard. The coat is duller and paler (more sandy-yellow) in ground colour, and the spots on the head are sparsely distributed, mainly on the forehead and cheeks, extending back from the eyes in a line towards the cheeks. From the front corner of each eye runs a narrow dark line (like a tear mark) to the upper lip, where it broadens out. The hair of the coat is rough and wiry, and the numerous blackish spots are distributed widely (in single, oval or circular form) over the back, flanks and quarters, becoming largest on the hindquarters and down the legs. The spots are 'solid', i.e. not formed in a ring in groups, but scattered singly. The chest and abdomen are very sparsely spotted, more or less white, as are also the chin and throat. The long tail is spotted for the greater part of its length, the spots gradually uniting to form bands near the rather bushy tip, which invariably is white. The sexes are alike, though the males grow larger and have a more pronounced 'ruff' or slight wiry mane above the shoulders.

A very handsomely-marked aberrant colour variation of the cheetah, the 'king cheetah' has been known to exist in the far northern and eastern Transvaal, the eastern and south-eastern parts of Zimbabwe and eastern Botswana. This animal used to be considered a separate species but has recently been bred in captivity from normally marked parents and has been shown to be an aberrant form of the single species of cheetah. The 'king cheetah' is marked with thick black, mostly longitudinal, stripes, blotches and loops, set off against a creamy-buff background, and it has

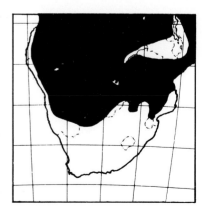

shoulder height: 85 cm
weight ♂: 54 kg
    ♀: 43 kg
length: 2,0 m
running speed: 75 – 80 km/h
sexual maturity: 2 years
gestation: 3 months
number of young: 1 – 5 cubs (av. 3)
birth weight: 275 g
weaning: 3 months
longevity: 16 years

Order: *Carnivora*
Family: *Felidae*
Subfamily: *Felinae*

the same conspicuous black tear lines running from the eyes as in the common type. It is truly a most striking animal.

King cheetah

Distribution and habits

As a result of the demand for spotted skins in the world's fur trade, cheetah have been exterminated over large parts of their former range. Southern Africa is no exception in this regard; formerly widely distributed across the subcontinent, cheetah are today restricted to the less developed northern parts and to certain areas where they have been re-introduced.

Cheetah still occur widely across Africa and in parts of Asia. They are absent from the more densely wooded regions of Central and West Africa and most of the the Sahara Desert.

Cheetah move about singly, in pairs, or in small groups of up to six individuals. These groupings consist of litters of cubs (with or without their mother) or of bachelors. The males in these bachelor groups tend to stick together for long periods and very strong bonds exist between them.

Although cheetah may move over large home ranges of up to eighty square kilometres, it is unclear whether or not they actively defend territories. Most evidence suggests that they are territorial to some extent at least, with the females appearing to be more strictly territorial than the males. Males mark areas with urine and faeces but it is unclear as to how long these marked areas are defended by the cheetah. Males are attracted to females in oestrus and under such conditions vicious (and sometimes fatal) fights between the males can ensue.

Cheetah are largely diurnal but will move and hunt on moonlit nights to some extent. They lie up when it is hot, frequently choosing a cool spot with a clear view of the surrounding landscape. At such times cheetah may climb into trees but they are not good climbers and spend most of the time on the ground.

They are most active very early in the morning and during the twilight hours. Most of their hunting also takes place at this time: there is still enough light for them to see obstacles in their way while charging at breakneck speed, but it is poor enough to allow them to get closer to their prey without being seen than would otherwise be the case. They might be said to combine the hunting methods of the dogs (to some degree) with the grace and stealth of the cats. They usually creep or stalk as close as possible to the quarry (usually up to about 100 m) and then rush straight at it, seizing it by the throat and strangling it, sometimes knocking it down first in order to do this. The cheetah's initial burst of speed is so great that its victim at reasonably close quarters has little chance of escape, unless it jinks cunningly from right to left or darts away at abrupt angles. This is particularly true if two cheetah (they often hunt in pairs) chase the prey simultaneously. There is some contention as to what a cheetah's top speed is. It has been estimated to be able to achieve up to 120 km/h but the fastest recorded speed (set up on a dog race track) is just under 90 km/h. This still allows it to retain its worthy title of fastest mammal on earth. Top speed can only be maintained for up to about 400 m and if the prey has not been caught within this distance, the chase is usually abandoned. In the past cheetah were often killed after being chased on horseback until they were totally exhausted and unable to escape.

A cheetah extending itself to the full in the chase must surely be one of the most awe-inspiring sights in nature — the animal keeps its head almost dead still, its eyes locked on the prey, while its long graceful limbs propel it forward with apparently effortless ease. As the terrified victim senses that it is losing the race, it often attempts to escape by swerving and jinking; the cheetah attempts to anticipate these movements, swerving in unison, the long tail sweeping expertly from one side to another in order to keep the mammalian missile on balance and target. The *coup de grâce* is usually delivered with a swipe of a forepaw which bowls the animal over, or it is grabbed and restrained with both forepaws until the jaws can be brought into play to deliver the death bite. The exertion of the kill often leaves the cheetah too exhausted to start eating for some time, but once it has started eating it devours the carcass hastily and nervously, knowing that if other predators become aware of the carcass it may well lose its meal. The bones, skin and intestines are normally left uneaten.

Cheetah prey on medium-sized or small herbivores, preferring animals of up to 60 kg in weight. These include impala, springbok, steenbok, duiker, reedbuck, warthog, and the young of other antelope species. Waterbuck, kudu, tsessebe, wildebeest, zebra and even buffalo, gemsbok, young giraffe and even larger species may be taken when several cheetah band together in the hunt. During the course of such a hunt, a cheetah may be injured by the prey with subsequent disastrous effects for the carnivore. In addition to the above they also hunt smaller animals such as hares, porcupines and ground-living birds such as guinea fowl and francolin. In drier areas, such as the southern Kalahari, cheetah are able to get sufficient water from their prey and do not need to drink. Should water be available, however, they will drink readily.

Because the cheetah usually hunts during the day and because it prefers fairly open, lightly-wooded country where visibility is easy, it is seen far more often than is the leopard. As it is a large 'spotted' animal, it is very frequently mistaken for a leopard by the inexperienced, and is often reported as such! In fact the two creatures are very different, quite apart from distinctive form and colouration. The cheetah is of mild disposition, rarely aggressive, even when wounded or cornered. It is more sociable than the leopard but less so than the lion. As a result of its relatively few numbers in any one locality (it can nowhere be said to be common) it hardly ever becomes a serious menace to stock, and it can never be regarded as a menace to human life, as it is far too timid and retiring, and in fact makes an excellent, affectionate pet. It has no vicious hooked claws like true cats, and rarely bites except in self-defence. It is therefore a sad fact that it is now so scarce, and that its extermination over much of Africa seems likely unless it is strictly protected in these areas. Unfortunately high prices are still paid for its beautiful skin, like that of the leopard, although it is illegal to trade in them in most countries today.

The cheetah is a silent creature, only occasionally uttering a curious sort of 'chirruping' when excited or when greeting others of its group. They also purr loudly in contentment and when angered or frightened will growl deeply or hiss or cough. When seen indistinctly at a distance, in longish grass or scrub, the spots merge into a general tawny hue, and a cheetah may then easily be mistaken for a small lioness.

Although man is undoubtedly the cheetah's most serious enemy, they are often attacked (and even killed) by lions and leopards and even spotted hyaenas will maul them if they can catch them. Cubs may be killed by many carnivore species or larger birds of prey. Their unaggressive nature often results in their being robbed of their kills, off which even vultures have been known to drive them.

Breeding

Courtship is a delicate and sensitive procedure with cheetah. About a week or two before a female comes into oestrus she begins to tolerate males in her vicinity, whereas at other times she reacts aggressively to their presence. The males become increasingly excited, sometimes mock

charging the female, scraping up earth and urinating or defecating on top of her. They also spray urinate frequently. When the female comes into oestrus the males near her may become extremely aggressive towards each other and intense fighting may occur. Although they may manage to mount the female quite frequently, successful copulation often does not take place and this may result in the female coming into oestrus two or three times immediately after each other until conception takes place. Although the female may invite copulation by crouching, she is very aggressive towards the male when he mounts her. This aggression, as well as inter-male aggression is essential for a successful mating.

The young are born at various times of the year in different areas, and it is not certain whether or not cheetah are seasonal breeders. The female usually goes to a well-secluded spot before giving birth to about three dark golden, blind and helpless cubs. By the time they are two weeks old their eyes are open and they follow their mother from about six weeks of age. Before this time the mother frequently moves the cubs to new hiding places in order to avoid their being discovered by the many carnivores which prey on them.

The cubs begin to eat meat once they start to follow their mother and they participate in kills from about eight months of age. They are clothed with a thick mantle of long bluish-grey hair along the back from head to tail, which conceals the immature spots. This mantle is evident up to about three months. Once they are a year old they move off on their own and the mother begins to raise another litter. They may remain together as a group for some time after becoming independent of their mother.

Leopard

Panthera pardus

Luiperd

Descriptive notes

The leopard is gracefully and powerfully built, with a long body and comparatively short and stout legs. The general colour is bright yellowish-tawny on the head, outer parts of the limbs, back, flanks, quarters and tail, paling to white round the lips, chin, throat, chest, underparts and insides of the limbs and underside of the tail. The whole body is marked with closely-set markings in the form of groups of four to six black spots, right down to the toes. Those on the head are small, solid and very closely set, stopping short of the upper portion of the muzzle and the muzzle itself, which are unmarked and tawny-yellow. The spots become larger round the cheeks, and across the throat and upper chest form broken horizontal bars. The spots on the shoulders, body and quarters are set more widely apart in symmetrical rows, and combine in rosette-like clusters of five or six spots more or less encircling an area usually slightly darker in tone than the surrounding fur. These tend to become solid again, though larger, on the hindquarters and abdomen.

The long tail is irregularly spotted in more or less rosette fashion, and the upper surface of the tip (which is not bushy) is usually, but not always, black. The ears are black above, with whitish tips. The eyes, which are fierce and baleful in expression, are pale greenish-yellow, and the white whiskers are very long and bristly. The teeth and jaw are more powerful than those of a cheetah and the leopard does not have dark lines in front of the eyes as does the more slimly-built and singly-spotted cheetah. Also unlike the cheetah (which has blunt, only partially retractile claws) the leopard is a true cat which can sheathe its powerful curved claws when they are not in use.

Black leopards are rare in Africa but very dark animals quite often occur, as well as a number of variations in the size and distribution of the spots (or rosettes) and in the ground colour and size of the animal as a whole.

Distribution and habits

Leopards are found throughout sub-Saharan Africa except in the interior of southern Africa and also occur in Asia,

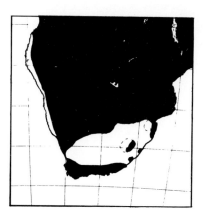

shoulder height: 75 cm
weight ♂: 60 kg (up to 90 kg)
♀: 32 kg (up to 60 kg)
length ♂: 200 cm (max. 292 cm)
sexual maturity: 2,5 – 4 years
gestation: 3,5 months
number of young: 2 – 3 cubs (max. 6)
birth weight: 55 g
weaning: 3 months
longevity: 20 years

Order: *Carnivora*
Family: *Felidae*
Subfamily: *Felinae*

Sri Lanka and Malaysia.

As a result of its secretive and shy nature, its nocturnal habits and solitary dispostion, the leopard today has a wider distribution than any of the other large cats. They can exist for years in suitable country without any obvious indication of their presence, until or unless they begin to kill stock; hence their ability to survive in comparatively well-populated areas where lions have long been exterminated.

The leopard is essentially a lover of fairly dense bush, frequently in rocky or mountainous surroundings. It is mainly a nocturnal hunter – spending the greater part of the day lying up in dense cover or undergrowth, in caves among rocks, or sometimes extended along the branch of a tall tree, well screened by the foliage. Although lions can climb fairly slanting trees, they do so comparatively rarely, their greater weight no doubt providing a formidable handicap. Leopards, however, are perfectly at home in trees of almost any kind and can climb with the facility of lesser cats. When looking for leopards, therefore, it is always a good idea to keep an alert eye on the foliage-covered branches of the great trees bordering river banks etc., where the vegetation is usually lush and rank. Very often the first thing that will draw your attention to a leopard lying along a tree branch is the sight of a long spotted tail hanging below the level of the branch. From such vantage points they are able to keep a good look-out for potential prey.

Whereas lions like to sleep and bask right in the open, and are consequently often quite easily seen, leopards only emerge from dense cover for very brief spells at a time.

They are most often seen in the very early morning, when they may bask for a while on rocky outcrops or large ant-hills or *sidwalas* (the slabs of flat, basaltic or granitic rock which constantly outcrop in the veld). Likewise, in the late afternoons, as they begin to stir in anticipation of the evening or nighly hunt, they may be seen wending their way, or sitting up, among the vegetation of river or stream banks. In most game reserves they are becoming more confident of motor cars and are fairly often seen by tourists, although the sighting of a leopard is always to be taken as rather unusual good luck.

Leopards also frequent rocky, boulder-clad hills, as well as the precipitous rugged cliffs and ravines of the large mountain ranges (with their almost inaccessible bush-crowded valleys and gullies), and in such surroundings they exist largely on baboons and dassies (hyrax), klipspringers and other rock-haunting creatures. They can be found throughout the thorny savanna bushveld; particularly haunting the dongas and sandspruits and clumps of denser bush. They are accomplished swimmers and although they avoid getting even their feet wet unnecessarily, they will take to water readily if the need arises. Finally, they often occur in the great primary forests.

Leopards are generally solitary creatures but sometimes move about in pairs or with subadult offspring. They are, on the whole, rather silent creatures, particularly where they have been much persecuted. Where unmolested, however, they soon reveal their presence by their curious, rasping 'sawing' grunts, usually heard in the early mornings, late afternoons and during the night as they are moving about. This is an extremely harsh-toned coughing grunt, uttered several times in fast succession. After each grunt, the air is drawn in huskily, producing a double effect very aptly compared with the sound of sawing coarse wood. This might be likened to: *'Grunt-ha! Grunt-ha! Grunt-ha!'* usually uttered six or eight times in succession, and often ending in a harsh, sighing note. Both sexes have this call, the voice of the male being deeper and harsher than that of his mate and they will sometimes repeat the call between them as they move. An angry leopard growls and grunts in the same 'explosive' tones as a lion, though with somewhat lesser volume, and it may also give a brief roar.

Males and females scentmark by spraying urine and the

males rake their fearsome claws on tree trunks, perhaps advertising their presence in this way. The male also patrols and defends his territory from other males but may tolerate a number of females, each with her own territory, within his area. Fighting is rare as leopards usually avoid each other except when courting or mating. When fighting does occur it can be very intense and aggressive, especially between males.

The leopard's senses are extremely well developed, particularly its sight and hearing. It obtains prey by stealth and ambush, and quite frequently watches a game trail from a tree branch, pouncing onto its prey from above. More often, though, leopards will use even the most meagre cover to the full, expertly stalking their prey, with their bodies held close to the ground, and with breathtaking skill and singlemindedness of purpose, until they are in a position to make the final dash and pounce. Although extremely quick over a short distance, the leopard lacks stamina, and will soon give up the chase if the prey is not caught quickly. Small victims are simply swatted with a paw and killed, while larger animals are gripped with the front paws around the forequarters. The killing bite is then delivered at the base of the skull or neck, or the prey may be grabbed by the throat and strangled or the jugular vein severed. As it is a solitary hunter, it is essential that the leopard kills its prey as quickly and efficiently as possible before injury from flailing hooves or horns can take place.

Large prey is frequently pulled high up into the branches of trees in order to keep it out of the reach of other predators such as lions, hyaenas and wild dogs. Leopards frequently drink the blood of their prey and will pluck the feathers from birds or the fur of smaller mammals before commencing with their meal.

The leopard's prey consists of mammals as small as mice right up to antelope as large as adult kudu and wildebeest. The choice of prey depends largely on its availability in the particular area in which the leopard lives. The principal food normally consists of small or medium-sized mammals such as canerats, dassies, porcupines, hares, impala, springbok, bushbuck and baboons, or the young of waterbuck, kudu, giraffe, zebra etc. They also frequently take game birds and rodents whenever the opportunity arises and will eat fish and reptiles as well.

The varied range of its diet has undoubtedly assisted the leopard in surviving in areas where most other 'game' has long since disappeared. Leopards are well known for their taste for the flesh of all members of the dog family, and their audacity in this respect is astounding. They have been known to creep up and literally snatch a dog from under its master's chair in a bush camp, and to take dogs from the verandas of houses. If you value your dog, keep it well enclosed after dark in leopard country! In spite of their partiality for dog flesh, leopards will always run from dogs in the daytime, and they are very easily 'treed' by a few dogs — even the meanest mongrels.

Monkeys and baboons will often betray the movements of a leopard; vervet monkeys will follow it in the branches overhead, coughing and chattering raucously, doing their best to keep the hated enemy in sight. Two leopards will sometimes co-operate cleverly in this manner: one concealing itself in the branches, and the other strolling along in full view below, thus attracting the attention of the monkeys. Baboons behave similarly when a leopard is viewed, barking defiantly, and scrambling to places of refuge, whence the predator's movements will be watched and followed as closely as possible. When a leopard succeeds in snatching one of a troop of baboons, absolute screaming, raging pandemonium breaks out, and the leopard usually quickly seeks a safe retreat in which to devour his victim. If he is not quick enough, the infuriated powerful males may attack him and, in spite of his strength and slashing claws, nearly tear him to bits from sheer force of numbers, thus forcing him to turn tail and flee.

For his size and weight, the leopard is probably among the most dangerous of animals. The words 'savage' and 'fierce' are infinitely more suited to the leopard than to the lion (speaking very generally of course) and it embodies all the most striking attributes of the cats. The small flat head with its baleful eyes, and the sinuous graceful, yet intensely muscular, form suggest the killer in its every movement, and yet even where common, leopards are rarely seen, and they will seldom deliberately attack man if escape otherwise is possible. In spite of his shy elusiveness where man is concerned, the leopard is a bold and very courageous creature, and should he fancy himself to be in danger and his escape cut off, he will not hesitate to charge directly at an intruder or hunter. There seem to be good grounds for the oft-repeated statement of hunters that you can pass close by a hiding leopard, or gaze right up into the branches in which he is crouching, and, unless your 'eyes meet' he will allow you to pass. But the very instant he is aware that you have noticed him he will probably flee, or if wounded or cornered he may attack. As his spotted form easily harmonises with the play of shadows of leaves or herbage, it is (perhaps fortunately) very easy to overlook a leopard. Once he is committed to a full attack, however, very little will stop a charging leopard except a fatal bullet (whereas a lion may often be turned by a shot, and more frequently charges in bluff). He comes very fast, is low on the ground, and his method of attack is to 'scalp' his opponent with the frightful hooked claws, knocking him down and mauling him with teeth and all four clawed feet. In certain parts of Africa (and quite often in parts of India) leopards have become man-eaters, preying mainly upon women and children who are always killed by a bite in the throat. But there are exceptions to the general rule and a leopard will nearly always retreat when confronted by humans unless it or its offspring are threatened.

Breeding

The leopard normally gives birth to two or three cubs in a sheltered place in a cave, a crevice among boulders or rocks, or in dense reeds or thickets. Blind at birth, the cubs open their eyes by about ten days. They are very similar to the kittens of domestic cats, playing with each other and inanimate objects with great exuberance and frequency. When they are about six weeks old the mother regurgitates food for the cubs, and later may carry food back to the lair for them. They may be frequently moved by her, particularly if disturbed.

The young move with the mother from about four months and remain with her for almost two years. When away from the mother, cubs are very vulnerable to other large carnivores, particularly lions, and stay near to a place where they can seek refuge.

The mother may teach the cubs hunting skills, and reunions between her and them may take place after they have left her.

Lion

Panthera leo

Leeu

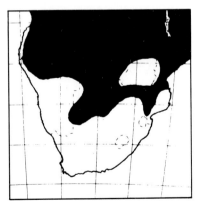

Descriptive notes

The general appearance of the African lion is sufficiently well known to require little description. The body colour varies from an ochre-tinted silvery-grey to dark brown above; the underparts always being lighter (also insides of limbs) — almost white in lionesses — darkening to buffy-ochre in adult male lions. Black marks form a conspicuous band across the back of the ear, and the black tail tuft conceals a horny spur at the tip of the tail. There is also usually a suffusion, more or less, of blackish hair down the back of the hind legs just above the hocks, most pronounced in males. The overall colour of lions varies substantially, with some individuals being almost black whereas others are white. The best known of these are the white lions of Timbavati in the Eastern Transvaal, but such extremes in colour variation are rare. In general southern African lions are darker in colour and larger than lions elsewhere in Africa.

The size, colour and extent of the mane in the male varies a great deal, and subadult males usually have a tawny or yellowish mane, but this can blacken with age, resulting in the lion taking on a very impressive and regal appearance. Mane colour varies between an almost silvery blond, through various shades of ochre or yellow, almost rufous, dark brown to pitch black — the last always being considered the most handsome, especially as the body colour of a real 'black mane' is usually richer and darker than that of a lighter-maned animal. In all cases, however, the long hair in front of the ears, depending from the cheeks, and usually most of it immediately over the forehead, is most often ochre-yellow. Both dark- and fair-maned lions may be born in the same litter, and the commonest colouring is a mixture of dark and light colouring, the darkest portions usually covering the throat and chest and the back of the neck to the ridge along the withers. In rare cases adult lions either have very small manes or no manes at all, as in the case of the man-eating lions of Tsavo in East Africa. The mane is a sexual signal to females and may protect the lion's neck during fights as well.

The lions which formerly inhabited the temperate Cape Province (the last of which were exterminated by the latter half of the last century) were magnificent beasts; the males grew huge luxuriant manes, mostly black or blackish in colour save for the yellowish-ochre fringe round cheeks and forehead, which completely covered the shoulders but apparently stopped short as a rule on the chest. The forepart of the belly was bare of long hair, but a thick growth traversed the latter end of the abdomen to roughly between the hind legs – such an extension of long hair is very rarely seen in even the best wild lions in other parts of Africa today.

shoulder height ♂: 120 cm
  ♀: 105 cm
weight ♂: 180 kg (up to 235 kg)
  ♀: 130 kg (up to 200 kg)
length ♂: 280 cm (up to 334 cm)
  ♀: 240 cm (up to 270 cm)
walking speed: 4 km/h
sexual maturity ♀: 2,5 years
gestation: 4 months
number of young: 1 – 4 cubs (up to 6 recorded)
birth weight: 1,5 kg
weaning: 7 – 8 months
longevity: 20 years

Cubs are marked with vertical brindlings along the body and light ochre-coloured rosette-like spots and bars along the flanks and limbs and a dark line down the centre of the back from the nape. The tail tuft is barely distinguishable in a small cub, and the hair of the coat is much more woolly than that of an adult. The cubs' ears are proportionately enormous. Young male lions soon begin to grow noticeably longer hair on throats and cheeks, and budding crests on the top of the head, and in this way they can soon be distinguished from young lionesses, as the latter, even when fully grown, never grow longer hair on cheeks or chest, nor indicate any crest. The young male soon develops pronounced side-whiskers of budding mane, and his head is always broader than that of a lioness. It takes four to five years before his mane reaches reasonably full development.

The lioness is a good deal smaller and more lightly built than the lion; she is whiter about the throat and almost pure white along the abdomen – an adult male lion being

Order: *Carnivora*
Family: *Felidae*
Subfamily: *Felinae*

young male

darker along the flanks and more rufous-buff along the abdomen. She may also have indistinct dark spots or rosettes on the belly and tops of the hind legs.

Distribution and habits

The lion has been mercilessly persecuted by man throughout history, largely because it competes directly with man and his interests. Once found over most of Europe, Asia and the whole of Africa there are only about 200 left in Asia (the Gir lions of north-western India). They have been extinct in Europe since shortly after the death of Christ, and in Africa they are no longer found in the north and south of the continent, generally being limited to the areas between about 12° north and 24° south, with the exception of the forests of Central and West Africa. In the Cape Province they used to be found as far south as Cape Town up until about 1720 but had been exterminated in this province and in most of Natal 150 years later. They have since been re-introduced into the Umfolozi-Hluhluwe Reserves in Natal.

As a result of their wandering and nomadic tendencies, lions still occasionally pitch up in unusual places, far from their areas of regular occurrence. Places where these sightings have been made include the metropolitan areas of Windhoek (Namibia), Gwelo and Harare in Zimbabwe and Heidelberg in the Transvaal. They also frequently wander out of the Kruger National Park into the adjacent agricultural areas, as far as Louis Trichardt, and out of the Kalahari Gemsbok Park into the farms in Namibia. The lion is currently being driven from areas of its range probably faster than any other mammal species in Africa. Although they live in almost any habitat except forests, they seem destined to be tragically banished to protected areas which are often too small to allow the 'Kings of Beasts' to live in the style which they deserve.

heavy maned male

Lions are most active at night and in areas where they are regularly hunted they become exceedingly elusive and nocturnal, even subduing their vocal utterances to occasional grunts, so that any direct observation of their habits becomes difficult. It has, however, been demonstrated that in the sanctuaries and national parks lions very soon regain confidence, fearlessly showing themselves at all hours of the day, and quite often hunting and killing their prey during daylight as well. In such areas the magnificent sounds of the lion's roar are freely audible at night. Apart from man, the lion has no natural enemy, and thus in areas safe from human interference he orders his way of life entirely to suit his own convenience. It is this 'return to the primeval' that makes the national parks of Africa so valuable to the scientist, as well as to the ordinary student of nature.

Except when hungry or thirsty, lions seldom stir from their shady retreats in patches of long grass, reeds, or under bushes, trees or thickets in the heat of the day, and as a rule they are not easy to notice over that period. They avoid the full heat of the sun and will not leave the shade at such times unless alarmed or driven by necessity. In really hot weather you can notice them panting, with widely sagging jaws, and although they will lie out in the open to bask and enjoy the pleasantly warm early morning rays, as soon as the heat becomes too powerful they rise and retreat to the nearest cover, where they may soon vanish from view.

After a good meal, at which they will gorge to repletion (instinctively providing against the uncertainty of when the next meal may be obtainable), lions invariably settle down to sleep heavily for hours at a time, and then, where accustomed to the sound of motor traffic, it is difficult to get them to raise their sleepy heads from the grass. They may spend up to fifteen hours a day sleeping, but if they are hungry, and hunting has not been successful, they may continue to wander and hunt throughout even the hottest part of the day, and kills may take place even at midday on scorching hot days. Lions may be met with in places like the Kruger National Park at almost any time, but by far the best period to seek them is from early morning until about 10 a.m., and again from about 3.30 p.m. onwards, depending on the weather and the seasons, and of course they are active for much of the night.

Lions are the most sociable of the cat family, associating in 'prides' which may consist of a dominant male and female and other animals of all ages and sexes. Sometimes there are no adult males present in a pride for a period and males may move alone, in pairs, or in small groups as well.

A male lion may mate with several lionesses as they come into season, and in due course they may introduce their offspring into the pride, and so its numbers increase. Such prides vary in number but have been found to average twelve in the Kruger National Park and East Africa, while only consisting of a maximum of about eight animals in Botswana. Quite often a fine but ageing male may be accompanied by an almost equally magnificent but younger and more alert companion of his own sex: the older beast, with superior experience, possibly supplying the strategy and tactics and the younger one the physical prowess.

Although most prides occupy territories which they normally defend against intruders, some prides or individuals are nomadic — wandering endlessly and avoiding confronation with territorial prides whenever possible. These prides are usually less prolific and successful than those with fixed territories.

The lionesses form the nucleus of the pride, whereas the lions may move more frequently from one pride to another or be displaced; a male may in some cases even 'rule' two prides at one time. The pride is in a constant state of flux with its members coming together and splitting up as they move over their territory; deaths and births mean that the dominant male and his 'henchmen' may be displaced by other stronger or younger lions. If this occurs while there are cubs in the pride, the new male or males often kill them. This induces the female or females to come into oestrus, thus giving the newcomer a chance to sire his own offspring sooner than would otherwise have been the case. Fights for the possession of a pride (and the subsequent right to mate) are vicious and may result in serious injury or death.

Scentmarking, roaring, and patrolling usually ensure that the pride's territory is not violated. Should interlopers be encountered, they will usually run for the safety of their own territory; actual confrontations under such conditions are rare and are usually played down. If they occur, however, they may sometimes escalate dramatically, especially when females are involved.

Lions eat almost any animal that they can overpower. Their prey ranges from insects to elephants (when young or injured). More often though, they will eat whatever prey species is most abundant and available to them, these being impala, zebra, waterbuck, kudu, wildebeest and buffalo in most parts of southern Africa. In the Kalahari they tend to subsist mainly on smaller prey species such as young antelope and porcupines, and in some areas giraffe are an important prey item. They will eat carrion of any age or stage of putrification and frequently bully spotted hyaenas off their kills. Some of the more unusual animals that lions have been known to kill and eat are: fish in drying up pools, termites, locusts, spotted hyaenas, leopards, cheetah, jackals, civets, honey badgers, caracal, crocodiles, hippo (when they are far from water) and rhino.

When lions hunt in a pride they are more successful than when they hunt on their own. They are expert stalkers, using any available cover to maximum advantage in getting as close to the prey as possible before launching the final assault. During the final dash they are unable to last for more than about 200 m before flagging, but are capable of covering 100 m in about six seconds when going flat out. Along the Sabi River near Skukuza they prey mainly on the swarming impala, and have learnt to take full advantage of lines of tourist cars from which to stalk and attack their normally alert and active prey.

The males of a pride usually drive the quarry onto the waiting lionesses which apparently do most of the killing, except where heavy, powerful animals such as bull buffalo are concerned. The males generally work round upwind of the prey to enable it to get their scent, but in certain conditions (such as when they are trying to stampede cattle out of an enclosure), if this fails they will grunt or roar loudly and the resulting panic usually has the desired effect.

Adult lions sometimes kill quickly and expertly, and beyond an occasional short strangled bellow the victim is in such cases usually dead before it can realise what has happened, often with its neck broken as it falls under the sudden weight and powerful clutching claws of its assailant. In other cases, however, death by strangulation may be a slow and traumatic process, and in the case of heavy, powerful animals such as a bull buffalo or giraffe, a prolonged struggle may take place with several big lions co-operating in eventually wearing their prey down.

Lions usually kill their prey with a bite in the throat from the front, or else by leaping onto the victim from the flank or rear, grasping its muzzle with one claw-extended paw and wrenching it down (the teeth meanwhile buried in the throat or the back of the neck), so that it crashes down, breaking its neck. Frequently the victim is licked all over for some moments before the meal begins, and then the body is bitten open at the flank or the belly and the stomach removed intact, its contents shaken out in a heap, then eaten, followed by lungs, liver and kidneys – all of which delicacies are usually eaten first (the entrails are usually buried under grass or earth). After these preliminaries, lions usually begin at the soft flesh of thighs and rump, eating towards the shoulders and head (leopards usually eat the head and foreparts first, after lapping and sucking the blood). The ears, lips, and sides of the head are eaten, together with the tongue. The flesh is mostly rasped off the bone with the rough surface of the tongue; smaller bones and tougher meat are bitten with the sharp carnassial teeth. Lions can crack only medium and smaller bones, the larger ones being impregnable to all but the specialised dental equipment of the hyaena.

Although the lionesses of a pride often perform most of the actual killing (the males generally playing their part in the driving of the game onto the already concealed and waiting females), the meal is seldom begun before the largest male or males have selected their favourite portions; until they have settled down to their repast the lioness and younger animals will not dare to join in. When game is plentiful and food not hard to come by, lions usually eat fairly peaceably, spread out along either side of the carcass, with only occasional arguments and mutterings taking place. But when times are hard and a large pride is very hungry, violent arguments and fights take place over the food, during which many of the younger beasts get killed and even eaten by their companions. Lions drink frequently, especially when eating on a carcass but are independent of water in some areas, obtaining the necessary moisture from their prey.

Skin and hair are bolted down with the meat, forming necessary roughage, hence the droppings of lions (and leopards) are usually full of the hair of the animals they have eaten. The enormous curved claws of lions are, like those of all true cats, withdrawn into sheath-like folds of skin for protection except when needed for clutching or self-defence, and so are not visible in the spoor (although they may be indicated in wet or slippery soil). Small grooves or irregularities in the teeth and claws of all predators (notably the felines) frequently retain fragments of decomposing flesh — hence the grave risk of wounds from them turning septic unless promptly treated.

As a rule lions do not roar or make other sounds while hunting. It is well recognised that it is when lions are quiet that they are most dangerous at night, and at night they are always more dangerous than during the day. Immediately after a successful kill, lions will often roar loudly and grandly; one begins in long-drawn vibrant notes, steadily increasing in volume, and the other gradually join in, creating a sublime chorus which finally subsists in a series of irregular, harsh grunts. It is a grand, thrilling sound, and it will indeed be a sad day if it ever ceases to be heard in the national parks of Africa. Both sexes roar alike, but the tones of a lion are always a good deal more rugged and harsh than those of a lioness. Young cubs utter a harsh kind of *'miaouing'*, and also an explosive sort of *'pook'*. At intervals while they are feeding at night, lions often roar, and later, as they return from drinking, they often roar again. At other times they roar when seeking mates (either sex) or when members of a pride are trying to locate one another. Soft moaning sounds are used as a means of individual communication also.

Sometimes individual lions, for some reason, may roar in an abnormal manner, which makes recognition of their individual movements easy. Maberly recounts the tale of one such lion which, when it had killed close to a little camp in the Kruger Park, had on one or two occasions permitted the camp attendant to approach very carefully and to cut himself a small steak with which he was allowed to retire unmolested! A mutual understanding and respect had apparently developed between lion and man.

Man-eating is fortunately quite rare, though it is certainly commoner in some parts of Africa than in others. In such localities one usually finds that the local tribespeople have superstitions about man-eaters (sometimes accrediting them with being the spirits of former chiefs) and so refrain from taking steps against them, so that the tendency is increased among cubs brought up on human flesh. Old or disabled lions may take to pouncing on humans outside their huts at night, and so learn how easily they can be caught. Otherwise the habit may be developed by accident, especially among young inexperienced lions which are still not always successful at normal hunting and have still not learnt respect for man. Generally speaking, it is fear and distrust of the human scent, rather than dislike of human flesh, that prevents the majority of lions from attacking man deliberately. In the majority of cases of unprovoked attacks on humans the explanation has been found in the discovery of broken-off nooses or wire snares deeply embedded in the necks of the poor animals causing unspeakable agony and gradual starvation.

Lions viewed from motor cars are rarely at all dangerous — even lionesses with small cubs. They are used to motor traffic in national parks, regard it as quite harmless, and the overpowering petrol scent drowns any human scent. They seem to be intrigued and puzzled as to what sort of creatures these buzzing monsters are, and lie watching with great interest which rapidly turns to boredom. But considerable danger is invited if you open your door, or attempt to get out close to lions, because they recognise the human presence, and the suddenness of the appearance adds to the shock of fear which may very easily prompt an attack in supposed self-defence. Many people simply will not realise this, and take the most reckless liberties with lions in order to get a better (so thought) photograph, but nobody who has any real knowledge or understanding of the temperament of the lion would do so. There is less danger in actually coming face to face with a lion in the bush than in suddenly appearing out of a motor car in front of him!

In assessing the emotional state of a lion or lioness the action of the ears and tail are of great importance. A really angry lion flattens his ears, crouches low, and whisks his tail ever more rapidly from side to side, meanwhile uttering a most nerve-racking series of coughing grunts and slurring growls. As his anger mounts, his tail is jerked stiffly up and down, and when charging he usually comes at a trot first of all. If the tail is twitching or jerking, but the ears are still cocked, the beast is probably merely nervous or excited, but not angry.

Lions, like other large felines, have a strong, acrid scent which is often quite perceptible at close quarters, and very often evident in herbage through which they have recently brushed.

Breeding

When a lioness comes into season several lions often accompany her, but the dominant male will finally pair off with her, warning off his rivals, who may continue to hang about in the vicinity until or unless another alluring female arrives on the scene. A mating pair of lions enjoys a substantial 'honeymoon'. They will remain in practically the same spot for days on end, apparently not hunting or eating at this time, completely absorbed in themselves and with the male losing weight dramatically. The lioness tests the patience of her suitor to the utmost, and at this time the male is usually irritable and inclined to be aggressive towards all intruders, though exceedingly patient and gentle with his lioness. If a motor car is driven too close to such a pair the lion usually bristles and growls, lashing his tail angrily and crouching threateningly; and if this warning remains unheeded he may even make a short rush at the car, which in most cases has the desired effect!

The pair may copulate every fifteen minutes over a period of many hours, the female inviting the male by crouching and rolling in front of him. Although there may be snarling and the male may bite the female on the back of the neck during copulation, it is generally a much less aggressive and more symbolic procedure than is the case with most other carnivores. Most matings do not result in pregnancy; in some areas almost as few as one in four mating sessions results in fertilisation but females normally conceive every two years. Lions are polygamous, and as soon as a male has satisfactorily mated with one lioness he may mate with another which comes into oestrus. Maberly watched a male lion sharing his attentions with two lionesses at the same time, all apparently in quite a friendly spirit; and occasionally two males, old friends who have long hunted together, pair in turn peacefully with the same lioness, but such happenings are rare.

The cubs, from two to four as a rule, are born in thickets, reedbeds, patches of long grass or among clumps of dwarf palms etc., and they are born with 'their eyes at least partially open' (Stevenson-Hamilton). They may be born at any time of the year, with the mother leaving the pride to give birth. Sometimes another lioness assists the mother in guarding and caring for the cubs; the two of them take it in turns to hunt for food, one always remaining on guard while the cubs are very small and helpless. Without such a 'nursemaid' or 'auntie' being available, the lioness has from time to time to leave her cubs concealed while she seeks prey, and then the risk of their being attacked by hyaenas or other predators is great.

In the same way one will sometimes see a lioness accompanied by two sets of cubs obviously of different ages; the mother of one set is probably away hunting. The lioness is a very dangerous animal indeed when her cubs are small, and she will not hesitate to charge anything, no matter what size or species, which she fancies is threatening them. The most beautiful, peaceful-looking spots along the banks of rivers or spruits, so tempting for a picnic, and apparently so quiet and safe, may very easily harbour a lioness sleeping with her cubs, and one always needs to be alert to this possibility in lion country.

After about a month or two the lioness rejoins the pride with her cubs and, provided they are not eating, the big males usually seem affectionately disposed towards the youngsters, allowing them to gambol about all over them, play with their tail tufts and so on. However, the cubs are in grave danger if they attempt to approach an adult male lion when he is eating, and many cubs get killed, or at least badly mauled in such circumstances. If there are cubs already with the pride which are older than three months then the mother will normally not join the pride with her young cubs. Since mothers will suckle any cubs in the pride the younger cubs would not be able to compete against the larger ones.

The cubs remain dependent on their mother until they are about two years old, as before that age they are still insufficiently trained to fend for themselves. Consequently a lioness normally only breeds once in two years, a factor in the natural regulation of lion populations, to which is added the comparative delicacy of lion cubs among which infant mortality from various causes is very high. In most cases over half of the cubs born do not reach maturity.

When the lionesses have to travel far and wide in search of prey, many families of small cubs die of exhaustion or starvation; or get killed and eaten by hyaenas etc., in the absence of their mothers. In addition to the above, a certain number get killed annually in courtship fights, quarrels over food, territorial rights, accidents in hunting and so on. Lions are usually infested with ticks, and the famous lioness Elsa died of a tick-borne disease akin to biliary, known as *Babesia*. Many wild lions, particularly if in poor condition, also succumb to disease.

The cubs are carefully trained, and even while comparatively small the lioness throws down half-killed smaller and fairly harmless victims for them to tussle over and practise upon, later holding down creatures such as warthog and smaller buck for them to 'kill'. This is gruesome and painful to watch, but essential training. The milk canines are not replaced by strong adult teeth until the cubs are about a year old. Those of young lionesses are replaced earlier than those of males, and even at an early age the young lionesses display more hunting initiative than their brothers. When about ten or twelve months old, the young lions learn to assist in driving and stalking game, and to attack and kill prey.

At first they probably only worry at animals already in

their death throes, or at least partly put out of action by their elders, but from a year on they seriously try to tackle game themselves. They are now practically as big as, and in the case of males possibly heavier than, their mothers, but clumsy, inexperienced hobbledehoys. As may be expected, a good deal of ghastly blundering takes place at this age as the young lions have to learn the vital spots before they can kill as quickly and efficiently as adults. In many cases the victim struggles free, and many a young lion has had to flee with an infuriated old wildebeest in vengeful pursuit! A lion's training is a hard one, and it has to amass considerable knowledge of the habits and movements of the game on which it lives if it is to survive.

Caracal

Felis caracal

Rooikat

Descriptive notes

This large wild cat has short, sleek fur which is more or less grizzled-rufous; in some specimens a beautiful rich bright rufous-bay, in others duller and more grizzled — but always distinctly reddish in hue. Above it is completely unmarked, but along the abdomen there are a few brownish spots. The chin, throat and upper lip (latter bordered with black) are white. There is a black spot above each eye. The narrow and pointed ears are black but white-fringed in front; they are decorated with conspicuously long narrow tufts of hair at their tips — these tufts frequently droop down like tassels. The tail is short and slender, reddish like the rest of the body. The size and bright reddish colouring of the caracal render it liable to be mistaken for a steenbok when observed indistinctly in longish grass or in the shadow of bushes. The eyes are very brilliant rich amber-yellow, sometimes greenish in tint.

Distribution and habits

Although more widely distributed, and on the whole more plentiful in southern Africa than farther north, the caracal is not very often seen by day, and it can nowhere be said to be very numerous. In the Cape districts it is often accused of causing damage among lambs and many thousands of caracal have been killed in these areas; but in the wilder country of the Transvaal and further north, it is seldom plentiful enough anywhere to inflict other than occasional damage among small domestic stock such as poultry. It is found throughout Africa, except in the desert and heavily forested regions, and also in southern Asia as far west as India.

This is a remarkably beautiful cat: graceful, though powerfully built; its small, roundish face is strikingly dominated by the long tufted ears whose pencilled tips sometimes droop heavily downwards, or at times are cocked upwards. It is almost exclusively solitary, only associating with others when mating or in the case of mothers with young kittens. Although largely nocturnal, the caracal is more partially diurnal than the majority of the smaller felines and is thus more frequently observed; however, as a

shoulder height: 45 cm
weight ♂: 15 kg
  ♀: 11 kg
length ♂: 117 cm
  ♀: 109 cm
gestation: 2,5 months
number of young: 2 – 4 kittens (sometimes 5)
longevity: 14 years

Order: *Carnivora*
Family: *Felidae*
Subfamily: *Felinae*

result of its shy nature and expertise at camouflage and concealment there is little known about the natural habits of this animal.

Caracal are principally terrestrial but can climb very well if the need arises. They are expert hunters and killers, being extremely quick, agile and powerful, and equipped with heavy, curved claws and a very powerful jaw which carries long sharp teeth. They are able to snatch birds out of the air as they come down to drink and large numbers may be caught in this way. They normally kill by stalking, pouncing and then biting larger prey in the throat or hitting smaller prey with their forepaws. Their principal prey consists of small or medium-sized animals such as birds, the young of larger antelope, dassies, hares, rodents, lizards and smaller species of antelope such as steenbok and duiker. Even large birds of prey such as tawny and martial eagles may be killed while roosting at night, and sitting adult ostriches are said to be taken. Prey is sometimes taken into trees to be eaten and although it is usually plucked of feathers or fur, it is not disembowelled as would be the case with a leopard. Caracal do not take carrion and can become a problem as a result of their killing sheep and goats in certain areas. These cases are usually isolated and involve specific individuals; most caracal prefer natural prey where it is available.

In temperament the caracal is savage, and a dangerous opponent when wounded or cornered. At one time it was described as 'untameable', but there have been several records of caracal becoming affectionate with their owners, as pets. When cornered they growl and spit but otherwise are reported to call with the rasping saw-like sounds of the leopard, though pitched in a lower key.

The caracal's social system is probably much like that of the leopard, with the males defending territories within which a number of females will have their own territories.

Breeding

Caracal kittens are born mainly during the summer months in thick cover, holes in trees or in disused antbear holes which are lined with fur and feathers. They are blind at birth and the eyes open after about ten days. The female has the entire responsibility of rearing the two to four kittens, as the male separates from her shortly after mating. The offspring may remain with their mother for as long as ten months.

Small Spotted Cat
(Black-footed Cat)

Felis nigripes

Klein Gekolde Kat
(Swartpootwildekat)
(Miershooptier)

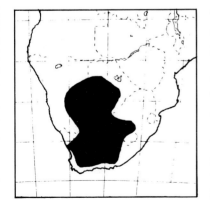

Descriptive notes

The former name of black-footed cat is being phased out since it is something of a misnomer. The feet are only black underneath, a feature which is not peculiar to this species.

This species may be confused with the African wild cat but is smaller and more stockily built and is also very much more spotted and barred, the wild cat being almost unmarked except for banding on the legs.

The small spotted cat is a little smaller, but taller, than a domestic cat. Its general colour is tawny in the northern parts of its range but a rich cinnamon-buff in the south. It is lighter on the underside of the body, in particular the chin, chest and insides of the legs which are white, and is profusely marked with black spots which tend to run into lines on the shoulders, back and neck. There are two conspicuous black bands on the cheeks, and there are a number of irregular black stripes which run round the front of the fore and hind legs. The markings on the lower parts of the body are well defined and extremely black whereas those on the upper parts and in older individuals are more brownish and less distinct. The tail, the same colour as the back, is comparatively short — about 20 cm — and is confusedly spotted for most of its length. The top of the head is darker than the rest of the body and the ears are uniform dark grizzled-brown.

Distribution and habits

This species is confined to the arid central parts of southern Africa, and is not found anywhere outside the sub-region. It is nowhere common and is rarely seen.

It is strictly nocturnal and very shy and for this reason very little is known about it. It will quickly seek shelter when caught in the beam of a light and only tends to become active a few hours after sunset.

Small spotted cats, despite their minute size, are extremely vicious and aggressive. They are virtually impossible to domesticate or tame even if captured when extremely young, tending to retain a fear and distrust of man. They lie up in disused holes in the ground, in termite mounds or in trees during the day.

These little cats have heavy, broad skulls and long, sharp canine teeth, but on account of their size are unable to take prey much larger than young hares and francolin-sized birds. Their prey generally consists of smaller rodents, birds, reptiles, insects and spiders. They can survive without drinking water.

Little is known of the breeding habits of these cats except that one to three kittens are born in midsummer.

shoulder height: 25 cm
weight ♂: 1,5 kg
♀: 1,0 kg
length: 50 – 60 cm
gestation: 2 months
number of young: 1 – 3 kittens

Order: *Carnivora*
Family: *Felidae*
Subfamily: *Felinae*

African Wild Cat

Felis lybica

Vaalboskat

Descriptive notes

This wild cat is rather similar to the domestic cat and is thought to be one of the forebears of our feline pets. It will, in fact, interbreed with domestic cats if given the opportunity but the progeny can be distinguished from pure wild cats by their shorter legs and the absence of the rufous colour behind the ears. The back of the ears of interbred individuals is black or dark grey. The main difference between the African wild cat and the smaller spotted cat is that the latter is much smaller, shorter legged and is profusely marked with black spots. The colour of the back of the ears and the very much longer legs of the wild cat distinguish it from the domestic cat.

The overall colour of animals from the drier parts of southern Africa is a light sandy-grey, whereas those from the wetter eastern parts are very dark grey. There are rather indistinct, wavy, vertical stripes (sometimes broken up into indistinct marks) along the body, more pronounced along the upper part. The upper portions of both limbs are marked with broad dark bars — more distinct than those on the body. There are conspicuous black bands round the legs, and tabby-like markings on the face (including long dark lines extending across the cheeks from the outer corners of eyes). The foreparts of the chest and underparts are much paler and spotted, but the rear half of the underparts is unspotted and yellowish-buff. The proportionately shortish tail usually has a dark tip and two clearly-defined dark rings near the tip — the remainder being marked indistinctly.

When walking, this animal's long legs give it a very different gait to the domestic cat; not unlike that of the cheetah. When sitting it is almost vertical — again the result of its long legs.

Distribution and habits

This cat is found throughout Africa, although it is absent from the deserts and tropical forests.

The wild cat is another nocturnal and shy creature which, though often numerous in a locality, is very rarely seen by day. Little is known of its habits in the wild as a

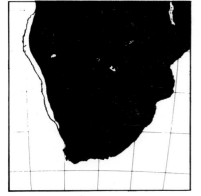

result. However, occasionally — especially in the game reserves — it may be observed quietly padding along one of the roads (particularly in dull weather, or near dawn or dusk) but as a rule as soon as it hears a car it slips into the grass and trots off or bounds away in great leaps. It can easily be recognised, as it looks very like an ordinary domestic tabby, but the tail is slightly shorter, the backs of the ears (if you are close enough to see) are always sandy-rufous, the legs are longer and the gait is quite different. It occurs in all types of country, though prefers slightly wooded surroundings or at least plenty of long grass. It is solitary except when mating and although primarily terrestrial, it can climb well when chased or when hunting.

It preys primarily on rodents when these are available but supplements its diet with birds up to the size of guinea fowl or geese, reptiles, insects, spiders and wild fruits. This wide range of food enables it to live in a diverse number of habitats — from swamp to semi-desert. Near settlements it can become a bad poultry thief. In settled areas it interbreeds freely with domestic cats, and its rather harsh 'miaou' is similar, though deeper in tone (more of a *'Mwa! Mwa! Mwa!'*), and it utters the same screeching and caterwauling serenades when mating. Kittens, when tamed or crossbred with wild parents, seldom become really tame, but tend to remain rather fierce and untrustworthy. They do, however, become much more tame and affectionate than the small spotted cat ever becomes.

Pure wild cats are in danger of becoming hybridised over most of their range as a result of the spread of domestic or feral cats which interbreed with them. They are preyed upon by the larger birds of prey and carnivores such as leopard and caracal.

shoulder height: 35 cm
weight ♂: 5 kg
♀: 4 kg
length: 90 cm
gestation: 2 months
number of young: 2 – 5 (normally 3)
longevity: 12 years

Order: *Carnivora*
Family: *Felidae*
Subfamily: *Felinae*

Breeding

Most kittens are born in holes which are in the ground, in trees or in termite mounds. Sometimes they may also be born in dense cover or grass thickets or in rock crevices. They are normally born in the summer months. The mother appears to raise the kittens on her own and frequently moves them about, carrying them by the scruff of their necks.

Serval

Felis serval

Tierboskat

Descriptive notes

The serval is a large, leggy and elegant, tawny-yellow wild cat richly marked with large, rather widely-spaced solid black spots which tend to run in the form of bars along the back and around the chest. It is lanky and tall on the leg, with very long upstanding and oval ears, a small rounded face and a relatively short tail which is more or less ringed with black. Its colouration − to a certain extent − resembles that of the cheetah, but the spots are more widely separated. The backs of the ears are black with buffy-white patches. It is nearly as large as a caracal but is longer in the leg and less powerfully built.

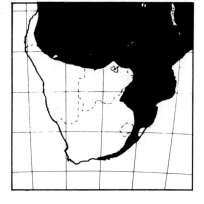

Distribution and habits

The very attractive and delicate serval is a lover of fairly dense vegetation, such as the luxuriant growth of reeds, grass and thickets which usually borders streams and larger rivers; it is rarely found far from the neighbourhood of water and such growth. It is thus restricted to the wetter eastern side of southern Africa and is absent from the

Sahara and the forests of Zaire and West Africa. It is otherwise found over most of Africa in places where there is suitable habitat.

The serval is normally solitary except when mating. The female and her offspring, however, appear to remain together for a long time. It is predominantly nocturnal and runs quickly for a long distance when caught in the beam of a light. It may occasionally be seen in the early morning or late afternoon as well.

It generally uses a system of paths when moving about and may hunt in watery, swampy terrain at times. It is (where numerous) a noisy species at night; its very distinctive and curious ringing, high-pitched call – 'How! How! How!' – is often audible in its haunts. It preys largely upon guinea fowl and other game birds, rodents – particularly canerats – hares, and smaller creatures of all kinds. The serval uses its large ears to locate smaller prey and then pounces, striking downwards with both its front paws simultaneously in order to immobilise the animal.

Although fairly powerfully built, the serval is lighter and more mild-natured than the caracal, with a temperament more like that of the cheetah. They are not dangerous to domestic stock and only very rarely kill poultry. The track, like that of the cheetah, may show slight indications of claw marks; it is otherwise cat-like, about as large as that of a terrier.

shoulder height: 55 cm
weight ♂: 12 kg
　　　♀: 10 kg
length: 110 cm
gestation: 2 months
number of young: 1 – 3 kittens

Order: *Carnivora*
Family: *Felidae*
Subfamily: *Felinae*

Breeding

Litters of one to three serval kittens are usually born during the summer months with a possible peak towards the end of this period. The mother usually finds a site where there is thick grass or other cover in which to give birth. The young are greyer and less distinctly marked than the adults and remain with their mother until they are quite mature.

Bat-eared Fox

Otocyon megalotis

Bakoorvos

Descriptive notes

This dainty little fox is unmistakable on account of its relatively enormous ears which are oval-shaped, black-tipped and rufous-based behind. The distinctive bushy tail is blackish above and at the tip. The animal's overall colour is greyish-brown above, tinged with ochre on the upper part of the tail and flanks. It is paler below and has a rather short but pointed muzzle and a black face below the level of the eyes. The coat is very soft and thick and the sexes are alike.

Distribution and habits

Like the black-backed jackal, the gemsbok and a number of other species, the bat-eared fox occurs in two discrete areas — the one in southern Africa and the other in East Africa. In days gone by, these two populations were linked, but with the onset of wetter times and a subsequent change in the vegetation of the intervening area, they have been separated.

These quaint and attractive little animals, however, are not true foxes at all. They occur in open grassland or semi-arid scrub areas and may be diurnal or nocturnal, depending on the amount of disturbance to which they are subjected. In the Kalahari they are mainly diurnal during winter, but change to a nocturnal activity pattern during the hot summer. They are usually seen in small family parties of between four and six. The male and female in a pair remain together for many years — perhaps for life. When resting, they lie up in holes in the ground which they either dig themselves or modify and enlarge once the previous owner (usually an aardvark) has left. They may also lie up at the base of larger bushes or other vegetation. They are not uncommonly observed basking near the entrances to their burrows in the early mornings and late evenings.

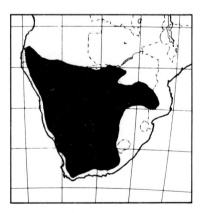

When foraging, bat-eared foxes walk about fairly well spread out, each individual concentrating intensely on locating its prey. The nose is pointed downwards and the ears are tilted forwards, listening intently for the slightest sound which will betray the presence of a small animal either above or below the ground. They turn their heads from side to side in order to determine the precise location of the prey as accurately as possible and then dig rapidly with their front feet to uncover the prey which is then snatched up in the mouth. Insects and other prey are also caught on the surface but may be missed if they do not move. The fox seems to rely largely on its very keen sense of hearing when hunting. Its diet consists mainly of adult insects and grubs, but mice, small snakes, lizards, geckos, scorpions, spiders, wild fruits and millipedes are also eaten. The prominence of the various items in the animal's diet may vary substantially between the seasons.

Bat-eared foxes are subject to predation by most of the larger carnivores and the large eagles. When chased they dash off, dodging and jinking from side to side through the vegetation with their large tails being flicked about rapidly in a way that adds to the confusion of the pursuer.

They may be playful and boisterous, and are very agile when involved in such antics. They may at times growl, but their normal note is a rather melancholy, long-drawn, but not unmusical, whine or a shrill repetitive 'who-who-who'.

Breeding

Bat-eared foxes are strictly seasonal breeders; between four and six pups are born in holes in the ground during November or December. Many of the pups die or are killed while young, and usually only two or three survive at least to a reasonably mature age.

The pups are born blind. Their eyes open at about nine days and they may leave the burrow for brief periods after about two or three weeks, and are weaned from about four weeks. Both the male and the female bring food to the pups at the den, attend to them and are very protective towards them if threatened. The young are, however, very alert and dash for the burrow at the slightest sign of danger.

shoulder height: 30 cm
weight: 4 kg
length: 80 cm
gestation: 2 months
number of young: 4 – 6 pups
birth weight: 120 g
weaning: 4 weeks
longevity: 11 years

Order: *Carnivora*
Family: *Canidae*
Subfamily: *Otocyoninae*

Wild Dog
(Hunting Dog)

Lycaon pictus

Wildehond

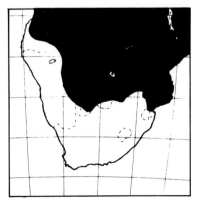

Descriptive notes

These unmistakable African carnivores are about the size of an Alsatian dog and are built rather like hyaenas but without the prominently sloping back. Most characteristic are the large upstanding ears, with decidedly rounded or oval tips, and the (generally) white tip to the fairly long bushy tail.

Occasionally the tail tip is dark, but always there is a fair amount of white in the tail, which is also marked with black and sandy-yellow patches. The blotched, irregular colouring of the body is equally remarkable. The upper part of the face, back of the neck, and irregular portions of the back, flanks, and usually the base of the tail are generally sandy-rufous or ochre (often with a dull orange tinge on the back of the neck). The lower portion of the face, chin and lower cheeks, muzzle and upper portions of the ears are dark brown. There is a fairly broad dark line down the centre of the forehead, and the long, ruff-like hairs on the front of the throat are usually dark brown to black. Irregular patches and flecks of black and white alternate with the yellow of the body and the tail; the size and distribution of these markings vary considerably in different individuals, even in one pack or family group. The limbs are for the most part white dappled with black. The coat is rather coarse and dry in texture, and there is usually a pronounced throat ruff. Although the species is notable for its individual variation, and no two hunting dogs are marked exactly alike, there definitely seems to be a preponderance of black or dark colouring in the northern and East African forms, whereas the southern forms become progressively yellower or whiter generally. The head is broad, with rather a short, pointed muzzle, very massive jaws and strong teeth.

Distribution and habits

The wild dog is also sometimes known as the Cape hunting dog, but now this name is a misnomer as they rarely, if ever, occur in the Cape Province today: a sad reflection of the wild dog's present predicament. Their disappearance from this entire area (they once occurred as far south as the

Cape itself) is largely as a result of their persecution by man, since they can become a serious problem to stock. Massive extermination programmes have been undertaken in various parts of the continent and the wholesale destruction of their prey species has also contributed to the wild dog's current precarious situation. Unfortunately the trend of development over most of Africa means that they will ultimately be confined to reserves: the important thing at present is to ensure that these are proclaimed early enough and are large enough to provide the species with the best chance possible for survival. There were only about 500 of these endangered animals in the whole of South Africa in 1983 and probably no more than 2 000 in southern Africa.

Outside of southern Africa, wild dogs are still found over most of the continent south of the Sahara but are not found in the dense forests of Zaire or West Africa. Their status is rapidly changing in many areas and across large parts of their range their continued presence is unlikely for a great deal longer.

This interesting mammal, unique to Africa, is in reality not a true 'dog' (as in the case of the wolf and jackal) because it has only four toes to each foot — lacking the fifth toe (or 'dew claw') present in all true canines. Hunting dogs are the most ruthless hunters, and in some ways the most interesting predators in Africa. Unfortunately many people have a strong dislike of these animals as a result of their apparently bloodthirsty hunting habits and they have even been systematically wiped out in some of Africa's game reserves as a result of this feeling. This attitude has largely been fostered by the rather short-sighted (even irresponsible) writers of earlier times who built these animals up as vicious, wanton killers in the minds of the public. It is important not to judge the actions of predators by standards based upon our own perspectives and feelings; these wild animals survive by behaving in an innocent, natural way which has evolved over time. In places where they have turned to domestic stock this is usually as a result of man's wanton killing of the game in such areas; without their natural prey they will obviously turn to whatever is available in order to survive.

Wild dog packs do not defend territories but have home ranges which are between several hundred and several thousand square kilometres in extent. These wide-ranging

shoulder height: 70 cm
weight: 27 kg
length: 140 cm
running speed: 60 km/h
gestation: 2,5 months
number of young: 7 – 10 pups (range 2 – 19)
weaning: 3 months
longevity: 14 years

Order: *Carnivora*
Family: *Canidae*
Subfamily: *Simocyoninae*

habits must be taken into consideration when creating reserves if these are to afford the animals proper protection. The home ranges of neighbouring packs may overlap substantially and these are not marked except by urination. There may be mild aggression when wild dog packs meet but they are usually very tolerant of each other. This could be because many of the members of the two packs may be related since there seems to be a fairly large amount of interchange of members between packs.

Wild dog packs are extremely closely knit and unlike many of the more generally lauded social species, such as lions, they will very rarely fight seriously amongst themselves or allow the very young, very old, sick or injured to die as a result of the negligence of the rest of the pack. Whereas lion cubs are frequently killed or allowed to starve to death by the large males or other adults, wild dog pups are permitted to eat ahead of other hungry members of the pack which may have performed the kill in the first place. If the pups' mother is killed, the rest of the pack will bring food back for them. Food is also brought back for any sick or injured animals and for dogs which have remained behind to look after the pups while the rest of the group has been out hunting.

The tail plays a major part in social interactions during which it is held curved over the dog's back. When the wild dog is aggressive the tail is held upright, when scared it is tucked between the legs, and under normal conditions it hangs straight downwards.

In addition to the raucous, chattering *'kek-kek-kek'* cries which wild dogs utter when pulling down their prey, a number of other sounds can be associated with them. There is the hollow-toned abrupt bark which is rather hoarser than that of an ordinary dog (more like that of a bushbuck or some baboon notes) which is usually followed by a slurring growl — *'aough-urrr!'* — as when the animals are suddenly surprised at close quarters. When a dozing pack is so disturbed, they jump up and usually utter these rather sinister-sounding barks and growls, and then make off for a few metres before running around in circles, jumping up on to their hind legs to get a better view over the grass tops, big ears cocked forward, maintaining their singly-uttered hoarse barks or barking growls. They are notoriously inquisitive, and where not unduly persecuted will seldom go far before turning around again for another look. Finally, they usually gallop away, appearing very black at a distance, but with their white tail tips always very conspicuous. There are very few reliable records of wild dogs deliberately attacking man; though, if sufficiently hungry and desperate, they would no doubt be bold enough to attack a solitary traveller, particularly if they were encountered while very excited — during or just after a hunting attempt.

Another sound is the long-drawn rallying or communication howl, usually uttered several times in succession so that it resembles *'hoooo-hoooo-hoooo'* (at a distance it is remarkably like the succession of coos uttered by the green-spotted dove). This has a rather pleasing, clear, mellow tone especially when heard, as it usually is, on moonlight nights, or in the very early mornings, or in the evening. It is said to indicate the rallying of members of a pack, or communication during hunting, but it is not (generally at any rate) uttered during the actual chase. Wild dogs also whine at times.

Wild dogs are most active in the evening and morning and may hunt throughout the day on cool overcast days. On bright, moonlight nights they may be active well into the night. As a result of their hunting primarily by sight, they prefer open habitat such as plains, but may also inhabit fairly densely-wooded savanna, providing that the ground cover is not too dense and tall.

no fifth claw in wild dog

The members of the pack hunt in the most organised, clever co-operation. They will pick out a chosen quarry (where a herd or group of antelopes is concerned), and they will stick to that particular animal with the utmost determination. One or two of the lead dogs will run the prey pretty hard, usually mute, without calls or barks of any sort, while the remainder of the pack simply ranges out on either side, trotting along comfortably at their leisure. When the first dogs begin to tire, they fall back and others take their place, so that the victim is pressed relentlessly. The chase goes on for several kilometres at speeds of up to almost 70 km/h. Before long, as a result of increasing terror and fatigue, the prey's pace begins to falter, and the leading dogs race up alongside and, leaping at the flanks and belly, take snapping bites and mouthfuls of flesh, so that loss of blood adds to the weakening process. In a relatively short time (according to the stamina of the species) the quarry begins to stumble and fall, and immediately the dogs close in and pull it down in a matter of minutes. It is almost entirely consumed (an animal as large, say, as an impala) within about ten minutes. It is when they are actually closing in upon the doomed antelope that the first excited sounds made by the pack are generally heard — a curious high-pitched chattering chorus, quite unmistakable.

As they rend it limb from limb, tearing apart and bolting chunks of meat and skin, hunting dogs growl, snap and utter eager whines and dog-like whimpers. They wave their white-tipped bushy tails in their pleasure and excitement, and in no time the carcass is reduced to odd bony fragments. If the quarry is small and the pack large, they set out once more for a new hunt, and they are thus more or less constantly on the move. After a really satisfying meal, however, the dogs will roll and frolic about a while before choosing some shady spot under a tree or clump of bushes in which they will rest and doze briefly before moving on.

It is frequently asserted how utterly terrified game are of wild hunting dogs, and how they will usually panic and bolt at the mere sight of these bush brigands. This may be so as a general rule, but Maberly, amongst others, has noted that, as in the case of lions and other predators, herbivores seem to know perfectly well whether wild dogs are in a hunting mood or not. They are obviously so well attuned to the habits of the carnivores that they are able to pick up signs and indications of which we humans, with our less acute senses are unaware. Maberly recounts having seen a pack of twelve or more which, after trotting casually down the road ahead of his car, turned aside into the veld and, at the same casual pace, headed towards a point where three waterbuck cows and their young were standing watching them. These dogs had just pulled down and eaten an impala, and they were playful and obviously contented for the time being. One would quite have expected to see the waterbuck bolt wildly when the pack came towards them, but they did nothing of the sort. Moving slowly to one side they halted and watched, nostrils flaring and ears turned towards the hunting dog pack as it carelessly trotted past; but their behaviour suggested alert curiosity rather than fear, and there was no sign of panic. If, however, a pack suddenly arrives without warning in a certain neighbourhood, the game scatters at once, its nervousness being most noticeable. The desperate prey animals often even take to water or make for camps or settlements in order to shake off their attackers.

Wild dogs usually prey on medium and smaller antelopes — particularly impala, springbok and reedbuck where these are numerous — and the females and the young (occasionally solitary old males) of the larger species. Sometimes during the chase, smaller mammals such as warthog etc. are flushed out and are pounced upon and eaten. Selous records a single wild dog chasing a sable bull. They have been

known to chase a single lion from its kill — when desperate from hunger. Conversely, spotted hyaenas have been seen to chase wild dogs from their kill although the dogs are usually victorious in such encounters. In spite of their liking for dog flesh, leopards at once give way to wild dogs and take refuge in a tree, although both lions and leopards do sometimes kill wild dogs. Unlike the other carnivores, they rarely scavenge and normally avoid carrion, preferring to kill for themselves. They are able to survive without drinking and can obtain the necessary moisture from their prey in very dry areas.

Breeding

Wild dog pups are born in disused antbear or other holes which have been lined with grass and leaves. Most births take place in the dry winter months which indicates how important visibility is in the hunting procedure of this species: at this time of the year ground cover is sparse and they are able to see better and run faster, thus giving them a higher hunting success rate and offering the pups the best chance of survival. At birth the two to eight pups are blind and are black and white, lacking the yellow colour which becomes more prominent as they develop. The bitches leave the main pack at breeding time, and two or more usually give birth in one breeding earth with several entrances, hence as many as eight to ten pups have been found in one breeding earth, but these were probably the progeny of at least two bitches.

The pups are the most important members of the pack and will be readily adopted (or even kidnapped) by other females. They are guarded, cleaned, kept from straying, and fed on regurgitated meat by all the adults in the pack and, even if left behind during the hunt, they will be collected and taken to the kill to eat first. Apart from all this attention, the pups seem to be particularly susceptible to disease and mortality amongst them may be very high. From about two weeks the pups are fed on regurgitated food, but are suckled for about three months. They leave the den at about two and a half months and a number of quite young animals will always be noted in a pack (these being usually more brilliantly marked than the older animals).

Cape Fox

Vulpes chama

Silwervos

Descriptive notes

Cape foxes are true foxes and are rather smaller and more slenderly built than black-backed jackals. They are silvery-grey above and more reddish-yellow or buff below, with large pointed ears and a rather short but pointed muzzle. The bushy tail is typically fox-like and is very long with yellow and black hairs and a dark tip.

Distribution and habits

This is an exclusively southern African animal, occurring in open country — typically open grassland or semi-desert scrub — and often near rocky outcrops.

Cape foxes are nocturnal, being most active in the early evening and before sunrise. They move about alone or in pairs and lie up in thick cover or in disused antbear, springhare or other holes during the day — they may also dig their own burrows. Pairs do not appear to be very aggressively territorial although they do mark their home ranges with urine.

The call is a slurring scream or howl, followed by two or three yaps; sometimes the two animals in a pair will duet, the one uttering the first part of the call and the second replying with the yaps.

Cape foxes do not interfere with stock or poultry and it is shocking that they were accused of killing lambs in South Africa and, without hard facts to back up the accusations, were mercilessly persecuted: between 2 000 and 3 000 of these little creatures were killed annually between 1968 and 1976. The beautiful pelts are prized and one cannot but wonder whether this aspect did not have a bearing on the decision to hunt Cape foxes in such large numbers.

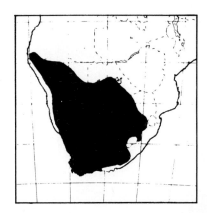

shoulder height: 30 cm
weight: 3,5 kg
length: 94 cm
gestation: 52 days
number of young: 1 – 5 pups
longevity: 10 years

Order: *Carnivora*
Family: *Canidae*
Subfamily: *Caninae*

Their principal food items are mice and insects although carrion, small reptiles, birds, millipedes, wild fruits and spiders are also eaten. They appear to eat the most abundant food items in greatest quantities and their diet thus varies seasonally.

Apart from man, the Cape fox's main enemies are the larger carnivores and birds of prey.

Breeding

The young are born in the burrows, probably during the early part of summer. They are grey with dark muzzles and tawny faces.

Black-backed Jackal

Canis mesomelas

Rooijakkals

Descriptive notes

This species, with its very handsome colouring, is the most widely distributed and often seen of the two southern African jackals. The upper part of the head is sandy-greyish, as the paler tips of the hairs become more sandy on the muzzle and cheeks. The backs of the ears are sandy, as are the outer sides of the limbs which become paler towards the feet. The abdomen, chest, front of the throat, chin and sides of the muzzle are white or whitish. The tail is moderately bushy, fairly long, and sandy, marked with darker hairs, and usually with a dark tip. The eyes are very keen in expression and yellowish in colour. The back is marked with a very distinct 'saddle' of white-tipped and black hairs imparting a silvery appearance at a distance. Male jackals are larger than females.

Distribution and habits

This species is found in southern Africa, southern Angola and East Africa, but is absent from the rest of the continent.

This is the jackal whose weird, wild voice is often heard during the night in areas where it occurs, as, unlike the side-striped jackal, it is a noisy animal. It has various cries, the commonest of which may be described as a rather abrupt screaming yell, followed quickly by three or four sharp yaps: *'Nyaaaa! ya! ya! ya!'*. The call is usually first heard shortly after sundown and its main function is probably to advertise the presence of a pair in their territory which they mark and defend aggressively against intruders. The call may also have sexual significance, being uttered more frequently by females when they are in oestrus.

Jackals, which are largely carnivorous, will discreetly follow hunting lions (keeping silent on such occasions) until the latter have successfully made a kill; and then you will hear the savagely wild, plaintive and almost agonised wailing chorus which the following jackals utter at such times, an almost siren-like *'EEEeeeaaaooouw'* which quavers fiercely on the night air, always fascinating to those who love the African wilderness. A subdued sort of grunting

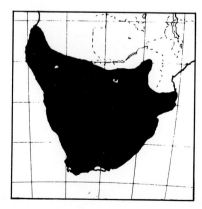

shoulder height: 38 cm
weight: 10 kg
length: 110 cm
gestation: 2 months
number of young: 1 – 6 pups
longevity: 10 years

Order: *Carnivora*
Family: *Canidae*
Subfamily: *Caninae*

bark is often uttered when lions are close at night; and they may 'chatter' when bickering with each other. They frequently utter their *'ya-ya-ya'* call almost continuously and without the long initial *'yaaaa'*, when following and mobbing their great enemy – the leopard.

Black-backed jackals are usually observed either singly or in pairs or family parties of five or six and may be active during the day or night: they tend to be exclusively nocturnal and very wary and shy in areas where they are persecuted, but become fairly tame and diurnally active in protected areas.

During the day, jackals usually lie up under bushes or among clumps of grass in the reserves; in rocky clefts and underground retreats in the settled areas. They tend to prefer more open country and are not found in thickly-forested areas. They move at a light trot, head slightly below the line of the shoulder, tail carried more or less horizontally, the tip drooping downwards.

Great numbers of them may gather at a kill made by lions or other carnivores and up to thirty may be found together on such occasions. While the lions are engaged at the carcass, the jackals will stand or lie about at a discreet distance, revealing stoical patience! Their anxiety is betrayed by the constant restless trotting back and forth, interspersed with stealthy approaches towards discarded titbits. Some of the bolder spirits may even worm their way (with a kind of jerky 'obeisance'!) fairly close to their formidable and dangerous hosts, snatch a mouthful, and dart hastily away. You can watch the same tactics displayed by any starving mongrel haunting the neighbourhood of a butcher's shop! As soon as the lions have moved away, the jackals – and probably hyaenas and vultures as well – close in on the remains, each snatching what he can for himself.

Apart from carrion and the 'leftovers' of predator kills, jackals eat mainly mice, insects and fruits. Young antelope are killed when they can be caught unawares or run down, and reptiles, eggs, and birds up to the size of guinea fowl are also eaten; in fact they may be accurately described as omnivores. I have seen a pair slowly wearing down a sick, mangy adult springbok over the course of a day. After harassing it and biting it until it eventually dropped down from exhaustion and loss of blood, they were able to finish their rather gruesome business. On the Namib coast these jackals occur in very large numbers around the seal colonies and mainly pick up pups that have died non-violent deaths or drowned in rough seas. They also scavenge from brown hyaenas, whom they often molest terribly: they nip the hyaenas' heels and bite their tails while they are walking or trying to sleep. These are, however, dangerous games which will result in the jackal's death if it is caught by the hyaena. In the Karoo districts their damage among lambs and sheep is well known. A pair of jackals will take it in turns to try to lure a mother antelope (even as large as a wildebeest) from her newly-born young, one defying her to charge so that the other can snatch the proposed victim.

The intelligence of the jackal is considerable, as sheep farmers will testify, and in spite of efforts to exterminate it, it still holds its own over much of the Cape Province. Jackals do not require drinking water and can survive on the moisture which they obtain from their prey.

The larger carnivores including caracal may kill and eat jackals; large birds of prey are capable of killing them, particularly the younger animals.

Breeding

Jackal pairs tend to remain together for many years. The litters, numbering about three, are usually born in late winter in disused antbear holes which the jackals modify, or in caves or rock crevices. They may be moved frequently and are fed with food carried back to them or regurgitated by both parents, or by 'helpers' from the pair's previous litter. These 'helpers' also guard, groom, teach and play with the pups, and substantially increase their chances of survival.

The pups may be seen out of the den from about three

weeks of age, are weaned at about two months and leave the den at about three and a half months. Younger animals are more drab and grey than adults.

Side-striped Jackal
Canis adustus

Witkwasjakkals

Descriptive notes

This jackal is about the same size and weight as the more common and colourful black-backed jackal, but its shorter ears, blunter muzzle and generally greyer colouring impart a more wolf-like aspect. Although the back is rather darker than the rest of the body there is no clear-cut dividing line, but along each side of the body runs a more or less distinct whitish stripe (bordered darker below sometimes) and hardly visible in some specimens. The muzzle, chest and limbs are more or less tan-coloured paling to whitish below. The tail, usually more bushy than in the previous species, is darker than the rest of the body (sometimes almost black) with usually a conspicuous white tip — though this also may be missing in some specimens. It is more nocturnal and shy (in reserves) than the black-backed jackal and prefers denser bush.

Distribution and habits

Although less widely distributed in southern Africa than the black-backed species, this jackal has a far wider distribution over most of Africa as a whole. It is found over most of the wetter parts of the continent but is absent in the forests of Central and West Africa.

This is a much more timid, solitary and nocturnal jackal than the black-backed species, and considerably less often seen — even in areas where it is fairly plentiful. It is also much more silent by nature, and when it does call, its voice is lower pitched and the cries more widely separated. Generally, it utters a single yap, followed by two or three in slow succession; sometimes it may precede the single yap by a long-drawn one. Whereas the black-backed jackal is quite often to be noticed trotting about by day, it is decidedly rare to see a side-striped jackal abroad at this time.

They are normally seen singly, in pairs, or in family groups of females with young. They are difficult to catch in traps, as are the wary black-backed jackals, and are able to run surprisingly fast when chased. They generally lie up in disused antbear or other holes during the day.

Like the black-backed jackal, the side-striped jackal is

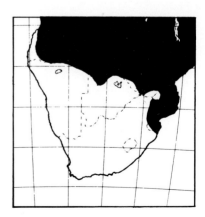

shoulder height: 38 cm
weight: 9 kg
length: 110 cm
gestation: 2 months
number of young: 4 – 6 pups

Order: *Carnivora*
Family: *Canidae*
Subfamily: *Caninae*

omnivorous, eating a great deal of vegetable matter and insects as well as small mammals, birds, carrion and reptiles. They are not stock killers and tend to scavenge to a lesser extent than the black-backed species.

Breeding

Pups are born in holes in the ground during the summer months. Litters usually number five and are initially looked after by the female only. The male assists later in regurgitating food or carrying it back to the den for the pups. Females will carry the young to another hole if disturbed when pups are present. The den has two openings, one of which can be used for escape if necessary.

Cape Clawless Otter

Aonyx capensis

Groot Otter

Descriptive notes

This otter is larger than the only other species which occurs in southern Africa, the spotted-necked otter. It is long-necked, sleek-furred and short-legged with a long, flattened but pointed-tipped tail which it uses as a rudder. Apart from the size difference, the Cape clawless otter can be distinguished from the spotted-necked otter by its overall darker colour, which is almost blackish-brown, and by its white throat, chin and upper chest, which are unspotted; the white extends along the side of the face under the eyes. This is the most obvious feature to use when telling the two species apart. Another difference between the two is that the spotted-necked otter is overall a reddish-brown in colour, the spots on the neck being creamy-white.

The coat of the otter has a beautiful silvery sheen as a result of the silver tips to the hairs. As the name suggests, the Cape clawless otter has no claws on the front feet and only two small nails on the hind feet. Only the hind feet are webbed. These features enable its spoor to be distinguished from that of the spotted-necked species which has sharp claws on all feet and whose toes on fore and hind feet are webbed. The male and female of the species are similar in size and appearance.

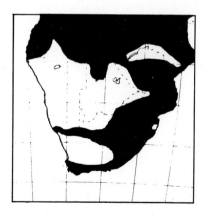

weight: 18 kg
length: 130 cm
gestation: 2 months
number of young: 2 – 3 cubs
longevity: 14 years

Order: *Carnivora*
Family: *Mustelidae*
Subfamily: *Lutrinae*

Distribution and habits

Outside of southern Africa, this otter probably occurs across most of Central, East and West Africa where there is water, but is absent from all of North Africa on account of this area's aridity.

These otters are mainly active in the morning and evening but may also move about at night or during the day. They dry themselves by rolling about and often shake themselves on leaving the water. They lie up under banks, in holes or in reedbeds and these places are known as holts. They are also very fond of sunning themselves on banks when out of the water; they may lie in all sorts of unusual, amusing and incongruous positions. Although these otters are more frequently seen than the spotted-necked ones they are alert, shy and retiring and normally keep to the more peaceful secluded parts of rivers, where there is less disturbance.

Primarily aquatic, clawless otters spend more time than their close relatives moving about on land. They usually walk about but may also bound or gallop in a rather 'see-sawing' and characteristic manner, being quite agile on land. They are seen singly, in pairs, or in family parties of up to five animals. They are exceedingly playful, and families may sometimes be watched swimming, rolling and playing in the water or along the banks, or 'tobogganing' down steep slopes to get to the water quickly. They favour specially selected deep pools where they may be encountered quite often – or at least their tracks may be regularly seen. Aquatic food, for which the animal may dive deep, is brought ashore to eat, as is indicated by the litter of mashed-up crab shells, fish-scales, etc., often visible on river banks and sand bars.

They normally defecate at latrines, but these are usually numerous and not very large. Where they live along the coast, these otters eat crabs, fish and octopus, and in inland areas they eat mainly crabs and frogs, together with some fish, insects, birds, reptiles, snails and rodents. Fish of up to 2 kg or more may be caught and are often played with in a 'cat and mouse' fashion before being taken to the bank to be eaten head first. Frogs are also eaten head first, but the spotted-necked otter eats its prey from the tail first. Food may be dunked in the water while being eaten and once the meal is completed, the otter cleans itself meticulously in the water. Where ducks are reared close to the otter's habitat and are not enclosed, the clawless otter may catch them. Prey is held in the forepaws and bitten, usually in the head, before being eaten.

These otters utter a harsh chattering cry when attacked and may also growl, hiss, squeak and whine. Crocodiles, pythons and the larger carnivores such as leopard probably prey on them. They are always charming little animals with appealing smug faces, and if lucky enough to see these shy creatures without disturbing them, one is invariably rewarded with a fascinating and entertaining sight.

Breeding

Two or three cubs are born in holes, in dense vegetation near water, or in hollows between overhanging tree roots etc. It appears that the young are born throughout the year and, interestingly, have to be taught to swim by their parents.

Spotted-necked Otter

Lutra maculicollis

Klein Otter

Descriptive notes

The spotted-necked otter is smaller and more slender than the Cape clawless otter. This otter also differs in colour from the previous species in that it is seal-brown or rich, reddish-brown, and lighter in places below. Its neck is mottled or spotted creamy-white as far back as the chest; the toes are webbed and they are tipped with long, sharp claws. (*See also* Cape clawless otter: descriptive notes.) This beautifully streamlined animal's coat has a lovely sheen which unfortunately means that it is greatly in demand in the fur trade. The males are larger and heavier than the females.

Distribution and habits

To the north of the subregion, spotted-necked otters occur in Central and West Africa but are absent from the northern and eastern regions.

They are much more closely associated with water than the clawless otters. On land they are clumsy, ungainly and subject to heat stress; a spotted-necked otter in the water is, however, an absolute joy to behold. In even the roughest surf conditions they are completely at ease and in still waters they gracefully glide and dive about, hardly making a ripple. Their speed and agility is breathtaking and they are master fishermen; once the prey is caught it may even be eaten (tail first, unlike the clawless otter) while the otter stays in the water, often lying on its back. They leave the water to urinate, defecate and groom themselves or each other, and sometimes to eat.

These extremely shy and rarely seen animals are mainly active around sunrise and sunset but may be nocturnal in places. They may occur in schools of up to six, but are usually seen singly or as a trio (an adult with two young). When not active, they lie up in holes, under banks or in other secluded places (known as holts) amongst the vegetation or reedbeds. They are normally silent but may chatter when excited, or utter various squeaks at times. Although their sight under water is presumably excellent, they cannot see well over longish distances out of the water, but their hearing and sense of smell are good.

They eat mainly fish, which are expertly caught, usually

played with and then, although not always, eaten; in some cases when the otter is well fed its prey is released. Crabs, frogs, insects and birds form a small part of the diet of this beautiful and graceful animal.

weight ♂: 6 kg
♀: 3 kg
length: 100 cm
number of young: 2 or 3 cubs

Order: *Carnivora*
Family: *Mustelidae*
Subfamily: *Lutrinae*

Breeding

Usually two cubs are born in the holt, at any time of the year. The adults teach the young to swim and hunt.

Honey Badger
(Ratel)

Mellivora capensis

Ratel

Descriptive notes

This thick-set, badger-like animal is unmistakable with its silvery-grey saddle, jet-black underparts and white crown. It is armed with stout knife-like claws with which it digs proficiently and the short, coarse fur and very loose skin protect it well from attack. The overall striking colouration undoubtedly acts as a warning to potential troublemakers, persuading them to keep away from this powerful little animal.

Distribution and habits

Honey badgers are found throughout Africa except in the Namib and Sahara deserts, and also occur in the Middle East and parts of Asia. They are solitary but are also frequently seen in pairs or threes — presumably these are family parties. They may be diurnal or nocturnal; in the Kalahari Desert the animal's behaviour is almost entirely dependent on the season; they forage at night in summer and during the day in winter.

Ratels usually occur in all types of country, both mountainous and flat, wet or dry. They trot along at an energetic jog-trot, head usually held fairly low, and short, bushy tail either drooping down behind or else waved upwards in the air above the back. They often huff and puff as they move along and also utter a harsh, grating rattle when disturbed or angry. They often move along tracks or paths, stopping frequently to scratch down a hole, in a bush or under a log, in search of prey. They are tremendously powerful and dig very well, an activity for which their long, sharp claws are well adapted. The large, moist muzzle enables them to smell their prey underground in their burrows and they can be heard blowing and sniffing into rodent holes, apparently to ascertain whether or not they are occupied.

The badger's diet consists of lizards, geckos, rodents, snakes, spiders, tortoises, scorpions, frogs, carrion, insects and their larvae, birds and their eggs, and bee larvae and honey. Huge amounts of earth may be moved in the pursuit of these items and although terrestrial, the ratel is capable of climbing very well in search of food. Social weavers' nests have been known to be literally demolished as the

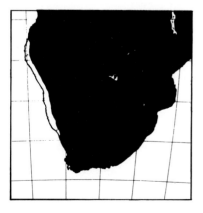

little tyrant searches for eggs and chicks. Pythons may be killed and eaten, fish are scooped out of drying pools, and unfortunately, honey badgers can be very destructive amongst poultry, even when this is enclosed. Commercial hives are also raided. There have been reported cases of sheep being killed and eaten, but these incidents are rare. The young of many of the medium-sized or smaller mammals are probably caught and eaten, and suricates are said to be dug up and devoured. From all this it appears that the ratel may kill and eat virtually anything that it can overpower, but usually sticks to smaller animals.

shoulder height: 25 cm
weight: 12 kg
length: 95 cm
gestation: 6 months
number of young: 2
longevity: 16 years

Order: *Carnivora*
Family: *Mustelidae*
Subfamily: *Mellivorinae*

Like all of the badger kind, the ratel is an admirable little beast of great character. By nature shy and retiring, and peacefully disposed towards all, it will not hesitate to fight gamely against the most impossible odds if attacked or interfered with; and once engaged in such a struggle nothing short of death will overpower it. Possessing a singularly tough and elastic skin, it can stand the severest mauling from attackers without apparent harm, meanwhile inflicting such punishment with teeth and claws on its adversaries that it quite often wins the day. Even lions battle to subdue this ferocious little animal and usually give it a wide berth. It will attack a human adversary in the same way, swarming up the legs and, it is said, very often attempting to attack the genital organs! In this connection Colonel Stevenson-Hamilton in the Kruger National Park records cases of blue wildebeest, waterbuck and even buffalo bulls found dead, with wounds of such a nature and, as none of the carcass was eaten in any case, he suggests that resentment at being disturbed was probably the reason for the onslaught. The testicles had been torn out and the animals in question had evidently bled to death. Even in captivity, although affectionate, honey badgers are liable to be very moody. They may use their anal scent glands when disturbed, but these are more often used to scentmark their territories or apparently to anaesthetise bees.

As its name implies, the honey badger is most fond of the honey and grubs of wild bees, and an underground or otherwise inaccessible hive will be dug out ruthlessly, even though the eager, determined little beast may be literally covered by the infuriated bees — each seeking to drive its sting home through the tough, mobile skin. The honeyguide probably originally learnt its trick of 'guiding' people and honey-eating animals to the site of a comb from the ratel. Bird and beast certainly co-operate here, for while the ratel's powerful claws dig out the honeycombs, the bird enjoys the wax, and what grubs and honey are left over by the ratel.

Breeding

There is virtually no information on this aspect of the honey badger's biology, but it appears that two young are usually born in a burrow or other refuge probably in early summer. The young probably accompany the mother until they are quite mature and are given prey items in response to a begging call which they may utter while crawling towards her.

Striped Weasel

Poecilogale albinucha

Slangmuishond

Descriptive notes

This jet black and white animal is rather small, narrowly-built and weasel-like in general appearance. It is much smaller, more slender and fine-coated than the striped polecat, the only animal with which it may be confused. Its tail is not as bushy as that of the polecat and its pure white 'cap' also distinguishes it from this species. The white on the body has a distinctly yellowish tinge to it, particularly near the rear, but the extent of this discolouration varies between individuals. The males are larger and heavier than the females.

Distribution and habits

Striped weasels have been recorded in many parts of Africa but are unknown much to the north of the equator. They are rare and shy and for this reason they are not often seen, resulting in a rather incomplete picture of their distribution.

These little animals may be active during the day or night and they tend to be found in grassland areas. They move about singly, in pairs or in family groups of about four animals; in the latter case the individuals may follow each other 'nose to tail', keeping contact with each other with the aid of their anal scent glands. They are principally terrestrial, moving about at a hunched walk, with nose to the ground, but may sometimes climb trees. Their calls include soft growls, grunts and snorts.

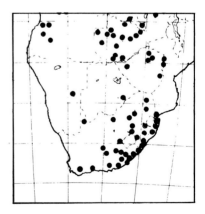

weight: 350 g
length: 45 cm
gestation: 1 month
number of young: 1 – 3
birth weight: 4 g
weaning: 11 weeks

Order: *Carnivora*
Family: *Mustelidae*
Subfamily: *Mustelinae*

They dig well and may even excavate their own burrows in which to lie up. Their food consists mainly of warm-blooded animals particularly mice and molerats. Insects, birds, and reptiles are also eaten. They probably hunt by scent, and with their lithe and narrow little bodies can follow rodents into their burrows and then kill them with a bite behind the head.

When disturbed they may run off at a gallop, with the back prominently humped, but will squirt a nauseating, oily discharge from their anal glands and give a loud bark if cornered. The hair on the tail is also raised in these circumstances. The conspicuous black and white colouring of the weasel is probably designed to warn attackers of this defence in order to prevent them even attempting to overcome it.

Breeding

Like the polecat, the striped weasel gives birth during the summer months in a burrow. The young are blind, pink and hairless but the dark pigment which will later produce black hair is clearly visible. Their eyes open after about seven weeks and they are capable of killing after about three months.

Striped Polecat
(Zorilla)

Ictonyx striatus

Stinkmuishond

Descriptive notes

This richly black and white striped, rather skunk-like creature is quite distinctive. It resembles a mongoose in general form, but has much longer and coarser hair; the black and white tail is very bushy. The only animal with which it may be confused is the striped weasel. The weasel is, however, much smaller, more slender and fine-coated than the polecat. The weasel also has pure white hair running from between the eyes, over the top of the head to the neck, whereas the polecat has a distinctive black band running from one ear to the other across the top of its head. The tail of the polecat is also more bushy than that of the weasel.

Distribution and habits

The striped polecat is found across most of Africa, except the very arid parts of North Africa (including the Sahara Desert) and the wet equatorial forests of Central and West Africa. Although widely distributed, it is nowhere common.

In spite of their striking and seemingly conspicuous colouration, polecats are very rarely seen by day as they are usually nocturnally active. However, they may sometimes be seen trotting along or across a road during the night, and then the brilliant white and black of their coats is conspicuous in a car's headlights; unfortunately many of them are killed on our roads, when they are blinded and confused.

Polecats occur in all types of country, and are equally at home among mountains, in waterless sand plains, karoo or bushveld, forests, swamps, the coast, or even in town gardens. They climb trees when chased, but normally move about on the ground. Occasionally pairs of females with young are seen, but most often they are solitary. This handsome little creature usually trots quickly along with back slightly hunched, and if disturbed, will gallop off and disappear down a hole. If cornered, angered or excited the long dorsal hairs on the back are erected and the bushy tail is fluffed out and raised and curved forward; at such times it utters a series of high-pitched screams, decidedly eerie

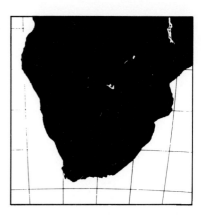

135

shoulder height: 12 cm
weight: 1 kg
length: 63 cm
gestation: 5 weeks
number of young: 1 – 3
birth weight: 12 g
weaning: 8 weeks
longevity: 5 years

Order: *Carnivora*
Family: *Mustelidae*
Subfamily: *Mustelinae*

and alarming to those who do not realise the origin of such sounds. Its main defensive weapon is the vile and powerful scent which it can eject — skunk-like — from its anal glands, and anything saturated with this (such as an attacking dog) will bear the scent for several days afterwards! Indeed, some assert that they surpass all other animals in this respect. Their aim is precise and the volatile oil they squirt can blind other animals. If caught, they may sometimes sham death as a last resort.

Polecats shelter in rocky crevices, under logs or in disused holes during the day but may also dig their own burrows in sandy soil.

They eat mainly insects and mice, but also take snakes, lizards, scorpions, birds and their eggs, frogs, spiders and millipedes. Most of the insects are dug up, or found under logs and rocks; smell is most important in locating these. Larger prey such as mice or snakes are pounced on and repeatedly bitten, with the claws often used to hold the prey down. Polecats may become poultry-killers if their access to this food source is not restricted.

Breeding

When mating, female polecats yap loudly. The young are born in the burrow or under shelter during the summer months. The hairless, blind young are pink in colour, with the chin already showing the black stripes of the adults. Their eyes only open after about five weeks and they are able to cope with most prey after about eight or nine weeks.

Tree Civet
(Palm Civet)

Nandinia binotata

Boomsiwet

weight: 2,5 kg
length: 93 cm
number of young: 2 – 3

Order: *Carnivora*
Family: *Viverridae*
Subfamily: *Viverrinae*

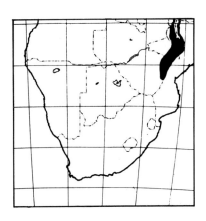

Descriptive notes

This animal looks very similar to a genet in overall build but is more thickset and heavily built, with smaller eyes and ears and a less pointed face. The long, thick and rather bushy tail has twenty dark rings running around it. The ground colour of the animal is buffy-brown but at a distance it appears dark brown on account of the dark brown or black spots which are present on its sides, rump and shoulders. It is also darker brown on the underside. The eyes and ears are both relatively small and dark. There is a small characteristic spot on each of the tree civet's shoulders.

Distribution and habits

Apart from its marginal distribution in southern Africa, the tree civet is found mainly in the forests of Central and West Africa but also occurs in a narrow band from Zimbabwe to Kenya.

The tree civet is also known as the palm civet and is always found in forested areas. They are nocturnal, solitary and almost exclusively arboreal, although they do sometimes venture onto the ground. They move more slowly and deliberately than genets and the tail is used to help maintain balance in the trees by being held upwards rather than horizontally.

During the day they lie up in holes in trees or in dense foliage. They are omnivorous, eating mainly vegetable matter (fruits in particular) but also taking carrion, birds and their eggs, insects and rodents. They can become a nuisance where poultry is not secured at night.

Little is known of this civet's breeding habits, but it probably gives birth to two or three young in holes in trees during July or August.

African Civet

Civettictis civetta

Afrikaanse Siwet

Descriptive notes

The civet is a rather long-bodied animal about as big as a medium-sized dog; the female is slightly heavier than the male although very similar in apparent size. Its legs are short and slender, with non-retractile claws, so that the track is dog-like, though narrower in form. Because its body is usually rather arched, with the head carried low, it appears taller on the leg than is actually the case. Its height at the back is emphasised, too, by the dorsal crest of shaggy black hairs which is erected when the animal is angry or alarmed.

Very conspicuous features are the black patches around eyes and cheeks which contrast sharply with the white around the muzzle and upper lip, and the very short, rounded and white-edged ears. The eyes are fairly small and are dark brown. The remainder of the body is clad in rather coarse wiry hair which is dark grey with a yellowish tinge, becoming black on the abdomen, throat, chest and legs, and the last third and tip of the long, pointed tail. Irregular, somewhat vertically-directed, black blotches mark the sides and flanks — becoming more like transverse stripes on the upper portions of the limbs. There are black bars along the sides of the neck. The tail, bushy at the base and becoming more pointed at the tip, is black marked with paler stripes along the basal half of the sides. The richness and contrast of the colours varies from one animal to the next, as does the detail of the marks and patterns but the striking black and white markings undoubtedly act as an effective warning to would-be attackers.

Distribution and habits

The African civet is found throughout the tropical, subtropical and equatorial regions of the subcontinent. It is, however, absent from the arid and semi-arid areas in the north and south of Africa. They are usually found near water in high grass or other thick cover.

African civets are often wrongly referred to as 'civet-cats'. They are, however, closely related to the genets and mongooses and belong to the *Viverridae* which, together with the hyaenas, come between the cats and the dogs.

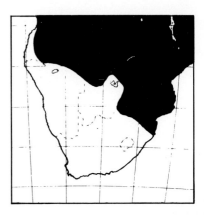

shoulder height: 40 cm
weight: 15 kg
length: 1,3 m
gestation: 2 months
number of young: 2 – 4
weaning: 5 months
longevity: 12 years

Order: *Carnivora*
Family: *Viverridae*
Subfamily: *Viverrinae*

A solitary, nocturnal creature, the civet is very rarely encountered by day, except by chance early or late, and sometimes in dull weather. Occasionally an adult and two young are seen together. Where plentiful, however, it may not uncommonly be encountered at night as it plods along or across a road (of which it makes great use), its vividly-marked, peculiar form rendering it unmistakable in the beam of a good light. It lies up by day in thickets, under thorny bushes, or in holes excavated by antbears, porcupines etc., and emerges for its nightly prowl around dusk.

Although the civet has been reported to kill young antelope, there are no confirmed records of this and it seems a very unlikely occurrence. The presence of parts of these animals in the civets' droppings is probably the result of their feeding off carcasses rather than executing the kills themselves. They kill their prey by repeatedly biting and shaking it, sometimes flinging it some distance in the process. This happens most often when civets are tackling more dangerous animals such as snakes, which may bite them if they hang on for too long. They are not very delicate feeders, simply ripping chunks of flesh, (including fur and feathers) from their prey while holding it in their paws.

This animal returns regularly to its chosen middens, often located next to its paths, for excreting: and such collections of the droppings (which contain seeds, hair and

A confirmed carrion-eater, the civet is extremely omnivorous in diet, eating a variety of vegetable and animal matter. Rodents, insects, wild fruits and reptiles form the bulk of its diet. It also preys on all kinds of small mammals (including domestic cats!) and birds up to the largest game birds; and is a confirmed killer of all poultry when it is accessible. Fortunately the civet cannot climb well, and cannot easily enter a strongly wire-netted enclosure, but brooding turkeys, which so often seek out hidden places where they are unprotected at night, fall easy victims. It also eats frogs, snakes, and even the large, terrestrial snails which abound during the rains. It is particularly fond of the giant millipedes which tortuously pursue their course all over the veld in the rainy season: it chews them up ecstatically with much champing of teeth. All birds' eggs of the ground-nesting types are taken, and bush fruits of many kinds are eagerly devoured.

small hooves and claws of mammals, portions of grasshoppers and other insects etc.) are clear indications of a civet's presence.

Civets mark their ranges frequently using anal glands. This scent is usually applied to flat objects rather than vegetation and was at one time used as a base in the perfume trade. Today it has been largely replaced by man-made compounds; this is fortunate for the civets which were often kept under appalling conditions and 'milked' of their secretion.

Its normal call, rarely uttered, is a series of low-pitched grating coughs, and, when cornered or angered it growls savagely. Civets also scream, mew, click their teeth and miaow under certain circumstances. On the whole, however, they are silent, retiring animals which tend to move quietly away or lie low when confronted. When frightened they may jump sideways from the source of danger and raise their long dorsal crest in an impressive display.

Breeding

Two to four young are born in disused antbear or other holes, or in rock crevices during the summer months when food is plentiful. They are coloured much the same as the adults but with shorter and rather darker coats. Like many of the other nocturnal and secretive smaller mammals there is little information, not only on their breeding habits, but also on most aspects of their socio-biology.

Small-spotted Genet

Genetta genetta

Kleinkolmuskejaatkat

Descriptive notes

This animal is a very long-bodied, short-legged, lithe cat-like creature which is closely related to the civet but is smaller and more arboreal. It has a rather narrow, pointed face, large ears and a long, fairly bushy but narrow, widely-ringed tail.

It is dull white above, with rather long fur. The sides are marked with dark brown spots, edged with rust (although they may be entirely rust-coloured in some specimens) and these are more or less arranged in several rows. The spots are smallish. The animal has a very characteristic and pronounced black band running down the spine from the shoulders to the base of the tail. This feature is unique to the species and is raised prominently when the genet is frightened. The tail has about eight white rings alternating with dark ones, and the tip is almost always white (in the large-spotted genet the tip is dark). The face is grey with white below the eyes, and a white upper lip and darker muzzle. The lower limbs are darker than the ground colour which tends to be lighter in individuals from drier areas. As with human fingerprints, every genet is unique in the detail of its spot pattern and colour combinations.

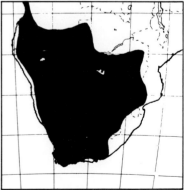

Using the above descriptive notes, a genet is unmistakable when clearly seen in the bush. Although there are many question marks about the precise number of species occurring in southern Africa, two can safely be said to exist, namely the small-spotted and the large-spotted. Further work and subdivision may result in others being recognised. The small-spotted genet can be distinguised from the large-spotted in the following ways:

weight: 2 kg (both sexes)
length: 94 cm (both sexes)
gestation: 10 – 11 weeks
number of young: 2 – 4
weaning: 2 months
longevity: 8 years

Order: *Carnivora*
Family: *Viverridae*
Subfamily: *Viverrinae*

1 The pronounced black band down the back can be raised to form a crest in the small-spotted species only.
2 It has more numerous, smaller and rounder spots which are arranged closer together and in a greater number of rows.
3 It has a white tip to its tail whereas the large-spotted genet has a black tip.
4 It has longer and coarser fur than the large-spotted genet.

The ground colour and the colour of the spots are not a good way of recognising the species apart since this varies greatly in both species.

Distribution and habits

Apart from its distribution across most of southern Africa (particularly in the drier parts) this species is found in a band across the continent between the Sahara and the wetter equatorial regions and throughout most of East Africa. It also occurs on the North African coast and in parts of Europe.

Small-spotted genets are strictly nocturnal, emerging an hour or so after sunset and remaining active until about 02h00. They are fairly common and are more often seen than many of the other smaller nocturnal mammals since they often stand and stare at a light, their large eyes reflecting brightly. They are usually solitary although pairs are sometimes seen. They will often ignore a light completely, and under such conditions they present a wonderful sight for the watcher as they literally glide rapidly about the undergrowth or through the trees with their long tails flowing out behind them and their delicate, lithe shapes boldly marked with dark spots.

They are principally terrestrial but will readily make use of trees when threatened or hunting, and they are good climbers. Although they do not dig, they make use of the abandoned holes of other animals when lying up during the day. They will also use rocky crevices, thick underbrush and holes in trees for this purpose. They tend to inhabit more open arid regions but require good cover and places in which to shelter during the day. The large-spotted genet favours more dense areas in wetter regions. Water is not an essential requirement for this species.

Genets are tigerish little animals and when hunting will carefully stalk their prey before making the final charge. Small prey is repeatedly bitten (often in the head) until it succumbs, whereas larger animals may be held between the front paws while being raked with the sharp hind claws. Although such large items as hares and guinea fowl are known to be eaten, it is not certain whether genets can overcome the adults of these species. Their diet consists mainly of insects, spiders, rodents, birds and reptiles; fruits, carrion, frogs etc. are eaten in smaller quantities when other prey is not available.

Their efficiency as rodent killers makes them invaluable to man as allies against the spread of plague and other rodent-carried diseases. Unfortunately they are among the worst of poultry pests, and the slightest gap or fault in the poultry run's wire netting will sooner or later be discovered by a prowling genet, and the ease with which it can squeeze its long, attenuated, lithe and snaky body through the seemingly most insignificant of gaps has to be seen to be fully appreciated. Once inside, a genet will slay ruthlessly — just as a leopard does in a goat kraal. It is a wasteful killer, seldom eating more than the head and fleshy portions of the breast, so that quite frequently one can eat a genet-killed fowl if, in other respects, it is a good one. When a female has young she will return night after night to a poultry roost which she can enter until she is destroyed (or unless, preferably, the run is repaired and rendered 'genet-proof'). They can climb with ease up the straightest wire netting if there is no 'roofing', and, if trees are closely adjacent to the run, will not hesitate to enter by that means. If threatened, a genet may growl and spit like an angry cat and it also releases a pungent odour from anal glands when stressed.

When captured young, genets make attractive, affectionate pets, and they are exceedingly intelligent. The eyes of a mature genet are amber-coloured, the vertical pupils contracting to thin lines in daylight. The Ancient Egyptians are said to have domesticated genets for household use (rodent killers) more than they did the African wild cats; the latter, being of religious significance to them, were used more in the temples.

Breeding

Genets give birth to between two and four young during the summer months. They may have two litters per year but this is not certain as yet. The young are born in disused holes or other sheltered places, and tend to remain dependent on these lairs for a long time (up to six months).

Large-spotted Genet
(Rusty-spotted Genet)

Genetta tigrina

Rooikol-muskejaatkat

Descriptive notes

As a result of the present confusion over the precise number of species which occur in southern Africa (and how they are defined) a number of possible species, such as the rusty-spotted genet, have been grouped together under the species group **Large-spotted Genet**. These animals are all different from the previous species in that their spots are larger, more rectangular or oblong, fewer, more widely separated and arranged in fewer rows. They also lack the crest on the back, have softer sleeker fur and have a black tip to the tail. (*See* Small-spotted Genet: descriptive notes).

The two species are very similar in all other respects except that the small-spotted genet has a black chin and black ankles and highly contrasting facial markings. The large-spotted species has grey ankles, a white chin and less distinct facial markings. The females of this species are very slightly smaller than the males.

Distribution and habits

This species is found in the wetter parts of southern Africa, being reliant on and often associated with water, unlike the small-spotted genet which prefers more open and arid country. It is widely distributed throughout Africa in suitable habitat. Because of the unclear situation with re-

shoulder height: 10 cm
weight: 1,9 kg
length: 100 cm
gestation: 9 – 10 weeks
number of young: 2 – 5
longevity: 8 years

Order: *Carnivora*
Family: *Viverridae*
Subfamily: *Viverrinae*

gard to this animal's subdivision it is not possible to indicate a detailed distribution pattern for it.

The habits and breeding of this species are very similar to those of the previous species, to which the reader is referred. Large-spotted genets do appear, however, to spend more time in trees than small-spotted genets and on occasions they eat aquatic animals such as crabs and fish. Both these features are not surprising in the light of the different habitats which the two genet species prefer.

Suricate
(Meerkat)

Suricata suricatta

Stokstertmeerkat
(Graatjiemeerkat)

Descriptive notes

Suricates are usually seen in small companies foraging or sitting up near their holes in open country or veld. They are stocky little fellows with shortish, slender-tipped tails, grizzled banded bodies, conspicuous black patches round the eyes and rounded, pointed-faced heads with closely-growing ears. Their general colour is grizzled — or tawny-grey with the indistinct bars on the back dark or reddish-brown. The ears are black and the lips, throat and cheeks are dull white. The males are slightly larger than the females. They are always active, alert and very inquisitive.

Distribution and habits

The suricate is found only in southern Africa. This jolly little animal, the true 'meerkat', was among the very first South African wildlife which Maberly observed on his arrival in South Africa in 1924. During the journey by train from Cape Town to Johannesburg he remembers the thrill with which, from the compartment window, he first noticed the numerous meerkats scuttling about, sunning themselves, and standing up quaintly on their hind legs to view the passing train as he journeyed through the Karoo and the plains of the Orange Free State.

They dwell in colonies or family parties of two to thirty animals and on cool mornings they love to lie basking in the sun not far from the burrow entrances, into which they will pop at the first alarm. Like ground squirrels, they will stand upon their hind legs to view a passer-by. The families of most Cape farmers invariably had pet meerkats among the rest of the household. They tame exceedingly easily and become most affectionate and devoted and, being extremely intelligent, are always entertaining. Even in the wild, once one has their confidence, meerkats become extremely tame. While studying and filming a group in the Kalahari we were eventually able to pick up and handle the animals as they went about their daily business. On one occasion we were even given the task of 'baby-sitting' at the burrow and were only relieved of our duty when we made it quite clear that we would not accept the responsibility by walking away; on seeing this

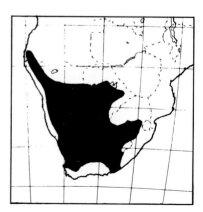

weight: 730 g
length: 50 cm
gestation: 2 months
number of young: 2–5

Order: *Carnivora*
Family: *Viverridae*
Subfamily: *Herpestinae*

one of the adults came running a few hundred metres back to the burrow, to take on the task which we had shirked!

F.W. FitzSimons wrote: 'It is most amusing to watch captive meerkats when the weather is at all chilly. The instant one is released from its cage or chain it runs out into the sunlight and lying upon its back, it spreads out its legs and flattens its body in order to absorb the maximum amount of heat. There it lies in an utter abandonment of delight, crooning and muttering to itself. If the garden is large and the meerkat has strayed, all that is needed is to seek out the exposed places where the sun is shining down upon the ground, and on one or other of them you will find the little fellow basking as usual. When the sun sets it races off, seeks out the kitchen stove, sits up before it and, spreading its limbs, toasts itself.'

Suricates often associate with ground squirrels and yellow mongooses in communal burrows which the first two are constantly enlarging and excavating. The different species appear to use different parts of the system although they may enter and exit by the same hole. The suricates regard the squirrels with obvious disdain and are clearly dominant over them. Even the small babies can sometimes be seen enjoying the power of chasing around an adult squirrel that is much larger than they are.

Suricates are strictly diurnal and will only set off foraging once it is warm, returning to the den around sunset. They may rest in the shade or in a hole during the heat of the day in summer but will remain active continuously all day during the winter months. In the morning before setting off and once they have returned to the burrow, usually exhausted, in the evening, the whole group will huddle together at the entrance or lie around. They take great delight in cuddling and hugging each other and much grooming takes place with both teeth and claws being used to scratch through their thick fur in the search for fleas and other parasites. At such times the young animals may play vigorously, rolling, wrestling and bounding about with great exuberance.

They prey mainly on adult insects, grubs, spiders, scorpions, and millipedes but may also eat rodents, lizards, geckos, snakes, eggs of ground-nesting birds and reptiles, snails, and certain plants. They do not seem to be in the habit of taking larger vertebrates or poultry but I have seen a group catch and eat a baby hare in the Kalahari Gemsbok National Park.

When they are out foraging there is almost constantly one animal on guard for potential danger. The guard often takes up position on an anthill or other high point which offers a good view of the surrounding area. On occasions I have seen particularly conscientious sentinels scrambling up trees to a height of about 7 m above the ground. The little animals have phenomenal eyesight and can distinguish a potentially dangerous bird of prey when it is almost invisible to the human eye. A warning squealing bark from the guard sends the group hurtling down a nearby bolthole. Labour in the group is divided amongst the individuals, with certain animals specialising in guarding, scent-marking, baby-sitting, leading and defence.

These little animals have an extremely large repertoire of sounds in their 'language' including churrs, chatters, mews and whines and they are in constant communication while moving about foraging. When they sight danger or are angry they repeatedly utter a harsh barking sound which they may keep up for a long time (at least until the source of their chagrin has moved off). They are extremely industrious and in a single morning may dig several hundred holes in search of food, moving about fifty times their own bulk in sand!

During the course of a day's foraging they may travel up to 6 km and will normally return to the same burrow to sleep at night. There may be two or three such 'home-burrows' apart from the hundreds of smaller protective burrows in the suricates' territory. The high-ranking males mark the territory, using their anal glands. If two groups should see each other, the members of each will gather together excitedly and begin scentmarking on each other and the vegetation. They also leap up and down in a characteristic prancing fashion and create a cloud of dust by throwing soil into the air — scooping it out backwards with their front legs. Should this performance not intimidate the opposition, an attack may follow (again with the strange, arched leaping). Usually the smaller group retires but there may be some highly aggressive conflict in such a 'gang-war'. Solitary intruders are also chased in the same fashion and viciously attacked if caught.

The principal natural enemies of the suricate are the

larger eagles and hawks; the honey badger is also known to persevere in digging them out of their burrows and then devour them. Black-backed jackals also present a major threat to the suricate band. They attempt to surprise the meerkats by stalking them and making a final charge from behind cover in the hope of quickly dispatching any suricate which falters or does not reach a hole in time. Animals such as Cape foxes, chanting goshawks and venomous snakes would be more than a match for an individual suricate, but when the group encounters such a predator these plucky little animals immediately huddle together in a bristling mob and, by presenting a united front, are able to drive off the potential threat. Meerkats may sometimes

kill Cape cobras and other large, deadly snakes and they will harass these snakes and nip their tails until they are forced to seek the refuge of a tree or a hole. They have a very high immunity to snake venom as well as that of scorpions which are prized food items and which are dispatched by the suricate deftly nipping off the tip of the scorpion's sting before completely devouring it.

All in all these interesting little animals must certainly be amongst the most appealing, charming and endearing mammals in southern Africa and are always well worth spending some time watching when they are encountered, particularly when in game reserves where they are afforded protection from the senseless slaughter to which they are often subjected in other areas.

Breeding

Baby suricates are born during summer in the dens and are left at the burrow during the day in the care of a 'baby-sitter' while the rest of the group goes off searching for food. This task (which entails going hungry for the entire period over which the baby-sitter is on duty) is shared by the adult group members although some individuals may do more than others. The mother is excused all baby-sitting duty since she has the burden of providing her offspring with milk and can thus ill afford to go hungry.

When the young are a few weeks old they join the group on its foraging expeditions; at this stage of their lives all the members of the group help in feeding them with the softer and most palatable food items they are able to find. The babies keep up a continuous loud squeaking which enables them to be easily found if there is food in the offing. They may also follow closely behind one of the adults for long periods at a time as it forages. There may be fierce competition among the young for the particular adults which are known to hand over the most food – the mother being the most sought after animal in the group.

Selous' Mongoose

Paracynictus selousi

Kleinwitstertmuishond

weight: 1,75 kg
length: 76 cm
number of young: 1 – 4

Order: *Carnivora*
Family: *Viverridae*
Subfamily: *Herpestinae*

Descriptive notes

The whitish tail (becoming quite white at the tip) might cause this animal to be confused with the white-tailed mongoose, except that the latter is a very much larger, more shaggy-coated creature, blackish in colour, whereas Selous' mongoose is paler buffy or yellowish-grey. The white on the tail of the white-tailed mongoose extends the full length of the tail, whereas the tail of this species is only pure white at the tip. The top of the head is browner than the back, and the sides of the face are whiter; there is also some white on the forehead. This is a shy, nocturnal species about the same size as the much more commonly seen yellow mongoose which is diurnal. The sexes are alike.

Distribution and habits

This species is only found in Angola and Zambia apart from its distribution in southern Africa.

Selous' mongooses are nocturnal and solitary, although they may sometimes be seen in pairs. They are a savanna species, often preferring more open areas. They dig well and construct complex and deep burrow systems in which they seek refuge during the day and bring up their young. They do not climb trees, and invariably dive down a hole if frightened. They stand on their hind legs in order to keep a look-out for danger.

When moving about foraging, they keep their noses close to the ground, and smell, together with hearing, seems to be the principal way in which prey is located. Their diet consists largely of insects and other invertebrates, with rodents and reptiles only occasionally being taken. Most prey items are located underground and dug up – the mongoose being an avid digger and burrower, much like the diurnal suricate from the more arid regions.

One to four young are born in burrows during the summer months.

Bushy-tailed Mongoose

Bdeogale crassicauda

Borselstertmuishond

weight: 1,6 kg
length: 69 cm

Order: *Carnivora*
Family: *Viverridae*
Subfamily: *Herpestinae*

Descriptive notes

This is a medium-sized mongoose which is very dark brown to jet black in colour. Its only other distinctive feature is the very long-haired bushy tail which is always pure black.

Distribution and habits

Apart from its distribution in the far north of the subregion, this mongoose is found on the east side of the continent as far north as southern Kenya.

It is a very rare and shy nocturnal animal which is found singly or in pairs, usually in the vicinity of hills and rocky outcrops. It appears to eat mainly insects, but also takes other invertebrates, reptiles and rodents. They may lie up in hollow trees and the young are probably born in summer.

There is little else known of this species on account of its rarity and shy nature.

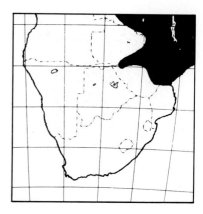

Yellow Mongoose

Cynictis penicillata

Witkwas-muishond

Descriptive notes

This is a smallish mongoose — the specimens from the southern parts being larger than those from the far north. Its colour is also variable, the northern animals being a grizzled-grey and those from the south being rich yellowish-brown. The hair of those in the north is shorter than that of the southern animals and the former may lack the very conspicuous white tip to the bushy tail, which is a useful feature in identifying this species in the more southern areas. The eyes are yellow and the head is very fox-like in many respects. There is a complete gradation between the features described above as one moves from the Cape up to northern Botswana or Namibia.

Distribution and habits

These mongooses are exclusively southern African.

They are commonly seen darting across roads alone, in pairs, or in small parties in the drier open parts of our area. They live in colonies of between about ten and twenty animals although they may on occasions be larger. The warrens may be occupied by suricates and ground squirrels as well, and all three species share in the maintenance and development, digging frequently. The yellow mongoose defecates in latrines near the warrens. Sometimes family groups of four or five may inhabit burrows on their own.

They are preyed upon by carnivores such as jackals, but their major enemies are birds of prey which take them frequently. When threatened they use holes throughout their home range, as do suricates and dwarf mongooses. They are extremely active and alert and can run very fast when the need arises. They are never seen in trees but may sit up on their haunches or stand on their hind legs to view a distant intruder.

Yellow mongooses are usually active by day but are sometimes seen early at night as well. They dig well and find a great number of insects, which form the bulk of their diet, in this way. They have more of a tendency to catch larger prey such as mice, small birds, reptiles and amphibians than suricates, and eat carrion and fruit as well. They may kill poultry if it is not secured behind wire,

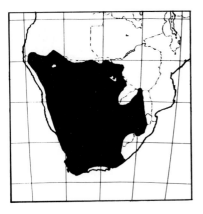

and are more aggressive and less easily tamed than suricates.

Breeding

Most litters (usually three young) are born in burrows during the summer months. Little else is known of the breeding habits of this species.

weight: 590 g
length: 50 cm
number of young: 1 – 5

Order: *Carnivora*
Family: *Viverridae*
Subfamily: *Herpestinae*

Large Grey Mongoose
(Egyptian Mongoose)

Herpestes ichneumon

Groot Grysmuishond

Descriptive notes

This is the largest of the African mongooses and quite clearly much larger than the other grey mongoose found in southern Africa. It has an elongated body and short legs, being about the size of a large cat. The coat is fairly long and coarse and is speckled grey in overall colour. The tail is densely-haired at the base and is the same colour as the body except for the thickly-haired black tip. The body may have a yellowish or rufous tinge, most evident round the animal's hindquarters. Like all mongooses, the grey species has scent glands at its rear, but these are never used in self-defence. The sexes are alike in size and general appearance.

Distribution and habits

To the north of the southern African subregion, this species is found widely across the continent, although it is absent from the more arid regions and the dense equatorial forests of Zaire. It is also found in Europe and the Middle East. The early Egyptians used to keep them as household pets to catch snakes and rodents. They were sacred and were embalmed and buried with their masters.

The large grey mongoose moves about in pairs or family parties of four or five animals. They are active both at night and during the day — the proportion of activity which takes place during the night or day depending on the area.

It seldom occurs far from rivers, lakes, swamps or dams and favours reedbeds, high swamp grass or other dense riverine vegetation. It lies up in burrows, crevices formed by overhanging banks, or under the exposed roots of trees. It is entirely terrestrial since its long claws do not enable it to climb. Although it may hunt in shallow water and can swim well, it does not often take to deep water except when threatened.

When moving about, pairs or families travel in lines, with the nose of each individual very close to the tail of the next animal in the line. The anal scent glands may have an important function in this behaviour, which is known as 'caravanning'. Although normally silent, they may growl or

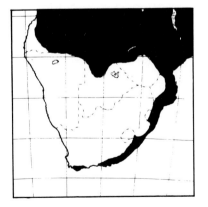

utter a harsh, high-pitched staccato rattling scream when frightened.

The diet of this species consists of mice, birds, reptiles, amphibians, crabs, fish and various insects. Birds' eggs are also eaten and the large grey mongoose is able to dig well if necessary. Although they may raid poultry runs, this behaviour is not very common — probably as a result of their largely diurnal habits.

weight: 3,5 kg
length: 110 cm
number of young: 2 or 3

Breeding

There is very little information on this aspect of the large grey mongoose's biology. Two or three young appear to be born in a burrow, hollow tree or similar refuge during the early summer months.

Slender Mongoose

Galerella sanguinea

Swartkwas-muishond

Descriptive notes

This diurnally active small mongoose is very commonly seen scampering across roads in the areas in which it occurs. It is very slender and stoat-like, and has a rather grizzled or speckled coat of fine wiry hairs which is brown strongly tinged with rufous or grey (particularly on the head and limbs), and its rather long tail is bushy at the base, tapering more at the tip, which has a fluffy black extremity. Its eyes are yellowish or straw-coloured. At a distance it looks a decidedly yellowish-brown creature, with a conspicuously black-tipped tail, although its overall colour is very variable and may be a rich red in some areas.

Distribution and habits

Slender mongooses are absent from the whole of North Africa, the Sahara and the Zaire forests, but are found widely elsewhere to the north of southern Africa.

These animals are mainly terrestrial, solitary and diurnal. They do, however, climb well when chased or searching for birds' nests etc. When moving about on the ground they often use roads and tracks and may be frequently seen in such places, characteristically flicking their prominent black-tipped tails just before reaching the cover for which they usually dash when disturbed. They move quickly when foraging — always appearing to be in a hurry and may often be seen with great regularity in very specific places. When encountered in the bush, the slender mongoose usually retreats into the herbage, whence it will watch the intruder, uttering a long-drawn growling sound. It is very inquisitive, however, and if you keep still sooner or later it usually advances cautiously in a series of little rushes (each advance followed by a stealthy jerky retreat), at the same time sniffing loudly. When suspicious they also often stand vertically upright and use their tails to keep their balance.

They eat mainly insects, lizards and rodents but will also take birds, snakes, frogs, various invertebrates and some wild fruits. Their method of hunting and killing is as for the other mongoose species: they stalk and pounce (where larger prey are concerned) and then bite the prey as fre-

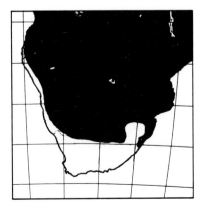

quently as required in order to immobilise it before it is eaten. Although of undoubted value in destroying quantities of rodents, insects and snakes, the slender mongoose unfortunately is a bad thief of young chickens and eggs, where the former are allowed to run free with no strong enclosure. It deals adequately with eggs by thrusting them backwards with its forepaws against a stone, so smashing the shells.

Birds of prey and the larger predators are the slender mongoose's main enemies. It will dive for the cover of thick undergrowth or a hole, at the first sight of a large eagle, and spends the night underground in disused antbear or other holes.

weight ♂: 640 g
♀: 460 g
length ♂: 60 cm
♀: 55 cm
gestation: 1,5 months
number of young: 2 or 3
longevity: 8 years

Order: *Carnivora*
Family: *Viverridae*
Subfamily: *Herpestinae*

Breeding

The young are born in holes in the ground, rock crevices or hollow trees or stumps, but little else is recorded of their breeding habits, except that the breeding season appears to be during summer. Although the young are initially carried by the mother when she wants to move them, they follow her in a procession when they are old enough to walk.

Small Grey Mongoose
(Cape Grey Mongoose)

Galerella pulverulenta

Klein Grysmuishond

Descriptive notes

This is a slender, smallish mongoose with a rather wiry coat of speckled grey. The face is darker than the back, more speckled above, becoming uniform around the nose. The throat, middle of the breast and middle of the underside are lighter and rather less speckled than above. It is a more stoutly-built animal than the slender mongoose, without the conspicuous black tail-tip of the latter, while its hair is longer and looser, and of course, greyer in colour. The females are much lighter in weight than the males.

Distribution and habits

The small grey mongoose is found only in southern Africa.

It is diurnally active and, although it may climb trees when chased or hunting, it is primarily terrestrial. It is quite a common species, especially in parts of the Karoo and is often seen on roadsides. It does not have the slender mongoose's habit of flicking its tail upwards just before diving for cover. These mongooses normally trot along fast with their heads held low and tails extended behind them, stopping to sniff and scratch for food every now and then. They sometimes occur in pairs although they are generally solitary, shy and elusive.

They do not dig well and usually lie up in thick vegetation, in tunnels, in piles of rocks or in holes in the ground which have been excavated by other animals.

The diet of this species consists largely of insects although it also eats mice, carrion, birds, various eggs and reptiles, including snakes. The larger prey is caught after a stalk and a pounce and then repeatedly bitten in the manner used by all mongoose species.

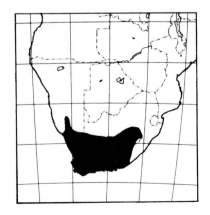

Breeding

Little is known about this aspect except that young are born from early to midsummer, probably in holes in the ground or trees, or in shelters in piles of rocks.

weight ♂: 900 g
♀: 683 g
length: 64 cm (male and female)
gestation: 1 – 2 months
number of young: 1 – 3
longevity: 8 years

Order: *Carnivora*
Family: *Viverridae*
Subfamily: *Herpestinae*

Meller's Mongoose

Rhynchogale melleri

Meller se Muishond

weight: 2,5 kg
length: 80 cm
number of young: 1 – 3

Order: *Carnivora*
Family: *Viverridae*
Subfamily: *Herpestinae*

Descriptive notes

This is a medium to large-sized mongoose which is grizzled light rufous-brown in overall body colour, with a brown, white or black tail. The limbs are darker than the body and the underside is generally paler.

Distribution and habits

To the north of southern Africa this species is found in Zambia and Kenya.

Meller's mongoose is uncommon, nocturnal, solitary and terrestrial. It is a savanna species which appears to live largely on insects, particularly termites, which it obtains by scratching amongst the leaf litter. It also takes reptiles and frogs.

Two or three young are born in summer but little else is known of this rare species.

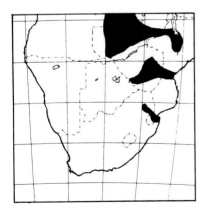

Descriptive notes

This large mongoose is only slightly smaller than the large grey mongoose. It is grizzled dark brownish-grey above and the underparts are blacker and the limbs almost jet black. The hairs of the coat are coarse and wiry and the most distinctive feature of this species is its bushy white or yellowish tapering tail which is usually carried low but may on occasions be carrried arched or erect like that of a cat. The contrast between the dark body and white tail is dramatic.

This species may be confused with Selous' mongoose, but the latter is smaller and does not have an entirely white tail, the white being restricted to a section near the tip.

The sexes of the white-tailed mongoose are very similar and cannot be distinguished apart in the field.

White-tailed Mongoose

Ichneumia albicauda

Witstert-muishond

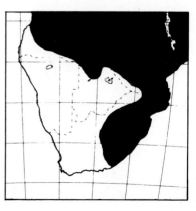

Distribution and habits

They are found in the wetter parts, right across the continent, being absent from the dense forests of Central Africa and from the desert or semi-desert areas.

White-tailed mongooses may be found in wooded savanna areas where there is a good amount of water. They are normally solitary and are active from a few hours after sunset through to the early hours of the morning. Family groups and pairs may be seen together. They are sometimes encountered along roads at night and in such circum-

weight: 4,5 kg
length: 110 cm
gestation: 2 months
number of young: 1 – 3
longevity: 12 years

Order: *Carnivora*
Family: *Viverridae*
Subfamily: *Herpestinae*

stances the glare of the car lights reveals the sharp contrast of the white tail with the dark grey body and renders identification easy. It usually carries its head and tail low as it trots along, giving it a slightly hunched appearance. When approached with a light they will hide in the undergrowth, only moving off when one is a few metres away.

The white-tailed mongoose frequents rather dense bush and lush undergrowth, particularly of the type bordering rivers, streams and vleis, and is seldom found far from a habitat of that type. It is common in the thickly-wooded hilly country of the north-eastern Transvaal. It feeds mainly on insects of various types, although rodents, reptiles, frogs, snakes and birds are eaten in varying quantities as well. Some fruit may be taken. Unfortunately it can become a serious poultry pest once it finds access to an enclosure. It is an excellent swimmer, though rarely taking to water unless alarmed or desirous of crossing a stream. Like all mongooses, it is very partial to eggs: it will roll an egg in line with a stone or other hard object, and hurl it backwards through its hind legs against this, thus shattering the shell.

When disturbed it may freeze and then stand up against an object in order to get a better look around (never sitting erect like many other mongoose species). When it is frightened the long hair may be raised, making it look even larger than it is. When attacked by dogs the white-tailed mongoose fights pluckily, exuding a powerful, musky odour from its scent glands. It occasionally utters a cackling sort of bark. When it lies up, it does so in holes, rocky crevices or under logs. Although it digs well, it never excavates its own burrow.

Breeding

The usual number in a litter is two. The young are usually born in a hole or in a rock crevice during the summer months.

Water Mongoose

Atilax paludinosus

Kommetjiegatmuishond

Descriptive notes

This fairly large mongoose is easily recognisable on account of its robust form, with rather coarse, shaggy coat and predominant dark grizzled-brown or black colouring. The long tail is shaggy at the base, becoming more pointed at the tip. The head is broad and rather blunt at the muzzle; the ears are short and rounded. The body hairs are actually ringed with dark brown or black and pale yellow, imparting a slightly grizzled effect, but the limbs are darker with wholly dark brown hairs. It is about as big as a small cat and the sexes are alike.

Distribution and habits

The water mongoose is found in most parts of Africa where there is permanent water, with which, as its name suggests, it lives in close association. The thick herbage, reeds and other marsh vegetation near water mean that the water mongoose is not easily seen as a rule. Sometimes it may be noticed crossing a road in such localities although more often its widely-splayed and pointed toe-prints are visible in mud or moist sand, together with the mashed up remains of the fresh-water crabs on which it often feeds. It is often solitary, but is quite frequently observed in pairs or family parties of three or four. It is active at dusk and dawn, lying up at other times in thick, dense reedbeds. It preys mainly on frogs, crabs and rodents but will also eat insects and fish. It probably also eats snakes and other reptiles as well as small animals associated with its very wet habitat. Colonel Stevenson-Hamilton noted that the water mongoose frequently scratches out and devours the eggs of crocodiles — in this respect rivalling the large monitor lizard (leguaan) in being possibly the crocodile's greatest natural enemy.

It is an excellent swimmer, taking freely to water when disturbed and may utter a high pitched cough or bark. The water mongoose has been accused of attacking poultry when the latter is unconfined at night near its habitat. Owing to its fairly large size and dark colouring, and its habit of taking to the water when pursued, it is sometimes

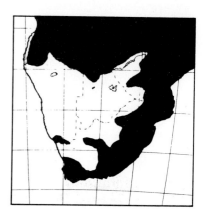

weight: 3,5 kg
length: 85 cm
number of young: 2 or 3

Order: *Carnivora*
Family: *Viverridae*
Subfamily: *Herpestinae*

mistaken for an otter. It may sometimes be noticed moving about by day along narrow stream beds or ditches when these are well concealed among rank grass and vegetation.

When foraging it moves along the water's edge, sometimes wading in fairly deep water. Distinct paths are used when moving from one feeding area to another. They may at times also move some distance from water while foraging or looking for new feeding grounds. Should the water dry up they will remain in its vicinity but switch to terrestrial species for their food. Water mongooses scoop crabs out of their shells, unlike otters which crush the carapace. Eggs, mussels and other food items with shells may be thrown backwards through the animal's legs against a hard object in order to crack them open or they may be thrown down with the front feet while the mongoose stands upright. Food is often dipped in the water while being eaten; this is done with the drier items in particular.

When cornered by dogs this mongoose puts up a fairly good fight, growling and exuding a powerful musky scent from its anal glands — as do most mongooses in such circumstances. When caught or trapped the animal becomes frenzied and panic-stricken and seldom, if ever, becomes tame, unless caught when very young.

Breeding

Two or three young are born in early summer. They are said to breed in burrows in overhanging banks, and also in floating masses of sticks, reed and other litter in the middle of dense reedbeds.

Banded Mongoose

Mungos mungo

Gebande Muishond

Descriptive notes

This smallish mongoose is usually seen in troops and is unmistakable as a result of the distinct banding across its back. The overall colour is grizzled- or dark brownish-grey and the bands are dirty whitish, alternating with others which are dark rufous-brown to black. The stripes run from behind the shoulders to the tail where they are most clearly defined. The coat is fairly coarse and the tail tapers towards the blackish tip. The sexes are alike.

Distribution and habits

Banded mongooses are found in the wetter savanna regions throughout Africa and as they are a thoroughly diurnal and gregarious species, they are frequently seen. They associate in packs, which range from a dozen or so individuals to as many as thirty or even fifty. These little animals hustle about with much rustling of grass and undergrowth, frequently uttering crooning sounds and high-pitched chirring cries when disturbed. Members of a troop sometimes follow one another so closely that at a distance the effect is that of a huge snake winding in and out of the herbage or crossing a trail. Individuals of all ages comprise such a pack, and they hurry about, incessantly searching for insects, grubs, pupae, snails, the eggs of locusts and ground-breeding birds, lizards and snakes as well as bush fruits and carrion. Birds' eggs (and snails) are thrown backwards (using their front legs) through their back legs against rocks and stones until they eventually break and the contents are then eagerly lapped up.

When searching for food, they dig and scratch under logs and vegetation but rarely dig very deeply (unlike the suricate which is constantly undertaking major excavations). They are very industrious little animals, constantly busy and active, using both nose and eyes to locate their prey. Prey is picked up in the mouth and chewed, if small, and is held in the paws and ripped up if larger. Such larger prey items may be violently shaken to kill them. The banded mongoose's method of dealing with millipedes, caterpillars and other animals which exude noxious substances or have stinging hairs is similar to that employed

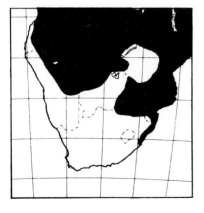

by the suricate: the animal is rubbed and rolled in the dirt with the forepaws until the offending substance or hairs have been removed, after which it is eaten. They are able to go for considerable periods of time without water, which does not appear to be essential to their survival. Banded mongooses often spread out widely while foraging, each member of the pack operating independently. Under such conditions they constantly churr and twitter in a bird-like fashion, in order to keep in contact with each other. They keep busy all day with a rest period over the hottest time of the day.

weight: 1,4 kg
length: 55 cm
sexual maturity ♂: 1 year
　　　　　　　　♀: 10 months
gestation: 2 months
number of young: 2 – 8
birth weight: 20 g
longevity: 13 years

Order: *Carnivora*
Family: *Viverridae*
Subfamily: *Herpestinae*

When danger threatens they all keep dead still and then may stand on their hind legs in order to get a better view. They may seek refuge in holes or thick undergrowth when pressed, but more often they quickly and quietly run some distance from the source of danger before regrouping and looking back to make sure they are not being followed. When threatened, the young are protected by the rest of the group which surround them before heading to safety. When there is no opportunity to flee banded mongooses will fight back gamely, growling and spitting and slashing with their teeth. They have a number of bolt-holes (often in large termite mounds or hillocks) scattered around their home range, and they remain overnight in the larger of these. Some dens may be used for long periods at a time whereas others are only used for a few nights.

Banded mongooses spend most of their time on the ground but if they are chased and are unable to get into a hole they will get into trees which are not too difficult to climb. They also climb to the tops of high termite mounds to keep a look-out for predators.

The social organisation of the group appears to be matriarchal but there is little conflict or aggression between group members. They scentmark with anal glands on prominent objects throughout their territory. If two packs happen to meet they will fight viciously (sometimes resulting in serious injury or death), with the larger pack usually emerging victorious. During such an aggressive encounter individuals of the different groups have been seen to mate with each other.

Banded mongooses are preyed upon primarily by large birds of prey such as martial eagles, and medium-sized carnivores such as jackals and wild dogs. They tackle large, poisonous snakes at times, the whole group co-operating in such an attack. These charming little animals are never known to menace poultry or other domestic stock and must do a great deal of good in keeping down insect and rodent numbers.

Many aspects of this species' social life and general biology are very similar to those of the suricate which appears to be the arid area equivalent of the banded mongoose. There are also many similarities between these two species and the dwarf mongoose.

Breeding

The females in a pack of banded mongooses come into oestrus at the same time. The female actively solicits and encourages the male in courtship and the pair may tumble about and play, with the male marking the female frequently with his anal scent glands. They chase each other about and there may be a number of mountings in each courtship.

The young are born in midsummer in the mongoose dens. Because several of the females conceive simultaneously, they give birth within days of each other and share the responsibilities of raising the offspring. These include suckling and baby-sitting at the den while the rest of the group goes off foraging. The other group members also aid in baby-sitting and also with protecting, grooming and transporting the babies.

The young are born blind and partly-haired. The eyes open after about ten days and they have the fully developed adult fur and patterning by about three months. They leave the den for short periods after three to four weeks and go off foraging with the adults after five weeks. Although packs may breed up to four times a year, fewer than half of the babies survive to the age of three months.

Dwarf Mongoose

Helogale parvula

Dwergmuishond

Descriptive notes

This is a very small mongoose of uniform dark grizzly grey-brown to dark brownish-slate colour. It is usually slightly more rufous-tinted round the head and chest and there are paler areas round the eyes. The nose of this robust little animal is pink and the tail is relatively short. They are gregarious — frequently seen during the day in small parties, scuttling actively about near termitaria, anthills or among rocks.

Distribution and habits

On the west side of Africa this species does not occur much further north than the southern African subregion, but in the east it is found as far north as northern Kenya. They often tend to be associated with rocky areas where there are termite mounds and fallen trees.

Dwarf mongooses are delightful little creatures and always a joy to watch as they scurry actively about, peering into every hole and cranny of an anthill, or clambering in and out of rocky crevices. Always they maintain an incessant conversation of bird-like musical chirrups and whistles varied with crooning notes. They always run in small packs, usually from about ten to as many as twenty or more. They are very inquisitive and not by any means timid.

They are strictly diurnal and will wait until it is quite warm before moving off from their permanent home in a termite mound, under or in a log, or in a rocky outcrop. They may sun themselves at the entrance on cold winter mornings. At these and other times they will groom themselves and one another meticulously, often showing tremendous pleasure in these activities. They also play a great deal, rolling, scrambling and gambolling about.

The members of the group are arranged in a pecking order or hierarchy. A dominant male and female which lead the troop have the privilege of being the sole breeders in smaller troops.

When out foraging dwarf mongooses are potential prey for many carnivores and birds of prey as a result of their small size. Although they may be accompanied by birds

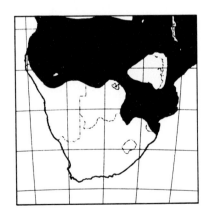

which pick up titbits, and warn them of danger in return, they frequently post a guard in a strategic position to keep a look-out as the rest of the group devote their time, attention and efforts to locating food. This guard duty is shared amongst the members of the pack but certain animals (particularly adult males) often do more guarding than others. Should the alarm be given the whole pack will scuttle for a bolt-hole or position of cover (which they often excavate or enlarge themselves) and disappear. It is usually not long before a small, inquisitive pink nose appears, soon followed by another and another. These temporary refuges can be distinguished from the permanent home by the absence of accumulations of scats, always present at the entrances to the latter.

weight: 300 g
length: 38 cm
gestation: 1,5 months
number of young: 2 – 4

Order: *Carnivora*
Family: *Viverridae*
Subfamily: *Herpestinae*

The diet of these mongooses consists mainly of mature insects or grubs. Earthworms, millipedes, scorpions, lizards, geckos, snakes and rodents, and birds are also eaten; birds' eggs are cracked and eaten in the same manner employed by the banded mongoose, with a quick flick through the back legs. Most food is obtained by scratching and digging under logs or in leaf litter, with both smell and sight playing an important part in locating the prey. Although water is not an essential requirement for this species it is often licked from the paws after they have been dipped in a puddle or stream.

Large snakes may be attacked and killed by the larger members of the group with the others assisting by distracting or biting the snake on the tail. The snake is immobilised by a bite behind the head and then killed with a bite in the head. The dominant female in the group always has priority when eating the carcass. Scorpions are eaten after being bitten on the sting in order to render them harmless;

the risk to the mongoose is reduced as it has substantial immunity to the poison of both snakes and scorpions. Rodents are caught with a pounce and killed with a bite in the head.

There are many aspects of the dwarf mongoose's biology which are very similar to those of the banded mongoose and suricate, to which the reader is referred.

Breeding

Only the dominant female breeds in small troops and the young are then looked after by the members of the troop. The female returns frequently to suckle them and she may move them about by carrying them in her mouth. The young are born in holes in termitaria usually during the summer months. They keep up a monotonous cheeping when not being suckled or attended and are at some risk from younger females who may carry them away from their den to starve unless they are retrieved by the mother.

NB:
In the following colour pages
the names of the animals are followed by a number in brackets,
which refers to the relevant text page.

Opposite page: Vervet monkey (24)

Opposite: Chacma baboon (20)   *Top:* Hedgehog (11)   *Bottom:* Porcupine (40)

Top: Lesser bushbaby (13)   *Bottom:* Thick-tailed bushbaby (17)

Top: Dassie rat (57)   *Bottom:* Greater canerat (55)

Top: Red squirrel (51)   *Bottom:* Tree squirrel (52)   *Opposite:* Ground squirrel (46)

Top left: Rock dassie (188)   *Top right:* Smith's red rock rabbit (37)
Bottom left: Riverine rabbit (39)   *Bottom right:* Springhare (44)

Top: Scrub hare (33)   *Bottom:* Cape hare (35)

Top: Aardwolf (58)   *Bottom:* Spotted hyaena (60)

Top: Brown hyaena (68)   *Bottom:* Caracal (99)

Top: Bat-eared fox (108) *Bottom left:* Wild dog (110) *Bottom right:* Cape fox (117)

Top: Black-backed jackal (119)   *Bottom:* Side-striped jackal (123)

Top: Cheetah (73) *Bottom:* Lion (86)

Top left: Small spotted cat (102)   *Top right:* African wild cat (105)   *Bottom:* Serval (106)

Opposite: Leopard (79) *Top:* Cape clawless otter (125) *Bottom:* Honey badger (130)

Top: Striped weasel (133) *Bottom:* Striped polecat (135)

Top: African civit (140) *Bottom:* Suricate (149)

Top: Small-spotted genet (143)   *Bottom:* Large-spotted genet (147)
Opposite: Small grey mongoose (162)

Top: Large grey mongoose (158)   *Bottom:* Slender mongoose (160)

Top: Yellow mongoose (156)   *Bottom:* Meller's mongoose (164)

Top: White-tailed mongoose (165)   *Bottom:* Water mongoose (167)

Top: Banded mongoose (170)   *Bottom:* Dwarf mongoose (174)

Top: Pangolin (31)   *Bottom:* Antbear (177)

Top: Elephant (180)   *Bottom left:* White rhinoceros (193)   *Bottom right:* Black rhinoceros (198)

Top: Cape mountain zebra (204)   *Bottom:* Burchell's zebra (207)

Top: Bushpig (211)   *Bottom:* Warthog (215)

Top: Hippopotamus (219) *Bottom:* Giraffe (225)

Top: Black wildebeest (230)   *Bottom:* Blue wildebeest (233)

Top: Lichtenstein's hartebeest (238)   *Bottom:* Red hartebeest (240)

Top: Impala (281) *Bottom:* Tsessebe (249)

Top: Springbok (259)   *Bottom left:* Blue duiker (254)   *Bottom right:* Grey rhebok (285)

Top: Red duiker (254)   *Bottom:* Grey duiker (256)

Opposite: Klipspringer (264)   *Top:* Damara dik-dik (267)   *Bottom:* Oribi (269)

Top: Steenbok (272)   *Bottom:* Sharpe's grysbok (277)

Top: Suni (279)   *Bottom:* Grysbok (275)

Opposite: Bontebok (244)   *Top:* Blesbok (247)   *Bottom:* Roan (288)

Opposite: Gemsbok (296)   *Top:* Sable (292)   *Bottom:* Buffalo (301)

Top: Kudu (305)   *Bottom:* Sitatunga (309)

Top: Nyala (311)   *Bottom:* Bushbuck (316)

Top: Eland (320) *Bottom:* Waterbuck (330)

Top: Reedbuck (325)   *Bottom:* Mountain reedbuck (328)

Top: Red lechwe (333)   *Bottom:* Puku (335)

Aardvark/ Antbear

Orycteropus afer

Erdvark

Descriptive notes

This animal is unmistakable in the field and virtually no description is required. Its colour is earthy-brown, sparsely interspersed with coarse reddish or brownish hairs. It is furnished with extremely powerful, bear-like digging claws, and these leave a very characteristic three-marked track. It is about as large as a medium-sized pig and is solidly built with short legs. The viscid, worm-like tongue is over 20 cm long and can be stretched to over double that length when probing for ants or termites. The sexes are alike and have genital scent glands which are used in marking.

Distribution and habits

Antbears are widely distributed to the north of the sub-region, being absent from the Somali Republic and parts of Ethiopia, most of the Sahara Desert and the forests of Central and West Africa.

This extraordinary mammal is strictly nocturnal and very rarely seen by day. Indeed it may be quite common in an area, but often the only indication of its presence will be in the great gaping holes, dug by its powerful claws as it searches for termites, which may arise overnight in the middle of narrow, private earth roads on farms. Such excavations in the veld quickly become overgrown by rank herbage, and many a horseman in the old days, and a car driving recklessly through the veld in modern times, has come to grief by crashing into one of these concealed holes.

Antbears are almost always seen alone except when one encounters a mating pair or a female with young. They are great walkers and may travel a distance of up to 30 km in a single night. They meander about while foraging and have extremely keen senses of hearing and smell, both of which are used in locating prey or enemies; but very poor eyesight. The antbear feeds almost exclusively on termites and ants, and it must be considered an extremely valuable mammal where termites are plentiful. It digs into the anthills and then projects its long, sticky tongue into the passages, thereby engulfing numerous termites at a time. It bends its long ears back against its neck in order to keep the sand

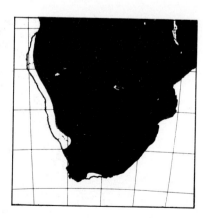

177

weight: 53 kg
length: 160 cm
length of tongue: 20 cm
(max. reach 40 cm)
gestation : 7 months
number of young: 1
(exceptionally 2)
birth weight: 2 kg
longevity: 12 years

Order: *Tubulidentata*
Family: *Orycteropodidae*

out when digging, and dense hairs in its nostrils keep out soil and insects. The seeds of wild melons are sometimes eaten, but the animal's very poorly developed teeth do not enable it to eat anything other than these soft food items.

The aardvark is a very powerful and muscular creature, and it can dig at such a rate as to completely vanish from sight within a few minutes. It can rarely be dug out of its burrow since it is capable of digging much faster than its pursuers are able to. It will simply dig itself a refuge when dawn starts approaching, and climb down the burrow to sleep for the day. The tunnel immediately behind it is blocked with soil once the antbear is inside. An occupied antbear hole invariably has a swarm of tiny flies buzzing around the entrance. Inside the animal sleeps, curled into a ball, with its tail and hind feet over its snout. These burrows are usually used as shelters by many species of small mammals (and other animals), which are incapable of digging their own holes, and the antbear unwittingly provides an invaluable service to many creatures with its industrious tunnelling.

The females have a main burrow system which is used as a permanent shelter and in which the young are born. This is a complex affair, with many chambers and entrances and it may extend deep underground.

Apart from being preyed upon by the larger predators antbears are frequently caught and eaten by blacks, who love their fatty flesh. They have never been heard to make any sound other than sniffing.

Breeding

A single young is born and the breeding season is probably early summer. The young leaves the hole to accompany its mother at about two weeks of age and digs for itself at about six months old.

Elephant

Loxodonta africana

Olifant

Descriptive notes

The elephant is well enough known not to require detailed descrpition. There are, however, a few points of interest that are worth mentioning. The animals have a very thick skin which is greyish in colour; in the wild, however, they take on the colour of the soil in the area in which they live since they are very fond of covering themselves with dust and mud in order to cool themselves and to get rid of ticks and other parasites.

Together with its enormous size (it is the largest land mammal) one of the most unusual physical features of the elephant is its trunk. This appendage is a combination of upper lip and nose and serves the huge beast well as a pair of 'hands'. Water is also sucked up into the trunk and then squirted into the rather small mouth before being swallowed; the trunk of an adult has a capacity of about nine litres. Tufts of grass are plucked, and bunches of leaves and twigs stripped with the trunk and the food is then passed into the mouth to be ground up by the huge molars. The tip of the trunk is extremely sensitive and mobile and is often held high in the air in order to catch a scent wafting past on the wind. It is also used for digging for water and for spraying water and dust over the animal.

The great size of the elephant makes it impossible for the animal to jump even one centimetre off the ground and it is also unable to cross relatively narrow ditches which smaller animals are capable of leaping across easily.

Elephants have massive ears which are very richly supplied with blood vessels; on hot days, as the warm blood from the rest of the elephant's body flows through these vessels the ears are flapped slowly and in this way they act as radiators, cooling the blood and the whole animal. The top edge of the ear is vertical in young calves and flops over as the animal ages.

Elephants' eyes are relatively small and are almost identical in size to those of humans. They are situated right in front of the massive head, thus giving the elephant a very limited view to the rear and making it particularly vulnerable to attack from this direction. The tusks are actually upper incisor teeth and are used for levering, stripping the bark from trees, and for digging. Bulls usually have larger and more massive tusks than cows. The tusks

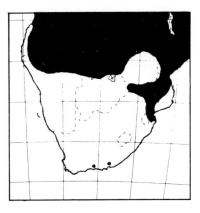

are often different lengths since individual elephants usually prefer to use either their left or their right tusks and this results in the so-called servant tusk becoming worn down or broken; the longer tusk is known as the master tusk.

Glands on the temporal region of the African elephant's head secrete a watery substance which runs down the side of the face. These glands are active in both sexes, and at any age and season. In the Asian elephant, however, the gland is only active in the male during a period known as 'musth'. The elephant is more aggressive during this period and it appears to have a sexual significance. The same has not been shown to be true in the African species and work currently in progress has shown that the bulls' male hormones are present at abnormally high levels when the gland is active and that only one bull in a bachelor herd usually has an active temporal gland at any one time. On the basis of this evidence one might speculate that the activity of the African elephant's temporal gland is related to social communication rather than to sexual phenomena of one sort or another.

The massive skull is reduced in weight by having a 'honeycomb' structure. Males have convex foreheads whereas females have foreheads which are concave in shape. The length of an elephant's life may be determined by its teeth: it has six sets of molars which progressively replace each other and only four teeth are in use at any one time. When the last tooth has been worn away at about the age of sixty years, the elephant is unable to chew its food properly and this results in its slowly losing condition and dying. These molar teeth appear at specific times during the elephant's life and they can thus be used to tell the age of a dead or immobilised elephant.

The elephant has thick layers of cartilage under its feet to cushion them from the massive bulk above. The soles are covered in cracks and these show clearly as a mosaic of ridges on the spoor. Elephants are able to move unbelievably quietly when one considers their size. Often the only sounds which betray the presence of a large group of elephants moving by quite nearby, are the occasional deep breath, the grinding of giant molars and the odd rumble. They are able to move literally without breaking a twig since their feet splay out and mould over objects

shoulder height ♂: 328 cm
　　　　　　　♀: 283 cm
weight ♂: 5 500 kg
　　　　♀: 3 700 kg
trunk capacity: 9 ℓ
walking speed: 5 – 15 km/h
running speed: 40 km/h
sexual maturity ♂: 10 years
　　　　　　　　♀: 11 years
gestation: 22 months
number of young: 1 calf (very rarely 2)
birth weight: 120 kg
birth height: 90 cm
longevity: 80 years

Records
height: over 4 m
weight: 6 569 kg
tusk weight: 107 kg
tusk length: 3,37 m

Order: *Proboscidea*
Family: *Elephantidae*

when weight is put on them, and then when they are lifted again, the foot contracts.

African elephants are of two major types: savanna elephants and forest elephants. Forest elephants are found only in the humid, equatorial forests of West Africa and the Congo. The elephants which live in the Knysna forest are not true forest elephants but are savanna elephants which have been forced into this area as a result of persecution by man. Forest elephants are smaller than savanna elephants, they have more rounded ears, and tusks that are slender and point more downwards rather than forwards.

The African elephant differs considerably from the Asian or Indian elephant. It is larger than the Asian, it has a more concave, saddle-shaped back, a more rounded forehead and much larger ears. Only the male Asian elephant grows tusks and these are much smaller than those of the male and female African elephant. The tip of the trunk is also quite different in the two species.

The closest living relatives of the elephant are the dassie and the dugong.

Distribution and habits

Elephants used to be found right across southern Africa but are today confined to the northern parts of the subcontinent, the Limpopo valley, the Transvaal lowveld, Tongaland and Mozambique. They were reported from as far south as the vicinity of the Cape Peninsula but, since the arrival of European settlers, years of persecution for their tusks and the destruction of their habitat have decimated their numbers and forced them into reserves and refuges which restrict their movements and result in severe ecological problems through overcrowding. The last remnants of the once numerous Cape elephants are now protected in the Addo Elephant National Park, with only three individuals tenuously surviving in the shelter of the dense Knysna forests.

Elsewhere in Africa elephants are found right across the continent, from about 12° north to about 18° south. Their numbers are, however, constantly dwindling and as a result of their destructive method of feeding, when they are offered sanctuary in reserves the effect on other mammal

Savanna elephant

species, and the ecology as a whole, can be disastrous, requiring drastic action in the form of culling programmes.

Elephants are gregarious, normally assembling in family groups of about five to fifteen animals. These groups consist of an adult female (the matriarch) and her offspring, or a number of related females with their offspring. They do not maintain territories and move over areas which are determined by the availability of food. At certain seasons, when subjected to heavy persecution, and for migrating in severe drought, the family groups may amalgamate into large herds numbering several hundred animals. These larger herds are also lead by a number of females.

When they reach puberty, young males leave the family groups to form loose associations with other males. Bulls only join the family groups to mate with females which are on heat. There may be aggression between the bulls over such cows, but conflicts rarely become very serious. Really old bulls are usually loners and seem to prefer solitude to the noise and activity sometimes associated with herd life.

Elephants browse and graze many different species of plants. They are almost constantly feeding, taking in about 300 kg of vegetation each day, and producing over 100 kg of dung. They feed mainly on leaves, grass, tender shoots, the pithy flesh surrounding palm nuts, reeds, papyrus bordering rivers and swamps, seed pods and wild fruits, various roots and bark. Trees up to about 1,2 m in diameter are broken or pushed over to get at the roots or foliage, and sometimes several individuals combine to push over a really big tree. The base of the trunk is used – sometimes with the assistance of a foreleg – in such manoeuvres. Although these habits can devastate areas where there are more elephants than the system can cope with, they are also very important in providing a habitat for the germination of seeds and shelter for small mammals; furthermore they play a very important role in stopping bush-encroachment and in opening areas up into grassland.

These massive creatures also perform a vital service to other animals in drier areas by locating water in sandy river-beds and then digging small wells with their trunks and forefeet. Once they have finished digging they stand patiently and perfectly silently until the clean, sweet water of which they are so fond, percolates through the sand.

There is no more fascinating sight than watching a herd of elephants come to drink. As they reach the water, prolonged vibrating rumbling sounds indicate pleasure, and these are varied with abrupt, squeaky sounds apparently made through the trunk, and the short, nasty screams of anger made by youngsters sparring or quarrelling, or angry mothers reproving disobedient infants (which they will not hesitate to lambast soundly with a blow of the trunk on a small, erring bottom). The adults are all invariably well behaved, affectionate towards each other, and dignified in bearing. Small babies gambol and disport like gigantic puppies, playfully chasing any other animals within reach. Water, drawn up in the trunks, is poured gurgling down thirsty throats, and later the great beasts wade gratefully into the depths, sluicing water over themselves right and left, and sometimes lying down more or less submerged and rolling over and over in the cool current. One, or more often, two or more cows will join in the task of thoroughly sluicing a tiny, protesting infant. Quite suddenly the herd decides to move, and in a moment they shuffle off in a mass, and silence reigns where a few minutes before the atmosphere resounded with gurglings, rumblings, squeaking and splashing.

Elephants drink about 160 litres of water a day and although they are normally tolerant of other species, they have been known to kill sable antelope, zebra, square-lipped rhinoceros and hippo and to chase off warthog and buffalo in situations where they are competing for limited water. They react nervously or aggressively to lions, which may be a threat to the calves, and kill crocodiles — especially when they are encountered travelling overland between one pool and another.

Forest elephant

Elephants' eyesight and hearing are not very good but they have an extremely acute sense of smell. They communicate with a deep rumbling which is produced in the throat; until quite recently this sound was thought to emanate from their cavernous stomachs. A group of feeding elephants is quite noisy as they snap off and tear up vegetation to stuff into their relatively small mouths. If they sense danger every single animal in the vicinity will immediately stop its activity, whether it be walking, chewing or pulling off leaves. Almost as if by magic, the message reaches every individual, there is certainly no signal that is audible to the human ear; perhaps when an animal stops rumbling it communicates the presence of danger to the others. The massive animals stand silently like frozen effigies, testing the air, until they are satisfied that all is well. Then as unexpectedly and suddenly as it all stopped, the activity and noise starts again as the animals commence their feeding and moving about; a sigh of relief being breathed by the cause of the interruption, sitting sweating in a rather puny bush nearby!

Elephants are well known for their intelligence. They have been known to fell trees across streams on purpose in order to create dams in times of water shortage and their efficiency in finding the easiest gradients over rugged, mountainous country caused many of the pioneer roads to be constructed along ancient, well-used elephant paths. They are normally quite placid and well disposed towards humans but if they are wounded, sick, have young calves with them or are subject to harassment or persecution, they are best treated with the utmost respect and should be given a wide berth. Bulls are usually better-natured than cows; young bulls are inclined to be 'playful' and mischievously inclined, and it is mainly they who are often wrongly accused of charging cars in national parks — though in most cases such demonstrations only consist of a few shuffling steps, sometimes accompanied by frightening screams, mainly with the object of driving the intruder away — possibly in order to see just to what extent they

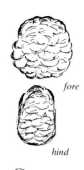
fore

hind

can get away with 'flexing their muscles'! When charging an enemy, the elephant, with ears flapping and trunk dangling, may utter a most nerve-racking series of loud, high-pitched, trumpeting screams.

A beast as powerful as an adult elephant has no natural enemies, apart from man, but there are records of young elephants being attacked and killed by lions — mostly of course when, for some reason they have become separated from their mothers or else have been seriously injured. There have even been occasional records of adult cows succumbing to a concerted attack by lions, but these are very rare. More than any other species on earth, elephants look after group members which are in need. An unweaned calf whose mother is killed will be adopted by other nursing mothers. An injured elephant may be helped to its feet and comforted by the others and they will continue to support, protect and keep it moving for as long as they are able. They may also defend the carcass of one of the group extremely tenaciously, remaining with it for many days. Sometimes the carcass will be covered with earth, leaves and twigs.

The story that elephants go to a 'graveyard' to die is a myth which probably arose from the fact that large numbers of bones have been found together in the past. These accumulations are most likely the result of natural disasters such as fires or floods. There is some truth in the story, however, since old elephants close to death often move to areas where the vegetation is softest since they are unable to chew hard foods with their deteriorating teeth.

Breeding

Although elephants tend to give birth in the early summer, in some areas calves may be born at any time of the year. The cow moves away from the rest of the group to give birth but may be accompanied by other cows which act as guards during this vulnerable period and assist with the immediate care of the new-born infant. As soon as it is able to stand, the calf suckles from the mother's two mammae which are situated between her front legs. It suckles with its mouth, the tiny trunk being bent backwards over its head. Elephants are most devoted mothers and cows have been reported to carry their dead calves around with them for a number of days; the rest of the herd waiting anxiously for her and her pathetic burden. The calf rarely moves more than a few metres from its mother during the first few months of life and for at least the first two years the mother protects it, squirts water over it, dusts it, and assists it in difficult terrain. It is unable to use its trunk for anything other than breathing for the first six months and has to learn how to use it skilfully as it matures.

Asian elephant

Rock Dassie
(Rock Hyrax)

Procavia capensis

Klipdas

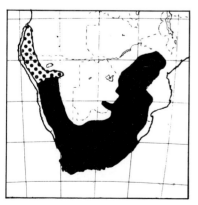

Descriptive notes

This is a small, plump and tail-less guinea-pig-like animal about as large as a big rabbit, which haunts rocky outcrops, hillocks and mountain cliffs. They are often observed basking on the rocks in family parties, which pop into crevices at the slightest alarm. To suit their rock-dwelling requirements, dassies have evolved specialised feet. These are furnished with pads below, and there are four very short toes without claws on the front feet, and three short toes with flattened nails (the innermost stronger and adapted for use in gripping sideways) on the hind ones. The soles of the feet, from the heel to the end of the toes are thickly covered with firm pads, about which Sanderson notes: 'The animals can draw up the central portion of their thickly-padded feet into a dome, thus making a vacuum cup, and have pads that are always moist. With these devices they can cling to almost perpendicular rock faces.'

Their colour is generally a warm speckly grey-brown, darker on the top of the head and the centre of the back, with pale-yellowish spots over the eyes. They are rather paler below and the animals from the south of their range are usually much darker than those in the north. There is a very dark brown or blackish dorsal spot on the back, under which there is a very glandular patch of skin. This spot is yellowish in the yellow-spotted rock dassie and white in the tree dassie. The yellow-spotted species is very similar in all other respects but never interbreeds with the rock dassie even where the two species live together on the same koppie. The females are slightly lighter and smaller than the males in both species.

Dassies are related to elephants and dugongs: some of the characteristics which they share are the continually growing pair of upper incisor teeth (the elephant's tusks), their skull bones are very similar, the males carry their testes permanently inside their bodies, females have hormonal similarities, their gestation periods are relatively long and both species have mammary glands on their chests.

Distribution and habits

The rock dassie is found only in southern Africa with the exception of a very small area in south-west Angola.

Although often plentiful among the slabs and boulders of koppies and the cliffs of mountains etc., careful inspection is often necessary in order to discern rock dassies. Their inert, rounded brownish-grey forms merge completely with smaller boulders and jags as they lie, usually quite motionless, basking luxuriously in the sun. It is worth scanning such places thoroughly with binoculars, and once you have picked out one such motionless form it is astonishing how easily you will notice the many others which make up a typical colony.

No other animal — save perhaps some lizards — seems to revel so wholeheartedly in the warm rays of the sun as does the rock hyrax. This is probably largely because dassies are very poor regulators of their body temperature which fluctuates a great deal; they therefore love an external source of heat such as the sun on cold days. The juveniles look exactly like pocket editions of their elders, and whole family parties may be observed joyfully baking themselves among the rocks; some lying quite motionless, others adopting all sorts of odd attitudes as they gradually expose various parts of their anatomies to the action of the rays. At the slightest cause for alarm every single one will instantly jump or drop into a sheltering crack or crevice; but, as you wait quietly and patiently, one head after another will cautiously be poked up — to be followed (if the surroundings seem safe) sooner or later by the whole animal as once again they resume their attitudes of lethargic enjoyment. Very quaint they look too; their rather smug little faces gazing straight ahead — even, seemingly, right into the sun. On the whole they are silent creatures, but when disturbed by a passing eagle or some other hostile form they will utter the most piercing chattering and vibrant screams.

They are largely diurnal but their activity is greatly influenced by temperature and they may be active after sunset on warm evenings. They feed at any time of the day but are most active in the morning and later afternoon, often moving some distance away from their rocky refuges or climbing high into trees in search of food. They feed on grass, bushes, roots, bulbs and almost any other vegetation they can find, using their cheek teeth for cropping and chewing their food unlike rodents which use their incisors for this purpose. The are poor diggers, spending most of

weight: 3,6 kg
length: 55 cm
sexual maturity: 17 months
gestation: 8 months
number of young: 1 – 6
birth weight ♂: 230 g
　　　　　　　♀: 165 g
weaning: 3 months

Order: *Hyracoidea*
Family: *Procaviidae*

claw

their time browsing or grazing, and in certain parts of the country where their major natural enemies — the leopard, caracal and larger eagles — have been exterminated, and they have increased unduly, they tend to cause serious damage amongst the pasture. They can rely on moisture in their food and do not have to drink.

Dassies have the rather unusual habit of huddling very closely together — all facing the same way — in order to keep warm. Sometimes up to twenty-five animals may pack together in a heap four layers deep in their efforts to keep warm. It is thought that the dark glandular patch on the dassie's back is useful under such conditions in order to recognise who you are lying on top of, when there is obviously no way of moving about near the bottom of the pile! The hair on this spot is also raised in aggression but serious fighting is rare, with such displays usually being sufficient to sort things out. Apart from their alarm call which is usually only given by a single specific individual in the group, they make many other sounds such as grunts, snorts, growls, squeals and whistles.

They can be very aggressive when cornered or threatened and under such conditions can put their sharp teeth to very good use. They regularly use latrines which may become very large over time, and the evidence of these among rocks is a certain indication of the presence of dassies.

Breeding

Most young are born during the wet season when grass is most plentiful, hence the breeding season of dassies varies from one area to another. Normally, two or three young are born in the rock shelters, at the bottom of crevices or in between loose boulders. Their eyes are open and they are reasonably well developed. The young are agile and active within a day and are soon eating solid food. They climb onto any adult's back when young and the scent from the adult's glandular patches is then transferred to them, thus making them recognisable as members of the colony.

Tree Dassie
(Tree Hyrax)

Dendrohyrax arboreus

Boomdas

length: 55 cm
weight: 3,6 kg
gestation: 8 months
number of young: 1 – 3

Order: *Hyracoidea*
Family: *Procaviidae*

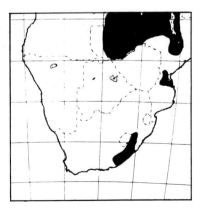

Descriptive notes

This dassie is rather similar in general size and appearance to the rock hyrax, though with rather longer fur which is more grizzled, as the brown fur is tipped with light grey. The dorsal spot (in the centre of the back) is pure white – instead of black as in the rock dassie or creamy-yellow as in the yellow-spotted dassie.

The ears are margined with white hairs and it is an inhabitant of wooded or forested areas only.

Distribution and habits

Apart from the two isolated populations of tree dassies in southern Africa, they occur in a band up eastern/central Africa from the Zambezi River in the south, reaching as far north as Uganda.

This forest dassie dwells entirely in trees, though it is also found among rocks in forested areas. However, the mere fact of a 'dassie' being observed in a tree does not necessarily indicate that it is of this species, as the rock hyraxes frequently climb into trees (Euphorbias and others) present in their rocky surroundings. The tree hyrax is completely nocturnal, sleeping in tree hollows throughout the day and only, usually, coming out to feed after dark; so it is rarely seen and data on its habits are scanty. At night, however, it is often extremely noisy, uttering piercing tremulous screams which begin with a few cackling notes and which are immediately answered from all sides.

Unlike the gregarious rock dassie, this species is solitary and is also rather more sluggish. They browse the shoots, leaves and fruit of trees, defecate in latrines and are less aggressive than rock dassies. The young appear to be born throughout the year.

White Rhinoceros
(Square-lipped Rhinoceros)

Ceratotherium simum

Witrenoster

Descriptive notes

The name 'white' rhinoceros is in fact something of a misnomer since this animal in fact has a grey skin which often takes on the colour of the soil in the area in which it lives. The so-called black rhinoceros is also not black and for this reason the colour of the animal should not be used to tell these two species apart.

The most readily apparent difference between the two is the shape of the head and lips: in the white (square lipped) rhino the head is *longer* and the muzzle wider and more *square* than in the black (hook-lipped) rhino. The white rhino is also larger and has a very *pronounced hump* on the neck just behind the head. The black rhino holds its head almost horizontally whereas the white rhino holds its head much lower. The folds in the skin are less evident in the square-lipped species and its horns differ more in length. The two horns of the rhinoceros are not true horns but are composed of a mass of tubular filaments which are similar to hair and are attached to the skin rather than to the bone of the skull. The front horn is almost invariably longer than the rear and there is normally a greater difference in the length of the black rhino's horns than is the case with the white rhino.

Distribution and habits

Today there are only two naturally occurring populations of the white rhinoceros: the one in East Africa and the other in Natal. In former times the animals were widespread, but persecution by man and climatic changes have reduced the species' range considerably. At one stage there were said to be only ten of these animals surviving in southern Africa and although this was probably an underestimate the species undoubtedly came very close to extinction in our area. This nucleus was carefully conserved by the Natal Provincial Administration and from it the white rhino has been re-introduced to many parts of its former range including the Kruger National Park (in 1961) where it is now well established.

Unlike the black rhino whose numbers have dwindled from 65 000 to 7 000 in the last fifteen years, this species'

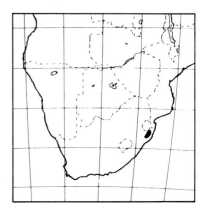

shoulder height: 180 cm
weight ♂: 2 200 kg
     ♀: 1 500 kg
front horn (average): 63 cm
         (record): 158 cm
running speed: 40 km/h
sexual maturity: 4,5 years
gestation: 16 months
number of young: 1 calf
(very rarely 2)
birth weight: 40 kg
weaning: 12 months
longevity: 45 years

Order: *Artiodactyla*
Family: *Rhinocerotidae*

numbers have increased from 35 000 to 40 000 over the same period as a result of the South African conservation effort. The population in East Africa is, however, in an extremely precarious and rapidly deteriorating position with large numbers of the animals being poached annually for their horns which fetch up to US$ 10 000 per kilogram in the East where they are used as an aphrodisiac, and in the Far East where they are used for medicinal purposes. There is also a great demand for rhino horn in the Yemen Arab Republic where it is used in the manufacture of traditional dagger handles.

Apart from its appearance the white rhinoceros differs in many important ways from the smaller and more widely distributed, though not more numerous, black species. Firstly, it is essentially a *grazing* animal, eating mainly short grasses which can be cropped to within a centimetre of the ground, and for which it is well equipped with its wide flat mouth. The black rhino is, however, essentially a *broswer*, eating leaves and shoots principally, hence its pointed, prehensile lip for grasping. As a result of its preference for sweeter grass it is often found in woodland or denser forms of forest in Natal where these grasses are most abundant.

In temperament the two species differ profoundly: the white rhino, in spite of its superior bulk and height, is gentle and placid and rather lethargic; whereas the black rhino is well known for its nervous, irritable and quite unpredictable disposition. Both are equally short-sighted so that poor vision cannot be the sole explanation for the latter's apparent aggressiveness. Provided the wind is in your favour (the animals have a very acute sense of smell and hearing) and reasonable care is taken, it is not difficult or dangerous to approach within a few metres of unsuspicious white rhinos, even on foot. Maberly recounts how, when visiting the Umfolozi Reserve, he was constantly amazed at the ease with which one could do this. As the beasts gradually became suspicious of his presence they stopped grazing or dozing, slowly raised their ponderous heads a trifle and stood listening intently, motionless except for the constant movement of the trumpet-like ears which swung slowly backwards and forwards to catch the slightest sound. Presently they would curl their tails in a loop over their rumps — a sure sign of alarm — and depart at a lumbering trot (with the graceful action of trotting cart-horses!).

The white rhino is more gregarious than the black rhino species and is often observed in groups consisting of a dominant or territorial bull, a number of subordinate bulls, and cows and calves. Player and Feely found that 'the ties between mother and calf are lasting, and females are regularly seen with the calf of the year and another three-quarters grown. Such groups frequently join up forming parties of from four to eighteen in number', but groups normally number between four and eight animals. Dominant adult bulls maintain territories which vary in size from less than one square kilometre to almost five square kilometres. The territories are demarcated by latrines which the dominant bull uses, and by his spray-urinating along the boundaries. If the bull happens to be outside his own territory then he will urinate without spraying, in the same way that subordinate bulls urinate. Before and after defecating, scratching movements are made with the hind legs; the droppings are large and rounded, not unlike those of an elephant. The type of vegetation consumed (grass or leaves and shoots) is clearly apparent on examination of the droppings and one can easily differentiate between white and black rhinoceros' latrines in this manner.

Rhinos must drink at least once every three or four days (usually at night); if water is not available in his territory, then a bull will leave it in order to drink. If he is encountered in another territory then he will normally avoid

195

a fight by returning to his own territory but if a female on heat is present then a violent confrontation may take place. A number of subordinate bulls are allowed to reside in the territory of a dominant bull and they usually remain in or near this area; cows, however, move over areas as large as twenty square kilometres and may overlap the territories of as many as seven bulls.

White rhinoceros communicate by snarling, grunting, puffing and squealing. A number of subtle displays such as pulling back the ears are also used.

Rhino calves are vulnerable to attack by lions and spotted hyaenas but the females defend them very aggressively. Only very occasionally are the adults killed by lions and there has been a report of elephants killing one at a waterhole in the Kruger Park. Most natural causes of death seem to occur from wounds inflicted in fighting; other causes are the result of such accidents as getting stuck in mud, falling over cliffs, drowning in floods and getting stuck between rocks.

White rhinos depend largely on red-billed oxpeckers to remove ticks and other ectoparasites from their vast hides; the birds also warn the rhinos of approaching danger. The rhinos frequently wallow in mud pools in order to rid themselves of ticks by coating their bodies with mud which is later rubbed off or falls off, with the parasites encrusted therein.

Breeding

A female on heat is detected by the territorial bulls which will then actively attempt to prevent her from leaving their territories with accompanying squeals and horn clashing. They will also keep subordinate bulls at bay and violent fighting may result in the combatants being killed or dying later of their wounds. Copulation takes place a number of times while the female is in oestrus. It is a lengthy procedure and males may stay mounted, with their legs stretched out and feet on the female's back, for over an hour. Calves are born throughout the year and can accompany their mother within twenty-four hours of birth. The female white rhino always follows close behind her calf, guiding it with her horn, except in the case of the very young which follows its mother; the black rhino calf always follows the mother. The calf begins to graze when it is about a week old; it suckles for about a year (during which time it moults the outer horny layer of skin twice) and eventually leaves the mother when it is between two and three years of age.

foot (both rhino)

track

Black Rhinoceros
(Hook-lipped Rhinoceros)

Diceros bicornis

Swartrenoster

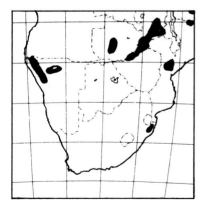

Descriptive notes

The 'black' rhinoceros is no more black than the 'white' rhinoceros is white. The animals' grey skins take on the general colour of the soil on which they live and the mud in which they frequently wallow. The hook-lipped (black) species is best distinguished from its square-lipped white counterpart by its pointed muzzle with prehensile, forward-curved upper lip. The animal is also less bulky and taller on the leg (though of lesser height and smaller size) and also has a shorter head which is held erect and more or less horizontal when walking or running. The neck is longer and the ears are shorter and rounder. The horns are composed of tubular, hair-like filaments which are attached to the skin rather than to the bone. The rear horn in the black rhino is usually nearly as long as, and often longer than, the front horn and there have been occasional instances of three-horned animals. The black rhino also does not have the hump at the back of the neck which is so characteristic of the white species. Cows are the same size and weight as bulls.

Distribution and habits

The black rhinoceros has historically had a much wider distribution than the white rhino. The coach of Simon van der Stel was upset by one near Piquetberg in 1685, and in Jan van Riebeeck's diary for 1653 he records it as 'common on the Cape Flats and on the slopes of Table Mountain'.

The reason for its wider distribution is no doubt on account of its *browsing* habit, there being a greater variety of bushes, leaves, and twigs available for it in more varied country than the comparatively few selected grasses essential for its larger counterpart.

Today, although the black rhino has a wider range than the white rhinoceros, most of this area (particularly in East and Central Africa) is inadequately patrolled and protected and, as with the white rhino, its numbers, which have been decimated in the past, are continuing to dwindle at an alarming rate. The world population of the black rhino was estimated at 65 000 in 1970 and in 1985 there were only

7 000 left. This species is also poached for its horn which can be powdered and easily smuggled past the authorities. The price of rhino horn is now up to US$ 10 000 per kilogram, almost thirty times as high as it was six years ago, as a result of its scarcity. Apart from its use as a supposed aphrodisiac in the East, it is also in great demand in the Yemen Arab Republic for making traditional Arab dagger handles.

In southern Africa, a nucleus of black rhino were protected in Natal just in time to save the species from extinction in our area. From this group they have established themselves successfully in Natal and have also been relocated in many parts of their former range where they are now afforded protection e.g. four animals were released into the Kruger National Park in 1961 after an absence of twenty-five years.

This rhinoceros tends to be solitary, with only occasional temporary associations between individuals taking place. Although the black rhino (like the white species) spray urinates and sometimes defecates at latrines, this behaviour is apparently to advertise the animal's whereabouts rather than to demarcate territorial boundaries as is the case with the white rhino. Their habit of kicking their dung about and spreading it around with their horns may aid in making their presence known. Since they do not have territories, black rhino bulls make every effort to avoid other bulls and for this reason confrontations are rare. An exception to this is when there is an oestrus female around: in these situations extremely violent fighting accompanied by a great deal of screaming, squealing, snorting and growling may take place. These fights frequently result in the death or serious injury of at least one of the contestants. Serious fighting may also take place between adult square-lipped and black rhino bulls, but this is the exception rather than the rule.

Calves may fall victim to lions and hyaenas but in most cases adult rhino emerge victorious from encounters with these predators. Most other mammals are ignored but conflicts between this species and buffalo and elephant do take place, normally when they are competing for water.

The black rhinoceros feeds mainly at night, and during the earlier part of the day and the late afternoon. It utilises a wide variety of woody plants and selects shoots,

shoulder height: 160 cm
weight: 800 – 1 000 kg
running speed: 35 km/h
sexual maturity: 6 years
gestation: 15 months
number of young: 1 calf
birth weight: 40 kg
longevity: 40 years

Records
front horn (southern): 105 cm
(East Africa): 120 cm

Order: *Perissodactyla*
Family: *Rhinocerotidae*

twigs or thorns depending on the plant species. As a result of this diet the black rhino is one of the few species which has its habitat improved by ranching, because of the overgrazing and subsequent bush-encroachment which usually occurs with this form of agriculture. Under wet conditions it will eat small quantities of grass and it spends the heat of the day resting in the shade, often lying down on its haunches or flanks like an enormous pig. Its dully greyish hide merges perfectly with the often dry, desiccated scrub or bush of its habitat and, provided the wind is right, to stumble on a deeply-sleeping rhino in such circumstances is not difficult — with often startling results! Fortunately, however, it is nearly always accompanied by its faithful guardians red- or yellow-billed oxpeckers, which cling incessantly to, or clamber about, its huge frame, eagerly extracting the ticks with which rhinoceros are burdened. Ever alert and watchful, at the first suspicion of alarm, these birds fly up with chirring cries, and the slumbering, dozing or feeding rhino is instantly on the alert.

Its eyesight is exceedingly poor (it probably cannot distinguish a motionless object beyond about 15 m), but hearing, and especially scent, are good. When suspicious, it will stand perfectly still, ears cocked and grotesque head raised with widely distended nostrils as it searches the wind. If its fears are confirmed, it will either utter a few piercingly loud, blast-like snorts, loop its tail over its rump and trot away through the scrub at a slinging, rather zigzag pace until it presently wheels about to stare and snort once more before finally vanishing from view, or else it may elect to come at a lumbering gallop straight for the cause of its alarm. Such 'charges' in the majority of cases are merely impulsive and confused rather than deliberately aggressive. In these cases the tail is not looped over the rump and provided there is time, the animals can usually be dodged or can be made to turn away by shouting loudly.

Nevertheless, in areas where rhinos have been much disturbed they can become exceedingly vicious and dangerous, and they should never be taken on trust, and should be given a reasonably wide berth. The rhino charges with its head held high in order to give it better vision and it is only lowered in the last few paces as it attempts to batter or throw the object of its rage with its formidable horn.

The final appearance of that battering-ram-like head lowered with the horns pointing right at you as he comes at an ever-increasing gallop is alarming enough — even if you are perched, with camera, on the back of a skilfully-manoeuvred jeep!

The average rhinoceros is an odd mixture of timidity, inquisitiveness, pugnacity and nervous irritability. They have been known to charge an oncoming train in Kenya twice in succession — in each event being the worse for the encounter. A young calf will guard the carcass of its shot mother with pathetic gallantry, repeatedly charging, with shrill squeals of rage, anything that approaches, regardless of size. Black rhinos differ greatly in individual temperament, and they also tend to vary locally in this respect: those in disturbed areas are invariably more savage and aggressively inclined than those in conserved areas. However, one has always to beware of the odd naturally truculent individual.

Every adult black rhino in Natal develops sores, normally on the shoulders, which discharge quantities of blood and fluid. Until quite recently these sores were thought to have a sexual significance but they have been found to be caused by a filiaria parasite. These lesions are found on the chest and sides of younger animals but occur behind the shoulders of adults. They are aggravated by the attentions of the oxpeckers and even occur on perfectly healthy animals.

Black rhinoceros normally drink in the evening or at night, sometimes travelling long distances to water. They are noisy and very quarrelsome. If they should gather at a solitary waterhole, they chase one another about and brawl over 'water-rights'. On such occasions they can produce some quite extraordinary sounds — ranging from deep hippo-like grunts or short roars to high-pitched squeals of indignation, and, of course, the usual locomotive-like snorts.

Breeding

Courtship in the black rhinoceros may last several hours and is a complex procedure. The ritual involves the squirting of urine by the female, horning of the cow by the bull, the cow attacking the bull at times and sparring bouts with the horns. The bull may mount the cow a number of times before successfully copulating; an act which may take thirty minutes or more, with the cow emitting periodic low-pitched squeals.

Female black rhinos drop a single calf at any season about once every three years. It can walk and suckle within three hours of birth and starts to browse after a few weeks. If they are separated the mother and calf communicate with each other with high-pitched mews and squeals. Many young rhino calves are killed by lions and spotted hyaenas but things are not always easy for the predators and a cow rhino has been known to kill a lion in defence of her calf. The calf will be rejected (sometimes violently) by the mother during her next pregnancy or when her next calf is born. The rhino is sexually mature at six years of age.

Cape Mountain Zebra

Equus zebra zebra

Kaapse Bergsebra

Descriptive notes

The Cape mountain zebra can be distinguished from the Burchell's zebra by the lack of *shadow stripes* on the hindquarters, the presence of a distinct *dewlap,* and the *'gridiron'* pattern of stripes across the top of the rump. In this species the black stripes do not go right around the body as they do in the Burchell's zebra. It also has larger ears than the Burchell's although it is a slightly smaller and lighter animal. These two species should not be confused in the wild since their areas of distribution are widely separated.

Distribution and habits

As in the case of the quagga, the reduction to the verge of extinction (the total wild population was probably as low as about thirty animals during the 1940s and '50s) of the Cape mountain zebra must be laid at the door of the early white settlers, who apparently hunted it for its meat. Fortunately, however, a number of farmers were sufficiently far-sighted and considerate to preserve herds on their properties, and it is entirely to them that we owe the survival of the species, since these animals have always been confined to the southern Cape mountains.

Cape mountain zebras normally live in groups of about five animals but these may number as few as two animals or as many as thirteen. As in the other zebra species these groups consist of a stallion, one or more females and their foals. Young stallions leave the herd voluntarily at about two years of age; they then form or join 'bachelor' herds in which they remain until they are able to establish themselves as lead stallions with a herd of their own. This may involve vicious fights with the current lead stallion, in which severe injuries are sometimes sustained through kicking and biting. The groups are, however, very stable and stallions have been known to remain in control of groups for up to fifteen years. A clearly defined hierarchy or pecking-order exists in the breeding and bachelor groups and the stallion is always dominant in the former.

The zebras communicate with high-pitched alarm calls, alarm snorts and squeals and, as with the Burchell's zebra,

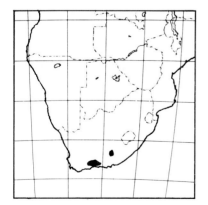

the stallion will allow mares with foals to run first if danger threatens, while he defends the group. These animals require a supply of drinking water in order to survive and prefer clear water to muddy water. Although they are predominantly grazers, they will occasionally browse from bushes and trees. Like all zebras, Cape mountain zebras enjoy dust-bathing and they also spend time grooming themselves and each other to keep their coats in peak condition. This species does not appear to associate with other antelope in the way that the Burchell's zebra does.

shoulder height: 127 cm
weight ♂: 255 kg
♀: 245 kg
gestation: 12 months
number of young: 1 foal
longevity: 22 years

Order: *Perissodactyla*
Family: *Equidae*

Breeding

Foals are born throughout the year but there is a peak in births in midsummer. Mares produce foals about every eighteen months. The foals are defended vigorously by the mothers (they even keep other group members at a distance), and are able to nibble grass at a few days. For about the first three months the foals nibble bits of the adults' faeces (particularly those of their mothers) and this behaviour probably enables them to obtain the microorganisms which they need to help in the digestion of plant matter. This behaviour also occurs in the Burchell's zebra.

Hartmann's Mountain Zebra

Equus zebra hartmannae

Hartmann se Bergsebra

Descriptive notes

The Hartmann's mountain zebra is not a distinct species from the Cape mountain zebra. The two are subspecies and are thus very closely related. This zebra is larger than the Cape mountain and the Burchell's zebras, the males standing 1,5 m at the shoulder and weighing approximately 300 kg.

Distribution and habits

Hartmann's zebras are found in more arid mountainous areas in Namibia and southern Angola as opposed to the Cape mountain zebra which is found in the mountains of the south-eastern Cape. They are less dependent on water, and migrate larger distances in response to food and water availability than the Cape species. As a result of the nature of the substrate on which these zebras live, they have extremely fast-growing hooves and are extremely agile under even the most treacherous and steep mountain conditions. The habits and social organisation of this species are generally very similar to their closely-related species except that they tend to form large herds when migrating.

They are also subject to predation by lions, spotted hyaenas, leopard and cheetah; these predators have, however, largely been eradicated by man in the Cape zebra's area. Hartmann's zebras defend their foals extremely aggressively and a stallion has been known to kick an adult spotted hyaena to death and then to continue mutilating the carcass by kicking it over a distance of about a hundred metres!

As a result of the heat in the areas in which they live, Hartmann's zebras tend to rest in the shade of thorn bushes during the hotter times of the day and are most active, grazing and moving, in the morning and late afternoon. They are extremely fond of dust-bathing and will also dig deep pits in order to find water in dry river beds.

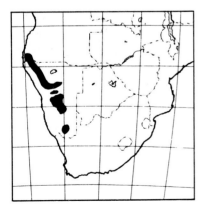

Burchell's Zebra

Equus burchelli

Bontsebra

Descriptive notes

Zebras are well known and easily recognisable by their characteristic stripes. Just as humans all have different fingerprints, so no two zebras have exactly the same pattern of stripes. General features can, however, be used in order to distinguish the different species apart. The Burchell's zebra, the most common zebra in southern Africa, differs from the less common mountain zebras in the following general ways: it has clear brownish or grey *shadow stripes* between the thick black stripes on the hindquarters (these are absent in the mountain zebras); it does not have the series of parallel stripes (or *'gridiron'*) which are found across the top of the rump and base of the tail in the mountain zebras; the *dewlap* (loose flap of skin under the throat) of the mountain zebras is also absent in this species and the black stripes continue right around the body unlike the mountain zebras which are pure white on the underside. Stallions can be recognised from the mares by their thicker necks but otherwise the sexes are alike.

Distribution and habits

Like almost all large mammal species in southern Africa, the range of Burchell's zebra has been considerably compressed since the arrival of the white colonists in the Cape. They probably used to occur across the subcontinent north of the Orange River. Outside southern Africa, they are today found across most of East Africa as far north as southern Sudan and Ethiopia. Apart from their occurrence in the game reserves of our area, small numbers have been re-introduced to a large part of their former range on private property.

Burchell's zebras are gregarious and live in family groups numbering up to twenty individuals, although in most parts of southern Africa, where densities are fairly low, the groups usually consist of four or five animals. These groups are composed of a lead stallion together with one or more mares and their foals. Other stallions are thrown out of the group and these may form 'bachelor' herds.

These animals are highly dependent on water and the

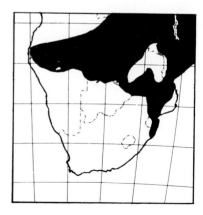

shoulder height: 136 cm
weight: 320 kg
gestation: 12 months
number of young: 1 foal
weaning: 11 months
longevity: 22 years

Order: *Perissodactyla*
Family: *Equidae*

family groups may assemble in herds of many hundreds when migrating during the dry season or in periods of drought. Such annual movements take place in the Nxai pan area of Botswana. Watching a few thousand Burchell's zebras congregating on these great plains is certainly one of the most spectacular wildlife sights to be seen in southern Africa. Such an experience immediately brings to mind the stories of the massive South African game movements which have tragically become chapters in our history books rather than features of our wildlife heritage.

The zebras' richly-striped coats always render them spectacular and they somehow always seem to look plump and in good condition even when the other game is in very poor condition. Possible functions of the stripes are to help camouflage the animals under specific light conditions and to confuse predators when they try to single out an individual in the group. They frequently associate with blue wildebeest or other sociable antelopes (sometimes even with ostriches). The reason for this may be that since the zebras prefer longer grass and the wildebeest short grass, by associating with the former, the wildebeest have a constant supply of their preferred food available. By forming larger, mixed herds each species benefits from the vigilance of the other and both are thus less likely to be caught by predators. Also, since wildebeest are the preferred prey of most of the carnivores, by staying near to them, the zebra are effectively decreasing their risk because the predators will usually attack the wildebeest in preference to themselves.

Zebras are noisy, restless creatures; and when alarmed or assembling at a drinking place, they constantly utter a very characteristic barking whinny. This usually begins with a whistling intake of breath, quickly followed by a succession of calls rather resembling: *'Kwa-ha! Kwa-ha! Kwa-ha-ha-ha!'* It is an excited, almost hysterical sort of cry, not without charm, and frequently audible at night where these creatures occur. By all accounts the cry of the now extinct quagga was practically identical, and from this it took its name among the Hottentots and Bushmen.

Since zebras are almost exclusively grass-eaters, they occur most plentifully in open, grassy plains, or in well-grassed, lightly-wooded savanna or thorn bushveld. Most areas of the Kruger National Park are thus marginal for them and they are severely affected by bush-encroachment; a phenomenon which is becoming alarmingly prevalent in many parts of southern Africa as a result of overgrazing. Young, sprouting grass is the Burchell's zebras' favourite food and they will move to recently burnt areas in search of such grazing. Where this is not available, they will eat longer grass and even browse twigs and shoots from trees and bushes to a small extent.

Although zebras are subject to heavy predation, and will normally flee when confronted by a predator, the lead stallion will defend his group courageously and females will not hesitate to do everything possible to defend their foals. The hooves and teeth are used in defence and attack; mares have been known to kill spotted hyaenas and Maberly recounts how the body of a poacher was found in a badly mutilated and disabled condition. From the tracks it appeared that he had killed a zebra foal and that the whole group had then attacked him and kicked and bitten him to death. Inexperienced young lions have frequently been beaten off and severely mauled by zebra stallions. When under attack the stallion will take up the rear while the group flees; in large herds the stallion groups move on the sides and at the rear in the same way. Rival stallions may also fight violently, often lacerating each other badly but never fighting to the death.

Breeding

The lead stallion ascertains whether the females in the group are in oestrus by urine sniffing and by exhibiting 'flehmen' (a characteristic behaviour in which the head is held high, the lips pulled back, and the nostrils flared while sniffing the rear of the female).

The foals may be born at any time of the year but most are born during the summer months. The female stays close to the group while giving birth and guards her foal very conscientiously until it is quite capable of looking after itself; she will even chase other zebras which venture too near. If danger threatens, the mare and her foal will run in front of the rest of the group and are thus defended by them.

Zebras will breed with donkeys to produce 'zebdonks'. These animals have stripes on the legs and sometimes up the rump, but are infertile.

Bushpig

Potamochoerus porcus

Bosvark

Descriptive notes

The bushpig is much the same size as the warthog but is a lighter animal which is more like a typical pig in general appearance. Bushpigs are also much less frequently seen because they are almost exclusively nocturnal, especially in areas in which they are in conflict with man; they also stick to very dense, thick bush which makes visibility difficult or impossible. They are covered in coarse, wiry bristles which form a mane-like erectile crest along the top of the head, neck and shoulders. This crest is usually dirty white in colour, contrasting with the reddish- to greyish-brown of the flanks and rump. The ears are tipped with long, pencilled tufts of dark hair as opposed to the warthog's bare-tipped ears. The tusks are short and knife-like and the tail is carried hanging down when running.

Distribution and habits

Although bushpigs are widely distributed across most of Central Africa and the eastern fringe of southern Africa, they require water and forests, thickets or reedbeds, and are thus patchily distributed within this wide range and are absent from most of our subregion which is either too arid or too open for them. They have taken advantage of man's crops where these are grown in 'bushpig country' and their numbers can increase dramatically under such conditions. They are also very difficult to control since they are cunning and wary and live in inaccessible and impenetrable areas and then move into the crops under cover of darkness.

These wild pigs are gregarious, living in groups, or sounders, of five to ten animals but occasionally coming together into groups of thirty or more. The sounder consists of a number of sows and their young offspring and a dominant boar and his sow which control the group with a rigorous discipline. Maberly once heard an errant youngster, which had lingered inattentively behind when the boar had warned the rest to depart from a mealie land on suspicion of danger, receiving decided chastisement (judging by his squeals) when he finally hastily joined his sounder! The boar leads the piglets to feeding grounds and

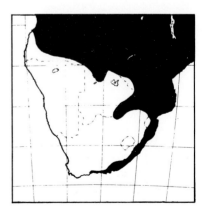

shoulder height: 760 cm
weight ♂: 62 kg
     ♀: 60 kg
tusks (average): 7 cm
    (record): 19 cm
gestation: 4 months
number of young: 3 – 8 piglets
birth weight: 700 g
longevity: 15 years

Order: *Artiodactyla*
Family: *Suidae*

courageously defends them if danger threatens. Boars (or sows with young) can be extremely aggressive but will not, as a rule, attack humans unless cornered, wounded or when with piglets.

Usually the boar emits at first an ominous-sounding, deep warning grunt and may charge dogs on sight. They can cause the most fearful slashing wounds with the ripping action of their knife-like canines, and many dogs have been killed or badly wounded by an infuriated boar. The boar sometimes follows up an intruder from concealment in cover, uttering his harsh grunt from time to time in order to see the object of his outrage 'off the premises'. The boars may compete for feeding grounds but these interactions usually take the form of threat display with little more than some jousting and head pushing taking place until one of the contestants decides to give in and turns and runs, with the rest of his humiliated sounder hot on his heels.

Even where plentiful, bushpigs are seldom seen by day, except in dull or wet weather, as they are strictly nocturnal feeders as a general rule – particularly in settled country. However, in the wilder parts, and in areas where they are undisturbed, they sometimes move about in the late afternoon, particularly when certain species of wild fruits are in season. Bushpigs sleep or rest during the day in any dense cover where they are unlikely to be disturbed, but remain alert to possible danger at all times. When flushed, the members of the sounder all rush off, with dorsal crests raised, through the undergrowth in different directions, regardless of how dense it may be; they frequently become almost hidden from view under masses of tangled vegetation caught up in their headlong flight. They then regroup once the danger has passed. Bushpigs usually emerge about dusk or shortly after, and often travel some distance (up to 4 km) to their feeding grounds along well-used, clearly-defined paths.

They root and dig with their snouts for various food items which they locate by means of their very keen sense of smell. Bushpigs are omnivorous, devouring grass, roots, seeds and wild fruits, insects, snakes and other reptiles, birds' eggs, the rhizomes of various forest or swamp ferns, and carrion of any age or quality. They will also kill small or young mammals and have been known to kill and de-your domestic stock. To all cultivated crops they are fearfully destructive, trampling and rending as much as they devour. They will tusk and scrape the soft stems of adult pawpaw trees until the tree falls over, so that they can get at the fruit, and they will deftly uproot small pawpaw trees to eat the roots. Bushpigs are known to associate with vervet monkeys, baboons and elephants in order to pick up food items which have been missed or dropped to the ground. While feeding, the adults in the group continually utter rather abrupt, soft grunts, presumably in order to maintain contact with each other.

Like warthog, bushpigs like to wallow in mud in order to gain protection from biting insects and to keep cool. They mark trees by tusking them and also by rubbing a scented secretion onto them from glands on the face. Their most deadly natural enemy is the leopard (which will pounce on a straggler and retire hurriedly to a tree until the infuriated sounder has gone); and where leopards have been exterminated, bushpigs often become a serious threat to cultivation. In some areas lions do kill bushpigs, but in general these pigs are not plentiful in typical lion country. In nature, they perform a valuable role by constantly snouting and turning over the soil, thereby helping to conserve water in heavy rains, destroying numerous insect grubs and larvae, and aiding seed dispersal.

Breeding

The sow constructs a nest in a remote, well-hidden spot where she is unlikely to be disturbed. The nests are made of long grass which is carried to the site by the sow and piled into heaps of up to 3 m by 1 m in size. She then burrows into this in order to give birth. Usually three to four young are born during the summer (although as many as eight have been recorded). The young are born dark brown with pale yellow or buff longitudinal stripes along the body. The stripes disappear at about three to four months and the piglets take on an orange-brown colour with a white and black dorsal crest and white side-whiskers, thus providing them with excellent camouflage in the dappled light of their forest habitat. The sow is capable of breeding every eighteen months and has very little to do with the piglets other than providing them with milk; the master boar is entrusted with their care and protection, a responsibility which he takes extremely seriously. This close association is terminated after about six months when both parents chase the youngsters off.

typical running attitude (tail down)

Warthog

Phacochoerus aethiopicus

Vlakvark

Descriptive notes

The warthog is the most commonly seen wild pig of the African bush. It is a dull grey colour and has a naked skin which is sparsely covered with a few tiny bristles along the back and flanks. The mane of long grey, brown or yellowish hair along the top of the neck and shoulders can be raised in excitement or alarm. The head is elongated and on the sides of the face there are long whitish bristles (more conspicuous in the young) which sprout backwards like 'side-whiskers'. Above these and just below the eyes are the enormous wart-like protuberances from which the name of the animal is derived.

The tusks in the warthog are canine teeth which grow so long that they protrude from the mouth. The upper teeth are extremely massive, widely-curved upwards at the tips and are used for digging out roots and bulbs. The lower tusks are sharper and shorter than the upper tusks and are used mainly for fighting and self-defence. The females have smaller 'warts' and shorter, smaller tusks than the males.

Distribution and habits

North of the southern African subregion warthogs are found in sub-Saharan Africa in almost all areas except where there has been extensive human development or in the forest and arid regions. Although they prefer open grassland they will also utilise open woodland and scrub.

Warthogs live in family groups, or sounders, of five to ten individuals consisting of an adult male, an adult female and her offspring. They also form maternity groups, consisting of females and their offspring; males join these groups briefly to mate with females in oestrus. Adult males often remain on their own or may join up to form temporary 'bachelor' groups. Warthogs are always most entertaining to watch, especially when a boar, sow, and their several young come trotting briskly along with their tails all stiffly erect. This habit probably helps the animals to see each other in long grass when fleeing, especially in the case of the young ones with their very limited vision.

Although warthogs do not defend territories they tend to remain in specific areas (home ranges) for long periods,

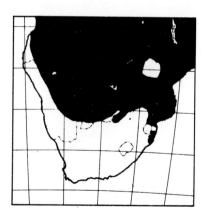

215

shoulder height ♂: 75 cm
　　　　　　　♀: 65 cm
weight ♂: 80 kg
　　　♀: 55 kg
tusks (average): 25 cm
　　　(record): 61 cm
running speed: 40 km/h
sexual maturity: 18 months
gestation: 3 months
number of young: 1 – 8 piglets (av. 3)
birth weight: 600 g
weaning: 9 weeks
longevity: 15 years

Order: *Artiodactyla*
Family: *Suidae*

if not for life. Group home ranges overlap extensively but groups will tend to avoid each other if possible and may defend a small area around their nesting holes. Several family parties may gather temporarily at a waterhole or mud wallow and there may be aggression on the part of the larger males towards the younger ones or the females, under such conditions. During the mating the males may also fight for control of family groups or females; these fights are not normally serious and take the form of head-pushing and various ritual displays such as pawing the ground and dropping to their knees.

Warthogs feed and forage for most of the day. They can often be seen digging and rooting around or grazing in the kneeling position. They develop large callouses on their front knees as a result of the large amount of time they spend moving around on them. They have the best of both worlds in that their legs are long enough to allow them to run away from predators but at the same time, by bending them and walking around on their front knees, they are able to get very close to the ground and thus utilise very short grass and exert a great deal of force in digging and removing roots and tubers. They are able to smell these 'bonus' dietary items under the ground while feeding on the grass which makes up the bulk of their diet. Warthogs will also eat wild fruits and bark on occasions and a number of cases of their eating carrion have been recorded.

Antbear and porcupine holes or other burrows play a very important part in the lives of warthogs. They use them at night as refuges in which to sleep in safety, they shelter in them from bad weather or heat, the females give birth in them and they are used as 'bolt' holes by the animals to escape from predators. Depending on the purpose for which they are used, the holes may be greatly enlarged underground into a whole burrow system by the animals, and the female may even carry grass in to line the nest on occasions. When chased, the young animals rush straight down the hole head first; the adults, however, execute a very rapid turn at the last moment before disappearing down the hole tail-end first. By entering in this way they are in a strong position to defend themselves with their sharp tusks, against anything that attempts to pursue them down the burrow. If you stand on top of a hole containing a warthog and stamp heavily, the pig will often come rushing out — to the detriment of anybody else standing in the way!

All the large African predators (including man!) seem to savour the taste of warthog flesh and they are subject to heavy predation pressure. They are also short and have a limited field of vision; for this reason they react extremely nervously to the alarm calls of birds (especially the calls of the oxpeckers which clamber over them searching for parasites to eat). Warthogs are, however, courageous and game fighters, even against the most impossible odds. They have been known to successfully defend themselves against a lone cheetah and against an attack from a pack of sixteen wild dogs. A young warthog fought bravely against an adult leopard for two hours before finally succumbing to its attacks, but not before the pig had chased the leopard up a tree and knocked it over a number of times. Maberly also saw a sow and youngster drive a jackal off a piece of meat before devouring it themselves.

On the whole they are silent creatures, occasionally uttering soft grunts to maintain group contact as they feed. They utter a long-drawn grunt of alarm when they are startled and about to run away and will snarl and snort when they are aggressive or defending themselves.

Breeding

The adult males follow oestrus females around and will chase off any other males, young or old, if they venture too close. Shortly before the young are born, the female leaves the group and chases off her present litter. Normally two to four piglets are born in the early part of the rainy season in a modified antbear hole which is often lined with grass by the mother. As many as eight piglets may be born but mortality of the young animals is usually high in these cases. They huddle together on a raised recess above the floor of the main chamber in order to avoid being drowned by heavy rains. The piglets are very susceptible to cold and damp and will die if they are not kept warm and dry. They start to leave the shelter of the burrow and graze at about a week old. They can be extremely comical at this age as they start to become confident on their feet: they run around in tight circles like puppies chasing their tails, or in short stop-start dashes, often colliding with each other or the adult warthogs and frequently missing their footing or tumbling down unseen banks or slopes. They seem to have endless energy for these antics which may carry on for hours at a time. A group of six or seven of these endearing little animals carrying on in this fashion is certainly one of the most amusing sights that the African bush has to offer.

The piglets are at great risk during the first six months of life and half of them are estimated to die during this period as a result of predation, starvation or sudden changes in temperature. The large litters which are often seen with female warthogs are probably a result of recruitment from other mothers — a common phenomenon in this species. The young leave their mother or foster mother after about a year.

Hippopotamus

Hippopotamus amphibius

Seekoei

Descriptive notes

The amphibious hippopotamus is easily recognisable by its huge size, its barrel-shaped body and short legs. Although the hippo is the second largest land mammal, after the elephant, the white rhinoceros exceeds it in weight. The four toes on each foot are capped with rounded hooves. There is webbing between the toes to assist in swimming and walking on soft mud; the toes splay out under pressure to further increase the surface area of the foot in contact with the substrate. The enormous head has a broad and square muzzle in which there are four large, curved, tusk-like teeth with sharp, flattened edges. Other notable features are the slit-like nostrils which can be closed under water, as can the small, rounded ears. The prominent periscope-like eyes protrude from the head, like those of the frog and the crocodile, to enable observation just above the surface while the rest of the body is submerged. Notable also is the short, laterally-compressed tail, its tip decorated with a few sparse bristles. The colour of the adults ranges from black to dark brown, with more or less fleshy pink around the eyes, sides of the face and the underparts. Although black at birth, the skin rapidly lightens and young calves are generally paler and pinker than the adults. The hairless skin can be damaged by lengthy exposure to bright sunlight and is protected by the secretion of a reddish fluid from glands in the skin.

Distribution and habits

Formerly plentiful in almost all the rivers and lakes or pools from southernmost Cape to Egypt, hippos are today found only in the very northern or eastern parts of our subregion. They used to be common in the vicinity of Cape Town and Van Riebeeck's diary of 1652 reports their presence in the swamp that is now Church Square. They occur throughout central Africa but have disappeared from the northern parts of their former range. This dramatic range reduction is partially due to the fact that these huge herbivores compete severely with man for his crops, which are often planted near to rivers and lakes to facilitate irrigation. This conflict has resulted in large numbers being ex-

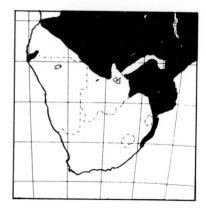

shoulder height ♂: 150 cm
　　　　　　　♀: 145 cm
weight ♂: 1 800 kg
　　　　♀: 1 400 kg
tusks (record): 105 cm
sexual maturity ♂: 7 years
　　　　　　　　♀: 4 years
gestation: 8 months
number of young: 1 calf
birth weight: 30 kg
weaning: 16 months
longevity: 40 years

Order: *Artiodactyla*
Family: *Hippopotamidae*

terminated. They have also been hunted relentlessy for their meat, fat and hides; over a thousand were killed in Chad in 1930 simply to feed railway workers. Their numbers and range continue to decline in the face of persecution even though they are now afforded protection in many parks and reserves. Although they are generally found in fresh water, hippos have been seen swimming between the African mainland and Zanzibar Island and also off the Natal Coast.

The aptness of the ancient Greek name 'river horse' can be appreciated when one looks at the upper parts of a hippopotamus's head as it appears just above the water. Actually, these creatures are more related to pigs than to horses, although they represent a family of their own containing one other dwarf type — the pygmy hippopotamus of Liberia and Sierra Leone, which is the size of a large pig and almost entirely aquatic.

Hippos spend most of the day either submerged or dozing in heaps (one head lying upon another) on rocks or sandbars, where they may be very easily mistaken for jumbled rocks at a distance. When completely submerged, they have to raise their nostrils above the surface to breathe every three to six minutes. Where much persecuted, they will project only the nostrils during the day, and then only under overhanging reeds or other cover. Actually hippos usually stand on the bottom (where shallow enough) or else float with their front legs raised until the head breaks the surface, the little ears wagging briskly. At such times an inquisitive hippo will often utter his cavernous, grunting bellow which sounds like a guffaw of cynical laughter *'Hsssh! Haw-haw-haw-haw-heee-haw!'* and not infrequently other members of the herd join in.

They are capable of moving surprisingly fast through the water, either by swimming or by walking along the bottom along clearly defined paths. They perform an essential function in certain areas by keeping waterways clear of plant-growth, thus allowing water to flow freely. Equally important in nature is the hippo's habit of defecating in the water, scattering his dung by vigorous tail wagging. In this way the hippo brings large quantities of valuable nutrients into the water which are of great benefit to the plants and animals living there.

Bull hippos mark off a territory adjoining the piece of

water in which they live. Territorial boundaries are demarcated by piles of droppings; they also whirl their flat tails rapidly as they are defecating, thereby spreading the dung over a large area and high into nearby trees and bushes. This action may make the territorial 'signpost' more prominent and has the added advantage of fertilising a wide area far more rapidly than would otherwise be the case. The territory is pear-shaped, with the narrow end at the water, and is usually about 3 to 8 km long. When food is scarce near the resting pool, however, hippopotamuses may move as far as 30 km per night to feed. A group of cows and their offspring, usually numbering ten to fifteen animals, live within the bull's territory.

When they reach sexual maturity, young males are violently driven from the herd (or school) by the bull. Although the hierarchy within the group is based on a matriarchal system, the bull usually leads the way on foraging outings and defends his territory and cows extremely pugnaciously, both on land and in the water, against other bulls which happen to trespass, especially during the mating season. During these violent and aggressive fights they often inflict terrible (not infrequently mortal) wounds upon one another by savage sideways slashes of the great shear-like canines, while uttering ear-shattering roars, screams and grunts. Most old bulls bear the healed marks of such wounds on their hides.

As a rule hippos emerge from the water at night to graze along the riverbank if food is available there, or to move inland to feed. In undisturbed areas they may wander about and graze during the cooler hours of the day. They prefer open areas of short green grass and crop it very close to the ground by plucking it upwards with the horny edges of the lips. An adult hippo may eat as much as 130 kg of green grass in a night. In areas where the density of hippos is very high, they can devastate the vegetation and cause severe soil erosion and general destruction. Under such conditions, culling of the animals in order to reduce their numbers, is the most humane and ecologically and economically sensible plan of action open to the management authorities.

Hippos follow regularly-beaten paths to and from their feeding grounds. The enormous four-toed tracks run parallel in a characteristic manner and can readily be recognised. On the whole they take very little notice of other species and will often bask on the same rocks or sandbars as crocodiles. These reptiles are a threat to hippo calves, however, and a mother will immediately drive them away from its neighbourhood. Lions may prey on adult hippos when they are caught alone away from water; normally several lions participate in such an onslaught but these occurrences are rare. Spotted hyaenas will also kill young or weak hippos. When the Savuti Channel in northern Botswana dried up recently groups of these carnivores literally ate the stranded hippos alive as they floundered in the drying mud.

Occasionally old bulls or cows with calves become truculent and attack watercraft passing their domains with devastating effect. This can also happen by accident such as occurred in the Okavango swamps. The unfortunate occupants of a motor boat had a hippo descend on them from the top of a three metre bank, after it had panicked at the noise and charged for the safety of the water (and the craft hidden below the bank!). Despite their huge size, hippos are amazingly agile (almost dainty) and fleet-footed on land. To get between a grazing hippo and his nearest retreat to the water is always a most dangerous action resulting, in some recorded cases, in the human trespasser being practically bitten in two.

Campfires built too close to the water's edge of a favourite pool often receive hostile attention from the resident hippo, particularly if it is a solitary bull. Generally speaking, though, the hippopotamus is a placid inoffensive beast when left alone. The hippo is also exceedingly inquisitive, and cannot resist the impulse to expose its head above the water from time to time to gaze wonderingly at the intruder.

Between 1927 and 1931 the famous hippo, Huberta, was in the limelight on account of her trek from Zululand to the Cape. En route she had a number of amusing (or hair-raising) encounters with local people — one such incident taking place in the streets of Durban where she inadvertently terrified many city folk before fleeing for the sanctuary of some nearby marshy reedbeds. Unfortunately she was eventually shot by three hunters near King William's Town; a tragic way to end such a tremendous trek.

Breeding

Hippos mate in the water, the female remaining submerged except when her head pops up for quick breaths. Calves are born throughout the year and the female moves away from the rest of the group, usually into a dense reedbed to give birth. The calf can swim within minutes of being born and the pair will remain apart from the rest of the group for a few months. When they return to the group the other females will look after the calf if its mother has to move great distances to find food. On land the calf stays very close to its mother and spends much of its time in the water riding on its mother's back to keep out of the way of roving crocodiles and to rest its legs which are often too short to reach the bottom. They are able to suckle above or below the water but need to come up about every minute or so for air.

Giraffe

Giraffa camelopardalis

Kameelperd

Descriptive notes

Giraffe are well enough known not to warrant a detailed description. They are the tallest animals in the world, standing the height of a double-decker bus (a specimen from Kenya measured almost 6 m). Their exceptionally long necks and legs enable them to reach the young shoots and leaves high up on the growing tips of branches and twigs. Their height means that they do not have to compete with other browsers (except perhaps elephant) which are restricted to the lower levels.

The giraffe has one of the largest hearts in the animal kingdom in order to enable it to pump blood some 3 m up to the brain. The jugular vein, carrying blood from the brain back to the heart, is supplied with a number of special valves which stop the blood from rushing back down to the heart and lungs under tremendous pressure. These valves also prevent blood from flowing back to the brain too fast when the animal lowers its head to drink. The giraffe has the same number of neck vertebrae as most other mammals i.e. seven; each bone is elongated, which accounts for the overall length of the neck.

The animal's coat is covered in a pattern of irregularly shaped brown patches on a light whitish-brown ground colour. Its overall colour tends to darken with age. Very often giraffes have severe skin lesions which form festering sores on various parts of their anatomy; these may be the result of a parasite. The oxpeckers which almost always cling to giraffes, running and flitting up and down their long necks, or over their shoulders, sometimes alighting on nostrils or ears (to be snortingly shaken off), frequently seem to worry unmercifully at such wounds, preventing them from healing.

A narrow, stiff, tawny-rufous mane runs down the length of the giraffe's neck and it has two large bony outgrowths from the skull which resemble horns. These 'horns' are covered with skin and hair which wears away at the tips in the adults. In adult bulls they grow up to about 20 cm whereas in cows they are shorter and tufted at the top with black hairs. In small calves the outgrowths are first indicated by large, tassel-like tufts of hair. In addition to the main 'horns', a prominent outgrowth of bone projects from the forehead more or less between the eyes, and in

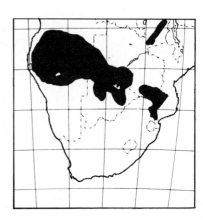

overall height ♂: 5 m
                ♀: 4,5 m
shoulder height ♂: 3 m
                ♀: 2,8 m
weight ♂: 1 200 kg
      ♀: 800 kg
running speed: 55 km/h
sexual maturity: 4,5 years
gestation: 15 months
number of young: 1 calf (exceptionally 2)
birth weight: 102 kg
birth height: 1,5 m
weaning: 7 months
longevity: 28 years

Order: *Artiodactyla*
Family: *Giraffidae*

older bulls, curious bony projections (also covered with skin and hair) stick out from the skull immediately behind and below the main 'horns'. In a large old bull the heavy eyelids and beautiful, long lashes impart a solemn, thoughtful expression, curiously set off by the heavy forehead prominence and the often numerous quaint tubercles projecting irregularly from the base of the horns.

The giraffe has a very long, narrow tongue and a mouth which is covered with a horny layer of skin. This enables the animal to reach the small leaves of trees such as acacias, and together with the very thick saliva which it produces, enables it to avoid being hurt by the sharp thorns. The nostrils are also thin slits which can be closed to keep out unwanted objects.

Huge splayed hooves up to 30 cm long allow the animal to move easily over all sorts of terrain and these leave a very large and characteristic spoor.

Distribution and habits

In former times the giraffe was found from the Sahara southwards down to the Orange River. Its range has been severely reduced since these times and it now occurs in widely-scattered, isolated pockets in the savanna regions of Africa. They are, however, not endangered and breed well where afforded protection and where the habitat is right. They are always an interesting and exciting sight for tourists or game-watchers and have thus been relocated onto private land and reserves in many parts of their former range in southern Africa.

Giraffes do not appear to have a very definite social or herd structure. Most herds comprise females and young, but mixed and bachelor herds are also found. All herds seem to be temporary associations and are constantly changing. The giraffe's whole approach to society seems to be very relaxed and 'laid-back': no clear leader can be identified within the herds; adult males are mainly solitary, wandering from one herd to the next; they do not defend a territory and the size of herds and ratio of males to females within them is highly variable.

Sometimes bulls may 'spar' in order to sort out dominance, by pounding away at each other's necks and shoulders with their massive heads. The contestants may stand side by side, but facing in opposite directions, swinging their heads to and fro but striking each other across the rump. Sometimes a third bull wanders up and seems to stand as an umpire, watching the contest. These interactions are rarely very serious or aggressive and there are no reports of animals being killed or injured while sparring, although they have been seen to be knocked down. With their long, graceful necks swaying and bending like giant snakes, sparring giraffes often look more as if they are involved in some sort of enchanting ritual dance rather than in combat.

Giraffes are predominantly diurnal but will also move about and feed to a limited extent at night. Contrary to popular belief, giraffes quite often lie down, though they usually keep their long necks upright. Sometimes they stand dozing with their heads supported in the fork of two tree branches. When a herd is resting (often in the shade during the heat of the day) they will lie orientated in differnt directions in order to watch for possible danger. Calves sometimes sleep deeply with their necks bent and heads resting on their rumps.

Apart from their usual diet of leaves which are plucked from even the loftiest thorny acacias, they also eat succulent twigs and shoots, but only rarely lower their long necks to eat grass. Giraffes are also very partial to salt licks and will often ingest large quantities of mineralised soil for its phosphorus; they also frequently chew old bones (especially in the winter) in order to obtain calcium. They drink fairly regularly when water is available but are able to do without it if necessary, obtaining their moisture from the vegetation they eat. Watching giraffes drink is a fascinating spectacle. In order to get their heads down to the water they have to spread their forelegs far apart, and getting into this incongruous position is achieved by a series of jerky movements, with the tall animal making sure that it maintains a sure footing at all times. Often when a giraffe is drinking it will have a companion standing nearby keeping a look-out for danger, and if suddenly alarmed when thus postured it can snap upright and flee very quickly.

The walking gait is very like that of a camel, with the two legs on each side of the body moving forward to-

drinking attitude

gether. An alarmed giraffe will snort loudly before 'galumphing' away in that ungainly but most extraordinary slow motion gallop: the hind limbs are brought well in front of the fore ones in a rhythmic motion, while the long-brushed tail is gracefully waved from side to side or else twisted in a loop over the immense hindquarters. In order to maintain their balance while galloping, the necks swing backwards and forwards in rhythm with the legs, giving the animals the overall impression of giant rocking horses. They are also capable of jumping fences up to 1,5 m in height.

The giraffe is normally a most gentle, inoffensive animal, in spite of its huge size, and its only effective method of defence is an extremely powerful kick. Females especially will defend their young boldly against lions, which are their only serious predator, apart from man. Leopards and spotted hyaenas may also occasionally kill small calves. When attacked by lions — several of which usually unite in such an attack — a giraffe will chop-kick with the front feet, strike with a stiff foreleg and swing-kick with the back legs. A single kick from a giraffe has been seen to kill a lion on more than one occasion. The giraffe will also gallop fast through the thickest bush it can find in order to dislodge its opponent. Its tough skin is impervious to the interlacing branches and in former days this toughness, together with the length of giraffe hide, made it ideal for the manufacture of long wagon whips. This factor certainly played a major role in reducing their numbers dramatically over most of southern Africa.

Giraffes have very acute sight, and their great melancholy eyes, heavily lashed, are among the most beautiful in the animal world. These animals also hear very well and use their noses to warn them of danger. Their great height puts them at a tremendous advantage in spotting lions and they are often, not surprisingly, accompanied by other animals. They are, however, extremely inquisitive and will often approach vehicles, or even lions, in order to get a better view. They can become very tame where they are not hunted and when approached will simply move behind a bush or tree in order to break their outline, while peering over the top. Giraffes were thought to be mute for some time, but they are capable of snorting or grunting when alarmed or harassed and often bellow and moo in captivity.

Breeding

Giraffes breed throughout the year but often mate about a month after rain. The female moves away from the herd to give birth, which she does standing up; the umbilical cord is broken as the calf drops to the ground. It can stand after about an hour and immediately drinks from its mother. For the first few weeks of its life the young giraffe lies hidden, normally resting for most of the time with its head down. The mother may move as far as 3 km from the calf which is extremely vulnerable to the attacks of predators at this time. One out of every two giraffes born in the Eastern Transvaal dies before it is a year old, and in East Africa the same applies to three out of every four calves.

Calves often gambol and play together. They leave their mothers at the age of about fourteen months, when the next calves are due, and frequently join nursery herds which are looked after by one or two females.

Black Wildebeest

Connochaetes gnou

Swartwildebees

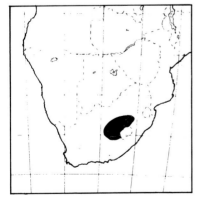

Descriptive notes

The black wildebeest is, in fact, very dark brown in colour but appears black at a distance. The most characteristic feature of this species is the long, yellowish-white tail which almost reaches the ground. The long hairs of the lower jaw and mane have whitish bases and black tips and the face is darker than the rest of the body. The eyes are very wild and goat-like, and the horns, which are present in both sexes are bent steeply downward, forward and upward. They are thinner and less robust in the smaller and more slender females. A fringe of long hair extends from the chest, between the forelegs, almost to the belly. These rather ungainly looking antelope have massive, humped shoulders and slender, lightly-built hindquarters and a sloping back.

Distribution and habits

Black wildebeest have always been found only in southern Africa. Their numbers have been severely reduced as a result of over-exploitation and the loss of habitat to agriculture. Once occurring in hundreds of thousands across the Orange Free State and adjacent areas they were on the verge of extinction during the 1960s, but with subsequent careful conservation and relocation to many of the areas from which they have disappeared, they are no longer endangered.

The bulls of this species establish territories which they inhabit throughout the year, although they tend to be most intense in defending and maintaining them during the rutting season. They have various glands with which to spread their scent around the territory and also use their piles of faeces and urine to demarcate its boundaries. They warn off potential intruders by uttering a very loud, two-syllabled bellowing call with a curiously metallic ring which has been described as *'ge-nu':* the name given to the species by the Hottentots. By pawing the ground as well as kneeling and horning it vigorously, territorial males are usually able to avoid having physically to deter other bulls which approach the territory too closely. Sometimes sparring and butting with the horns does occur but this rarely gets very intense before one of the two contestants gives up and moves away. The bulls also display by racing about, cavorting and plunging wildly, and tossing their heads and lashing their long pony-tails about.

Young bulls (usually up to the age of about five years) and old displaced territorial bulls form bachelor herds which offer them protection and within which there is minimal aggression. The female herds are far more tightly-knit and longer-enduring than the bachelor herds. The cows are accompanied by female subadults and male calves and the herds usually number between eight and fifty animals. They move about over the male territories but during the rut the territorial males aggressively herd them to keep them within the limits of their particular territories.

Black wildebeests' activity patterns vary according to the season and temperature. In summer they rest during the heat of the day and are active at night but in winter they remain active all day and are relatively inactive during the early morning and late evening. They are primarily grazers of short grass but also take a substantial amount of browse from bushes, especially during the dry winter months. They are antelope of the open plains; in former times they occurred in grassland regions and in the Karoo areas. It is likely that during these times they undertook large-scale migrations in response to changing environmental conditions.

When feeding, black wildebeest frequently kneel — a very unusual posture for an adult antelope. At first alarm, members of a herd walk uneasily to and fro, swishing their white tails from side to side with such violence that the whistling caused by this movement can be heard over a kilometre away. During this preliminary manoeuvre two bulls might very well begin to spar with their horns, and then with wildly lashing tails the herd will stampede away, cavorting, snorting and throwing their back legs high into the air. Before halting they will usually wheel round, strictly following the leader, and retrace their steps before coming to a halt, facing the real or supposed enemy with conspicuous white tails swishing. The vast herds of these appealing antelope which used to roam the endless plains of the highveld must have presented the early travellers with a fantastic spectacle — one which today we can unfortunately only imagine.

shoulder height: 120 cm
weight: 180 kg
horns (average): 73 cm
    (record): 83 cm
gestation: 8,5 months
number of young: 1 calf
longevity: 18 years

Order: *Artiodactyla*
Family: *Bovidae*
Subfamily: *Alcelaphinae*

Today there are very few predators left in the areas to which the remnants of our black wildebeest population have been restricted. In the past they would, however, probably have been preyed on by the same carnivores which today prey on the blue wildebeest in the grassland areas of its range. Like the blue wildebeest, this species becomes ferocious and untrustworthy in captivity, and its wild, staring eyes and grotesquely bewhiskered and tufted face lend it a forbidding aspect.

Breeding

The black wildebeest is a seasonal breeder. The precise timing of the births depends on the area, but most young are usually born around the months of December and January. The female remains with the herd and lies down to give birth to her calf. It can walk very soon after birth and remains close to its mother for the early part of its life. Most of the young black wildebeest survive through to adulthood, unlike the blue wildebeest calves which are subject to heavy predation.

Blue Wildebeest

Connochaetes taurinus

Blouwildebeest

Descriptive notes

The blue wildebeest is actually dark greyish-brown in colour; the coat may shine slatey, bluish-grey under certain light conditions. A series of more or less distinct dark brown or black vertical stripes extends along the neck and flanks but stops short of the hindquarters which are neat and rather small in comparison with the animal's fairly heavy, humped shoulders and thick neck. There is an upstanding black mane along the back of the neck which droops over the withers and a long, well-brushed, black horse-like tail. The massive head, with its black beard-like tuft below the chin, strongly whiskered nostrils and tufts of hair surrounding the large oval glands in front of the rather goat-like eyes, carries a comic, almost deranged expression. Both sexes have horns but they are more massive and widespread in bulls and more slender and sharply hooked in cows. The young animals are conspicuous in the herd by their fawn coloured coats and the long, russet tufts of hair on their foreheads.

The overall impression one has when looking at a blue wildebeest is that of a rather comic, clumsy and ungainly animal; the sloping back, comparatively thin legs, and small hindquarters make the animal look ill-proportioned, almost as if it had been put together from the leftovers, when all the other antelope had finished being assembled!

Distribution and habits

Although at one time common in the Transvaal, and ocurring as far south as the Orange and Vaal rivers, the blue wildebeest has been pushed northwards by human pressure. Today, apart from its distribution in southern Africa, it is found in a large, but separate area in East Africa. During drier times in the distant past this species probably occurred in the intervening area.

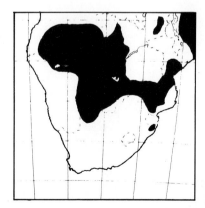

Blue wildebeest are gregarious, associating in large herds, sometimes numbering several hundreds or even thousands, but usually up to twenty or thirty. During the rutting season between one and three adult bulls may join forces and establish a territory which they will defend against intruding bulls with threat displays involving a

shoulder height ♂: 145 cm
　　　　　　　　♀: 135 cm
weight ♂: 250 kg
　　　　♀: 180 kg
horns (average): 58 cm
　　　(record): 84 cm
sexual maturity ♀:
15 months
gestation: 8 months
number of young: 1 calf
birth weight: 22 kg
weaning: 8 months
longevity: 20 years

Order: *Artiodactyla*
Family: *Bovidae*
Subfamily: *Alcelaphinae*

adult bull

characteristic see-saw gait and the rubbing of facial glands on the ground. If these displays do not prove sufficient in deterring the trespasser, then a conflict in which the contestants clash horns and butt heads, may develop. Injuries in these ritualised encounters are rare. The territorial bulls in a specific territory do not compete at all, but share the responsibilities such as defending the territory and herding the females to keep them within its boundaries. They also share the major benefit of their privileged position: the opportunity to mate with the females when they come into oestrus. More than one male might mate with the same female.

The females move about in stable herds with their yearling calves and wander over the various territories only as much as the possessive territorial bulls will allow. The young males which are not capable of holding a territory during the rutting season group together into bachelor herds which are not tolerated on the occupied territories. Where there are large concentrations of wildebeest at the time of the rut, there may be a continuous interchange of bulls between the bachelor herds and the breeding herds: as certain bulls retire from mating their places are taken by fresh individuals. Under these conditions territories are not formed but males will defend groups of females, or harems, from the attentions of other bulls.

Wildebeest are entirely grazing animals and will only eat short or very short grass. They are particularly partial to fresh, sprouting grass after rain or a burn. In some areas, such as the Serengeti or the Kalahari, huge migrations of hundreds of thousands of wildebeest may take place as they wander in search of seasonal grazing. These great nomads of the plains will also react, on a more local scale, to rain which they can hear and see falling up to 100 km away, and will often set off immediately to take advantage of the green flush which it will bring. They may be active throughout the day if it is cool, but on hot days they will often crowd together in the shade of trees. They usually require water regularly but in the Kalahari they are able to go without drinking for extended periods.

Old wildebeest bulls frequently dwell alone and are familiar figures of the bush landscape in areas where the species occurs; they also frequently accompany a herd of zebras or other animals. Wildebeest are, in any case, most sociable creatures which often associate with other game such as zebras (especially), impala, waterbuck, and even giraffe and ostriches. Their association with zebras is thought to benefit them since the zebras crop the longer grass down to a manageable length for the wildebeest. The two species are also mutually beneficial to one another since the larger mixed herds have a better chance of early warning of the presence of predators than is the case with smaller single species herds. The zebras also benefit by the association since wildebeest are the favourite prey of most carnivores and a hunting predator will usually take them and leave the zebras. Where numerous, wildebeest are a very common prey of lions. Rather stupid, they are very inquisitive and will stand staring at an intruder to their haunts, continuously snorting and blowing through their broad nostrils (producing a very characteristic *'Hshwa! Hshwa!'* sound), and occasionally galloping around in circles before halting to stare and snort again. Finally they depart in single file at a rather hunched, prancing gait (a weary-looking sort of gallop which can continue for miles on end), tails whisking wildly and heads down for some distance before coming again to an abrupt halt, and then repeating the whole process.

They usually walk or run in single file, and they drink twice a day — in the early morning and in the late afternoon. When gathering at water, and at other times, blue wildebeest call to one another with a rather solemn, resonant grunt which sounds rather like *'Kwang! Kwang!'* — oft repeated. The calves continually moo and bleat like domestic cattle, and a herd straggling along at leisure on its way to drink is often very noisy. Having arrived at the

young

cow

drinking place, wildebeest usually stand about for a considerable time, making quite sure that everything is safe, before advancing to the water — though they will unhesitatingly follow other animals who approach more boldly. At such times Maberly reports having often watched the elder members of a herd prodding the youngsters forward first — a most ungallant procedure!

Wildebeest are very tenacious and tough, and when wounded will charge dangerously. Like almost all animals they are naturally timid and inoffensive in the wild state, but are regarded as amongst the most dangerous and untrustworthy of mammals in zoos. They are naturally very courageous, in spite of their absurd and rather clownish appearance (which often results in their being referred to as 'the old fools of the veld'), and many a bull (or cow with her calf) has successfully beaten off a clumsy attack by a young lion — the latter frequently having to flee abjectly for his life or to escape serious injury.

These animals are also surprisingly fleet-footed when they are under pressure from a predator and can also often be seen, particularly after rain, leaping and prancing about, kicking their heels in the air and attempting all manner of aerial acrobatics in a most amusing manner. Wildebeest may suffer from so-called turning disease in which the affected animal loses its sense of orientation and balance and thus keeps turning and stumbling about in tight circles until it eventually dies. This may happen to hartebeest as well and is a result of bot-fly larvae which hatch from eggs which were laid in the animal's nose by the adult flies and which then bore their way through to its brain. One often hears wildebeest sneezing frequently in order to keep these irritating, and often lethal insects out of their noses.

Young wildebeest have a reputation for being extremely sound sleepers. I recall an occasion when we came across an apparently dead yearling lying on the side of the road while the rest of the herd fled from our approaching vehicle. On attempting to roll the animal over to determine the cause of death (and talking loudly all the while), we received a rude shock when it suddenly gave a bellow, scrambled to its feet and rushed off to a distance of about 100 metres, from where it stood and snorted at us for disturbing its sleep!

Breeding

Wildebeest rut around the month of April. The calves are born around November and December, thus ensuring that the nursing mothers have sufficient sprouting grass available after the summer rains. There are variations in this seasonal breeding pattern depending on local conditions and there may be two calving seasons; one early in summer and the other at the end of summer.

Females in oestrus move from one territorial bull to the other and may mate with several. During the rut there is a great physical strain on the territorial bulls and they often have to court a female for an extended period of time before being able to mate. The calf may be born near or away from the herd, with the female normally lying down. The calf is licked clean by the mother, can stand and run with her within a few minutes, and is a competent member of the herd at a day old. Notwithstanding their early maturity, wildebeest calves also suffer heavy mortality as a result of predation by many carnivores.

Lichtenstein's Hartebeest

Alcelaphus lichtenstinii

Lichtenstein se Hartbees

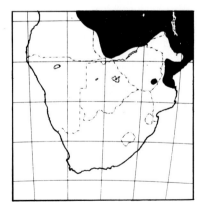

Descriptive notes

This antelope is very similar in build to its near relative — the red hartebeest — but the horns are mounted on a shorter pedicle, are much flattened at the base and are *strongly curved inwards* below the terminal backward inclination. Its colour is rich yellowish-tawny or red, becoming bright chestnut on the back, the upper part of the neck and the sides. The chin, fronts of the lower portion of the legs and the tail tuft are black, but the front of the face is not darker than the sides of the face as in the red hartebeest. There is a pale yellowish patch on the rump. The sexes are alike and the young are paler than the adults.

Distribution and habits

These hartebeest are found over most of Zambia, Malawi and Tanzania as well as north-eastern Angola, south-eastern Zaire and northern Mozambique. At around about the turn of the century they were still found in the lowveld of South Africa but were extinct in the Republic from then until 1986 when a number were re-introduced into the Kruger National Park.

Although Lichtenstein's hartebeest usually associate in small herds of about eight animals, they very occasionally form much larger temporary groups of up to eighty or more. A territory is occupied by a dominant male with a harem consisting of females and their young. The rutting season is a very active time for these animals as the males attempt to kidnap the females from surrounding areas; they also have to defend their own groups from other abductors and herd them to keep them from straying out of the territory. Prolonged and intense fighting can be seen between males at this time, and the young males of almost a year old are also chased from the groups by the territorial males. These join bachelor groups until they can challenge for a territory of their own.

The males are very protective of their harems and often stand on anthills or termite mounds as they look out for danger. They mark their territories by horning the ground, thus rubbing scent from glands near their eyes onto it. They also have dung heaps.

These animals are almost exclusively diurnal grazers, usually resting during the heat of the day. They are most often seen in open woodland or floodplain areas.

They are extremely swift like the red hartebeest and the tsessebe. When disturbed they may snort and then dash off; they also demonstrate the remarkable bouncing gait of their close relatives when not galloping at full speed.

shoulder height: 1,3 m
weight: 177 kg
gestation: 8 months
number of young: 1 calf
birth weight: 15 kg

Order: *Artiodactyla*
Family: *Bovidae*
Subfamily: *Alcelaphinae*

Breeding

The young are born in spring and are able to follow their mothers from birth. They usually lie near their mothers in the open but jump up to join them when disturbed. They suffer heavy predation from the larger carnivores.

Red Hartebeest

Alcelaphus buselaphus

Rooihartbees

Descriptive notes

The red hartebeest is an ungainly-looking, long and narrow-faced antelope with high withers and low hindquarters. The crooked, rather upright horns rise from a prominent pedicle on the top of the head. The animal has no neck mane and a shortish, moderately-haired tail. Its general colour is reddish-brown, darkening to almost purple along the back. The coat has an iridescent sheen in bright light which makes it look almost metallic as it reflects the sunlight. The face, chin, back of the unmaned neck, shoulders, thighs and tail are coloured blackish-brown whereas the lower part of the rump has a conspicuous off-white or pale yellowish patch. There is a tuft of hair under each wild and goat-like eye; a gland situated under each of these tufts exudes a waxy substance which the Bushmen value for its medicinal qualities. The sexes are alike but the bulls are stouter with more massive horns.

Distribution and habits

Apart from their occurrence in the north-western semi-arid areas of southern Africa, various subspecies of the hartebeest are found in a band across West, Central and East Africa just south of the Sahara. The position with regard to the survival of some of these subspecies is critical.

In our region, the red hartebeest has been persecuted to the extent that it has disappeared from most of its former range and is today confined to the drier and more hostile areas of the subregion except where it has been re-introduced to reserves or private land in small numbers. In the mid 1600s, Van Riebeeck reported them in the vicinity of the fort in Cape Town and at this time they were found across what is today the Cape Province, parts of Natal and the Orange Free State and the western half of the Transvaal. In South Africa today they occur naturally only in the far northern Cape Province.

Hartebeest herds usually number up to about twenty animals, but large herds of several hundred are not uncommon. In Botswana, particularly about November and December, aggregations of up to 10 000 or more may occur; these probably form in response to rain and food availability. Like the blue wildebeest of this area, they will also see and hear rain some distance off and then move in that direction in order to take advantage of the resultant green flush.

The social structure of the hartebeest consists of territorial males, nursery or harem herds (females and bull calves), and bachelor herds. The territorial males defend their territories against other intruding males by threat displays and vicious fighting may occur, especially during the mating season. A fight between two bulls consists of violent pushing and jousting, the two contestants usually keeping their horns interlocked and attempting to wrestle the opponent off balance and onto the ground. They frequently drag each other to their knees and the fighting may carry on for so long that both animals are virtually staggering about in exhaustion. Under such conditions they will ignore everything except their combat and one can approach to within a few metres of the duelling animals. Injuries are rare and the loser usually gives up before he is in serious danger, to flee with the victor hot on his heels, snorting, prancing and often spraying urine in order to express his dominance. A case was recorded in the Kalahari where two duelling males hooked their horns together inextricably; when they were found the one was already dead and its weak, exhausted rival was dragging it about hopelessly trying to escape from its death grip.

shoulder height: 125 cm
weight: 150 kg
horns (average): 53 cm
  (record): 71 cm
running speed: 65 km/h
sexual maturity ♀: 28 months
gestation: 8 months
number of young: 1 calf
weaning: 7 months
longevity: 16 years

Order: *Artiodactyla*
Family: *Bovidae*
Subfamily: *Alcelaphinae*

Apparently the two animals were parted with unbelievable ease by human hands, but had somehow been pulling and twisting in a way which had made escape impossible.

The bachelor herds consist of bulls which are either too young or too old to maintain a territory. They are forced to live outside the prime areas which are occupied by the territorial bulls and their harems.

Hartebeest are grazers and take in virtually no browsed material. They can live without drinking water, obtaining the necessary moisture from their food. They will, however, drink if water is available. When grazing, usually in the afternoons or mornings when it is not too hot, a watchful old cow often takes up a position as sentry on a piece of high ground or a termite hill in order to obtain a good view of the surrounding area. Their principal enemy is the lion although younger animals are probably often caught by cheetah, leopard, wild dog and spotted hyaena. Their sight does not appear to be as good as their other senses and they will often mill around after running some distance from the cause of flight. They are amazingly swift runners and can comfortably reach speeds of at least 65

km/h. They also have very good stamina which makes them difficult prey for spotted hyaenas and wild dogs. When displaying or confronted by a source of danger they will often gallop in a characteristic bouncing fashion with all four feet being lifted up to about half a metre off the ground at the same time, making them appear to be floating or running almost in slow motion. Young calves in particular, exhibit this type of gait and it may serve to advertise to the predator that they are aware of its presence and are fit and strong enough to be able to escape, 'so don't bother to try', in much the same way that the springbok's pronking does.

Like wildebeest, hartebeest may also die as a result of

bot-fly larvae burrowing into their brains after hatching from eggs laid by the flies in the animal's noses.

Breeding

The territorial bull ascertains whether the females in his harem are in oestrus by sniffing their rears. He then nudges them with his snout in order to prompt them to copulate. The cows drop their calves between October and December. Before giving birth the cow moves away from the herd to a secluded spot where she is well hidden. For the first few days the fawn-coloured calf lies concealed, while the mother grazes nearby and returns to clean and suckle it at regular intervals. She also licks up its urine and eats its faeces in order to get rid of tell-tale smells which may attract predators. If approached, the calf lies motionless with its ears laid flat in order to escape detection.

The calves join the harem herd with their mothers when they are strong enough. Initially they stay close to their mothers, but gradually become more independent until they are weaned at the age of about seven or eight months. They then form groups with the other calves within the main herd.

Bontebok

Damaliscus dorcas dorcas

Bontebok

Descriptive notes

The bontebok is a medium-sized, robustly-built antelope, which may be confused with the very similar blesbok. These two are, in fact, subspecies, and not separate species as was previously thought.

The bontebok is very richly and beautifully marked, with a pure white blaze down the centre of the face, white rump, base of tail, underparts and legs below the knees and hocks. The sides of the face, neck and body are rich purplish-brown, paler on the shoulders and middle of the back, and darker on the sides and upper portions of the limbs (becoming almost black on the quarters). This spectacularly contrasting colouring, coupled with the glossy sheen of its coat, make the bontebok more striking and handsome than the duller blesbok. The overall colour of the latter is reddish-brown and lacks the purplish sheen. The white blaze on the blesbok's face is divided by a narrow, transverse brown band between the eyes, and this subspecies does not have the clear white buttocks of the bontebok. Unlike the bontebok, the blesbok does not have prominent white stockings. The horns of the bontebok have a more pure black appearance than those of the blesbok, which are more straw-coloured. Both male and female bontebok carry horns which are slightly more upright than those of the blesbok. Bontebok males are slightly larger and heavier than the females.

Distribution and habits

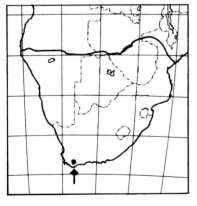

Bontebok have always occurred in the southern districts of the Cape Province, between Knysna and Caledon, and are found nowhere else in the world. They have practically the same distribution as the now extinct blue buck. The bontebok very nearly suffered the same fate, having been reduced, through over-hunting, to a population of a mere handful of individuals. As a result of the far-sightedness of a couple of farmers who preserved these last remnants, and, thereafter, the National Parks Board, which proclaimed the Bontebok National Park near Swellendam, the bontebok has been saved, and now surplus stock has been provided for re-introduction to parts of its former range. Even so, there are fewer bontebok than any other southern African antelope, with only over a thousand animals in the total population.

Bontebok are found in breeding herds consisting of females and male calves, in bachelor herds, or as territorial males. The latter advertise their presence within the territories by a series of complicated ritual displays involving numerous postures and behaviours. They also have latrines and scentmark from glands just under their eyes. These mechanisms are very effective in suppressing fighting and, at the most, two opposing males will kneel and prod at each other with their horns for a few seconds before moving apart; injuries seldom, if ever, result.

shoulder height: 90 cm
weight: 61 kg
horns (average): 38 cm
    (record): 43 cm
sexual maturity ♂: 3 years
    ♀: 2 years
gestation: 8 months
number of young : 1 lamb
birth weight: 6 kg
longevity: 12 years

Order: *Artiodactyla*
Family: *Bovidae*
Subfamily: *Alcelaphinae*

The males maintain their territories throughout the year and they may hold them from the age of about five years for their entire lives. They attempt to keep the breeding herds, which number up to about eight animals, within their areas by displaying and herding. They attempt to chase trespassing males off, but the bachelor herds of up to about thirty animals are sometimes too much for them, and then they have to patiently wait until the trespassers move off of their own accord.

The bachelor herds are very peaceful, with no aggression

or dominance behaviour, but members of the breeding herds enforce a strict hierarchy by doing battle with their horns.

These animals live on the coastal plains of the Cape and are almost exclusivly grazers. They prefer short grass and are always found reasonably close to water. Although they are most active during the cooler parts of the day, when it is hot they will often stand in tight groups with their heads held low and orientated towards the sun.

Breeding

Courtship is most frequent in bontebok during the rut, or mating season, in late summer, but may take place at any time of the year. The territorial male determines the female's sexual state by genital sniffing; he then displays to her with his head held low and his tail held over his back. The two may then move around in tight circles before copulation takes place. The male uses a similar display to keep the females tightly bunched in order to ensure that they stay on his territory.

The lambs are born in spring, the females remaining with the herd to give birth. Newborn bontebok stand within minutes and run with their mothers within half an hour of birth. The males leave the herd voluntarily when the next crop of lambs arrive, and join the bachelors, whereas the females may remain with their herd for life.

Blesbok

Damaliscus dorcas phillipsi

Blesbok

Descriptive notes

The blesbok looks very like its close relative, the bontebok, and the reader is referred to the descriptive notes on the latter to differentiate between the two. In general, the blesbok is slightly larger than the bontebok and is lighter and duller in overall colouring, lacking the latter's purple sheen and contrasting pure white markings on the buttocks and lower legs.

Distribution and habits

Like the bontebok, the blesbok is only found in southern Africa. It does, however, have a wider distribution than the bontebok, and today it is more widely distributed than nature intended as a result of its introduction onto many farms across the subregion. They are primarily a grassland antelope and, although they are not endangered, their numbers have been drastically reduced since former days when many thousands of them used to undertake dramatic treks in what is today the Cape Province. Although bontebok and blesbok occur naturally in totally isolated populations, they were probably continuous at some time before a climatic change separated them. After this separation, the differences between the two subspecies would have started developing in the two populations.

The habits and social system of the blesbok are very similar to those of the bontebok, with the exception of a few aspects: the males sometimes fight vigorously and fatalities can result, even though the fights are usually brief. The dung patches or latrines are also very important in the case of the territorial blesbok males; they are social rendezvous points and their presence on them signals occupation of the territories to other males. Blesbok females are less aggressive and intense in the manner in which they maintain their hierarchies. Large aggregations of blesbok of both sexes and all ages are found; these may number several hundred and form during winter. The males do not keep their territories throughout the year as male bontebok do; they are established towards the end of summer just prior to the rut. The female herds are also less rigid and more mobile in this species.

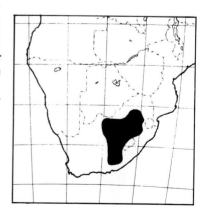

shoulder height: 95 cm
weight ♂: 70 kg
  ♀: 61 kg
horns (average): 38 cm
  (record): 51 cm
gestation: 8 months
number of young: 1 lamb
birth weight: 7 kg
weaning: 4 months
sexual maturity ♂: 3 years
  ♀: 2 years
longevity: 12 years

Order: *Artiodactyla*
Family: *Bovidae*
Subfamily: *Alcelaphinae*

Although blesbok mainly eat grass and are really true grassland animals, they will browse to a small extent as well. They are particularly partial to the short sprouting grass which follows a fire and they need fresh water. Botflies, which attempt to lay their eggs in the animal's nasal passages, irritate the blesbok and this results in the characteristic head shaking and sneezing which one associates with these antelope. Like the bontebok, blesbok are extremely swift runners with great stamina: some people maintain that they are even more than a match for the generally acknowledged number one athlete, the tsessebe.

Breeding

The peak of the blesbok lambing season is in midsummer. Courtship and lambing take place in the same way as with the bontebok. The lambs may form groups of their own within the herd and female lambs may remain with their mothers for two years, the males leaving the herd at about one year of age.

Tsessebe

Damaliscus lunatus

Tsessebe
(Basterhartbees)

Descriptive notes

The tsessebe is rather hartebeest-like with its long face, sloping back, and fine, silky coat with a reddish-purple sheen. It does differ in that its shoulders are not as 'humped' as those of the hartebeest, its horns are shorter, more lyre-shaped and do not project from a pedicle, and it has patches tending to black on the shoulders, hips and upper portions of the limbs. Although the rump is decidedly paler than the rest of the body, it does not have the very clear whitish patch which is so characteristic of the hartebeest. The tsessebe has unclear dark vertical markings on the sides of the neck and flanks and the tail is of moderate length, fringed with black hairs and tufted black. Some individuals have a yellow-fawn overall colour rather than being reddish-chestnut. The sexes are alike but the females are less robust and have lighter horns.

Distribution and habits

Although the tsessebe is not widely distributed in southern Africa today, in the past it was commonly found in the western Transvaal and in the northern Cape. Tsessebe occur throughout Africa south of the Sahara but have a scattered and discontinuous distribution across this range. They are not found in forested areas but frequently occur on the fringes of woodland areas where they have shade and open, medium length grassland for grazing. They also require open water in order to drink regularly. These specific habitat requirements have resulted in the patchy dis-

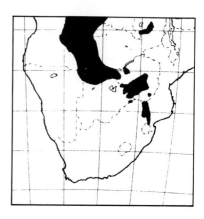

shoulder height: 120 cm
weight ♂: 140 kg
    ♀: 126 kg
horns (average): 35 cm
    (record): 47 cm
running speed: 60 km/h
sexual maturity ♂: 40 months
    ♀: 26 months
gestation: 10 months
number of young: 1 calf
birth weight: 11 kg
longevity: 15 years

Order: *Artiodactyla*
Family: *Bovidae*
Subfamily: *Alcelaphinae*

tribution of the species; overgrazing and subsequent bush-encroachment will invariably cause the rapid disappearance of these animals from an area. As a result of the dramatic decline in their numbers and their disappearance from many areas, tsessebe are today considered to be endangered over most of their range.

These antelope form herds of eight to ten which may either be composed of bachelor males which are unable to establish and maintain territories, or of females and young males which have not yet been evicted by the territorial bull. These bulls patrol their territories regularly and both males and females smear a secretion from glands under their eyes onto vegetation and onto the ground in order to demarcate their areas. Glands under their feet perform the same function and the bulls will often stand on termite mounds, not only to look for danger but also to make themselves clearly visible to would-be trespassers. Occasionally when fighting does break out, it takes a very similar form to that described for the red hartebeest.

The territorial bulls herd the females within their areas and young males are chased away from the group to join the bachelor herds when they are just over a year old.

Tsessebe only eat grass and prefer that which is of medium length or longish. At the end of the dry season they may form large aggregations, a couple of hundred strong on good feeding grounds. They need to drink regularly and also tend to move to areas where the grass has been burnt in order to take advantage of the new growth. They sometimes associate with zebra, wildebeest and other game.

When danger threatens, they move to an open area from where they have a good view and then rely on their speed to escape if necessary. Over a distance the tsessebe has the reputation of being one of the fastest southern African antelope, a fact not apparent from its awkward build. Like the hartebeest, however, its appearance is misleading, and once it breaks into that steady, bouncing gallop — body well stretched out and travelling at up to at least 60 km/h — it can continue, seemingly tirelessly, for kilometres on end, as all the old mounted hunters testified. Where not greatly disturbed, tsessebe are inquisitive, and will stare for some time before moving away. They are rather stupid animals and have suffered much from their inquisitive habit, but in places where they are hunted they become exceedingly wild.

Breeding

Tsessebe calves are born in early summer, and are able to join the mother and other members of the herd very shortly after birth. The calves tend to form groups of their own within the herd and tend to lie together with one female in attendance. If danger threatens, the other herd members will quickly move to the calves.

Blue Duiker

Cephalophus monticola

Blouduiker

Descriptive notes

This minute animal is the smallest antelope in southern Africa. Both sexes carry very small horns and the females are slightly larger and heavier than the males. They are greyish-brown in colour; browner above and greyer along the flanks, with more rufous-tinged legs and more-or-less white throat, chin and underparts. The rounded ears are white in front and dark grey behind; the fluffy tail is bordered with white and is white below.

Distribution and habits

Apart from its distribution along the east coast of southern Africa, this little antelope occurs throughout the forests of Central and West Africa, as well as in small, isolated areas on the eastern side of the continent. Like the red duiker, it needs very dense bush or forests, and water and is thus also distributed patchily over the above areas.

These very shy and timid animals are seldom seen in the thick forests or coastal bush which they inhabit. They move about alone, as mating pairs or as mother-offspring pairs and are most active in the early morning, late evening and at night.

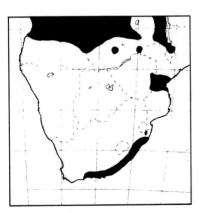

They often move into slightly more open areas to feed but need the dense forest and bush in which to hide or seek refuge. They frequently emerge onto the open beaches bordering dune forests in Natal, and even swim out to sea when hunted. They feed on a variety of leaves, shoots and fruits of the forest, and greedily devour wild figs and other delicacies extravagantly dropped and scattered by feeding monkeys overhead. They drink frequently.

Like all duikers, the blue duiker has a jerky, zigzag action as it darts through the bush, and being so small it can move freely *below* the level of the undergrowth. The ears are very short and rounded at the tips, and the short, hairy tail — brown above and white below — would normally be invisible except that its constant flicking, as the little creature moves about, exposes the white in tiny flashes. Unfortunately these little forest duikers leave well-marked trails or paths, so that the local snarer finds them easy prey. A snared or otherwise caught blue duiker 'gives utterance to pitiful, loud, strangely cat-like miaulings'. Their small cleft footprints are smaller than one's fingertip.

The forest-haunting crowned eagle preys on adults and young, and the skulls are often found beneath the nests of these great birds. Python, caracal, leopard and man are also enemies of this animal.

As in the case of the red duiker, few details are known of the blue duiker's habits or breeding. They breed throughout the year with a possible summer peak, and courtship involves the male prancing before the female and nibbling her as well as rubbing his head against her and presenting his horns.

shoulder height: 30 cm
weight: 4 kg
horns (average): 2 cm
       (record): 10 cm
number of young: 1 lamb
longevity: 10 years

Order: *Artiodactyla*
Family: *Bovidae*
Subfamily: *Cephalophinae*

Red Duiker

Cephalophus natalensis

Rooiduiker

Descriptive notes

As its name implies, this thickset, rather short-legged buck is bright foxy-red all over and is slightly smaller than the much more frequently seen grey duiker. It is somewhat paler on the underparts and the well-developed tuft of hair between the short horns (found in both sexes) consists of rufous and black hairs. The insides of the short, oval ears are whitish, fringed with black and the lower jaw and upper part of the throat are white. The short tail is rufous at its base and has long black and white hairs at the tip. There is a bare, dark glandular patch in front of and below the eyes.

Distribution and habits

These little antelope are found up the east coast of Africa as far as Kenya and also in the southern Sudan and Uganda. Over this range they occur only in forests where surface water is available and their occurrence is thus patchy and discontinuous. With the clearance of indigenous forest in many areas they are disappearing rapidly from many parts of their present range. Formerly they must have occurred throughout all the forests and moun-

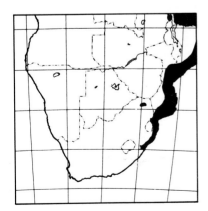

tain kloofs of the Drakensberg range and foothills in the north-eastern Transvaal, but today they have vanished from all but the most inaccessible areas, though still found here and there in wild, densely-wooded country.

As a result of its very shy nature and secretive habits,

there is little known about the habits of the red duiker. They are usually solitary or are seen in pairs or small groups. If they become aware of one's presence they bound away into dense bush almost immediately. Their cry is a curious 'sniffling' whistle and when caught or in distress they utter a deep rough cry, like that of a bushbuck, and not a hare-like squeal like that of the grey duiker. They use communal dung heaps and may be territorial. Wild fruits, leaves and twigs of shrubs make up their diet.

Their major enemies are probably crowned eagles, pythons, forest-dwelling wild cats (including leopards), and man with his merciless snares.

Virtually nothing is known about their breeding except that a single black lamb with a chestnut face is usually born at any time of the year. There is possibly a summer peak in births.

shoulder height: 43 cm
weight: 14 kg
horns (average): 7 cm
    (record): 10 cm
number of young: 1 lamb
longevity: 10 years

Order: *Artiodactyla*
Family: *Bovidae*
Subfamily: *Cephalophinae*

Grey Duiker
(Common Duiker)

Sylvicapra grimmia

Gewone Duiker

Descriptive notes

This small graceful but fairly thickset antelope is one of the more common small antelope and can be distinguished fairly easily from most of the other smaller buck (of which, apart from the oribi, it is the largest) by its uniformly greyish-buff tinge — though in certain localities it may assume a more warmly-rufous hue than in others. Since they are quite variable in overall colour, the name 'common' rather than 'grey' may come into more general use in time. The forehead is markedly dull rufous, in contrast with the rest of the body (both sexes), and a very consipicuous dark line extends from the base of the forehead to the nostrils, which are wide, black and moist. The ears are rather narrow and pointed and fairly long. Like all the members of the large, widely distributed groups of duikers, it has a pronounced tuft or crest of long hairs projecting from the top of the head (between the horns in the male), and this is present in both sexes. The front of the forelegs is dark brown or black. The tail is fairly short and narrow, ending in a slight tuft. Ewes are usually heavier than rams and old females occasionally grow stunted, short horns. There are well-marked and conspicuous, naked glandular lines below the front corners of the eyes.

Distribution and habits

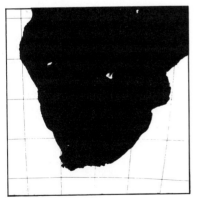

Grey duikers live in almost all habitats, except in deserts, where there are no vegetation-lined drainage channels, and in thick forest. They are thus found throughout Africa south of the Sahara, except in the forests of Central Africa and the West African coast and in most of Ethiopia and the Somali Republic.

Their distributional range has not been reduced even in the face of heavy persecution and development. They continue to survive in almost all areas where there is at least some bush or underbrush which provides them with food and cover.

These animals are usually solitary, but a male may be seen in the company of a female in oestrus, and females and their young move about together. They are almost exclusively browsers, only rarely taking in a little grass.

Their wide distribution must, to a large extent, be due to their extremely catholic diet. Shoots and leaves of almost all plants are eaten and they can cause damage to gardens and crops as a result of their habit of nipping off the growing tips of the plants, or stripping their bark. There are a number of records of their eating unusual items such as chicks, ducklings, lizards and caterpillars. They make good use of fruit dropped by feeding baboons but will also stand on their hind legs in order to reach fruit or choice bits of vegetation. The grey duiker is not dependent on drinking water and will rarely drink even when it is readily available.

As duikers stroll about at ease, they frequently whisk their short tails, and when mildly alarmed their first reaction is usually to squat in the grass. If they believe that they have been observed, they will then spring up and dart away, proceeding on a briskly zigzag course to elude pursuit, varied with very characteristic plunging jumps — hence the Afrikaans name 'duiker' (diver). Disturbed thus, duikers seldom go far before halting to glance back — a procedure which has often proved fatal for them!

This duiker is the royal emblem of the Khamas of Botswana and, according to the tribal tradition of the Bamangwato, this dates from one of the earliest chiefs who, fleeing from his enemies, took refuge in a thicket. After a while his enemies approached the thicket, but as they came close a duiker ran out of it. They therefore refrained from searching the thicket, feeling sure that nobody could have en-

shoulder height ♂: 50 cm
♀: 52 cm
weight ♂: 16 kg
♀: 19 kg
horns (average): 10 cm
(record): 18 cm
sexual maturity ♀: 8 months
gestation: 6 months
number of young: 1 lamb (rarely 2)
birth weight: 175 g
longevity: 12 years

Order: *Artiodactyla*
Family: *Bovidae*
Subfamily: *Cephalophinae*

ram

tered it without disturbing the duiker. Out of gratitude the chief adopted the 'puthi' as his family token.

Duikers are mostly nocturnal or crepuscular, lying up by day in patches of long grass or shady thickets, from which they usually emerge to feed in the cool of the evening, though in dull or cloudy weather they may move about and feed all day. The rams are plucky, attacking briskly with their small spiky horns when wounded or cornered, and in captivity they sometimes become untrustworthy.

They have extremely keen eyesight and a strong sense of smell and, when suspicious, utter a curious 'sniffy' sort of snort. When caught in a snare or by dogs, they scream pitifully. Duikers seem to be very easily caught in the cruel wire snares set by poachers, and, where the increase of such snares is uncontrolled, the species may be losing ground in areas in which it has hitherto held its own fairly successfully against other forms of hunting. The young are preyed upon by jackals, larger eagles etc. Adults are caught by wild dogs, leopard, cheetah, caracal, serval and python. Specimens with one horn missing or malformed are not infrequent, and albinos are not rare.

Breeding

Grey duiker lambs are born at any time throughout the year. The female hides in very dense vegetation before giving birth.

ewe

Although the young are initially hidden by the mother (who returns to suckle and clean them), they are well developed at birth and can run within twenty-four hours. If they sense danger, they will press themselves close to the ground with their ears folded back and their heads held low. They grow very quickly and are almost as large as adults by the age of six months.

Springbok

Antidorcas marsupialis

Springbok

Descriptive notes

This graceful, brightly-coloured antelope may be broadly described as the southern African representative of the gazelle group. Although there are a number of important differences between the springbok and the true gazelles, the species does have the characteristic gazelle-like face pattern and stripe down the side of the body.

The general colour of the upper-parts is bright cinnamon- or reddish-fawn, with the face, throat, underparts, inner sides of limbs and sides of the tail pure white. There is also a conspicuous white crest which can be raised along the middle of the back in a fan-like fashion, but this feature is not prominent under normal conditions. A dark chestnut streak extends from the eye to the angle of the mouth, and a broad dark chestnut band defines the fawn of the sides from the white of the belly. The moderately long and slender tail has a tuft of black hairs at the tip. Although both sexes have horns, they are narrower, shorter and straighter and only ringed at the base in the case of the female.

Very dark brown specimens occur in normally-coloured populations of springbok with a varying frequency depending on the particular area. They have an overall chocolate-brown colour with a white blaze down the front of the face. Predominantly white albinos also occur occasionally.

Distribution and habits

This very beautiful animal, the national and sporting emblem of South Africa, is found only in South Africa, Namibia, Botswana and in a very small part of southern Angola. In the past the animals were found right across the grassland and semi-arid regions of South Africa in huge numbers. Subsequently they were almost exterminated in the Orange Free State, the Transvaal, the Cape Province (except in the north) and they never occurred in Natal. Domestic stock farming, tremendous hunting pressure, the fencing of large areas of land, and rinderpest disease brought about this situation. It has, however, been remedied in part by the re-introduction of springbok to most of their former range, although on a minute scale when

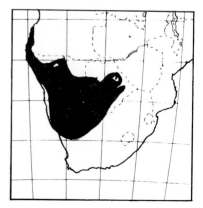

shoulder height: 75 cm
weight ♂: 41 kg
   ♀: 37 kg
horns (average): 35 cm
   (record): 49 cm
running speed: up to 88 km/h
sexual maturity ♂: 12 months
   ♀: 7 months
gestation: 5,5 months
number of young: 1 lamb
birth weight: 3,8 kg
longevity: 12 years

Order: *Artiodactyla*
Family: *Bovidae*
Subfamily: *Antilopinae*

ram

compared with the numbers which used to roam the plains in years gone by.

Springbok herds vary in size, depending on the season and the availability of food. In winter the groups tend to be more fragmented, whereas in summer large numbers of springbok congregate on good feeding grounds where there have been good rains. Like many of the plains-game, they are aware of rain falling great distances away and will move in its direction in order to take advantage of the resultant green flush.

Springbok also migrate in response to environmental conditions and up until the end of the last century one of the most unique and marvellous spectacles of the natural world used to take place in the interior of South Africa. This was the periodic mass migration of the 'trekbokke', when countless thousands of these antelope (very often accompanied by wildebeest, blesbok, quagga, eland, antelope of all sorts — many of which were simply engulfed by and forced along with the teeming masses of springbok) surged across the country from the Kalahari, over the Orange River, into the Cape Colony in search of better grazing. They were described as moving at a casual pace, feeding as they moved, but so densely packed that anything encountered was either trampled over by sheer numbers or else carried along by the host. When crossing hollows or rivers, those in the rear literally travelled over the backs of the slowed-up hesitant front ranks, and thousands of them were thus injured or drowned. The country behind them was completely devastated by the countless small hooves and teeth. These huge migrations were not regular but periodic (due to special circumstances such as severe drought) and Cronwright-Schreiner estimated that the

1896 trek occupied a tract of country 220 by 25 kilometres in extent. These dramatic treks numbered hundreds of thousands of animals or more, and on some occasions the springbok looked fat and sleek whereas on others they were thin and in very poor condition. When trekking they made a peculiar sort of grunting bleat and on reaching their destination the animals apparently disbanded and literally disappeared into the veld in all directions. The mass movements of springbok which take place today never reach anything like the proportions of those of yesteryear and are confined to southern Botswana and the far northern Cape Province.

ewe

Certain springbok males maintain territories which they mark off with dung heaps and advertise by standing in prominent positions. They do not remain on these territories all year round but establish and defend them as the mating season approaches. During the rest of the year they may join the bachelor groups, the breeding herds (consisting of ewes and young males), or they may remain on their own. When on their territories they herd the smaller groups of females to keep them within the boundaries, but when a large breeding herd decides to move away on to the next territory, the ram has no option but to let it go. When herding, the male stretches his head forward in a characteristic fashion with the tail held stiffly in a vertical or forward position. Territorial males urinate in a specific way, with their legs stretched out backwards and stomachs almost touching the ground. They also defecate in a crouching or squatting position which causes the faeces to fall in a pile, and therefore possibly maintain their odour for a longer period of time than would otherwise be the case. Other displays which draw attention to these rams' status are tail wagging, pawing the ground and horning bushes; pieces of vegetation often get tangled in their horns and they then parade around proudly, making no attempt to remove them. Occasionally the rams will indulge in fighting which may become very intense. Injuries and deaths are rare, with the weaker animal usually giving up before he is in real danger of being hurt.

The breeding and bachelor herds may number from two to several hundred animals. They keep contact by emitting a low, grunt-like bellow and although they normally move slowly, they can quickly break into a very fast extended

to show dorsal fan

trot. When confronted with danger or frightened, springbok will often start 'pronking' and it is from this behaviour that their name is derived. While pronking, the white 'fan' or crest on the back is erected and expanded. Cronwright-Schreiner compares it with the bucking of a horse. 'The head is lowered almost to the feet, legs fully extended with hooves almost bunched together; this arches the back and throws the haunches down making the legs appear unduly long. In an instant the buck seems to spurn the earth as it shoots up into the air to an almost incredible height, perhaps straight up; for an instant it hangs arched and then down it drops. It scarcely seems to touch the earth when it bounds up again like a rocket, perhaps with a prodigious leap forward and as high as before; then it touches earth again, only to bound up once more at a sharp angle to one side, then straight up, then to the other side, then forward, and so it goes on. Then it will set off at full speed, with the fan down, the neck extended, ears and horns laid back until nose and neck are almost in a straight line, with a wonderful stride and pace . . . when a buck is really racing his fan is not up.' Often one or two animals in the herd will start this behaviour and it then seems to infect the others which will also begin until the whole herd is racing and pronking about in a frenzied and almost lunatic sort of way. Yearlings and younger animals in particular will pronk at times when there is no sign of danger. This often happens after rain, early in the morning or late in the afternoon when it is cooler, and appears simply to be an expression of exuberance and sheer delight in life. The actual function of this energy-expensive behaviour is debatable, but it is probably performed in order to let the predator know that it has been seen, that the pronking animal is in command of the situation, and that the carnivore should not even bother to attempt a chase.

Springbok both browse and graze and are particularly partial to short fresh grass, new shoots and flowers. They will also dig out bulbs and roots with their hooves when there is little else available to eat. They are well adapted to very dry areas and can survive indefinitely without drinking water even if their food contains very little moisture. Although they will use salt licks and eat saline soil, they do this less than other species probably because of the high mineral content of their diet.

Black springbok

Springbok are preyed upon by cheetah and leopard to a large extent; lions and wild dogs will also catch them when possible. The lambs are also eaten by jackals and hyaenas if they are flushed from their hiding places when they are very young, and may also be caught by large eagles such as the martial.

Breeding

During the rut or mating season springbok rams will often be seen chasing each other about snorting and bellowing as they compete for the ewes. The territorial males will often tolerate other males in their areas during this time but will usually do the bulk of the mating. The ram will court a ewe by first exhibiting 'flehmen', and will then trot around after her in a very characteristic 'proud' manner with his feet being lifted off the ground. Before copulating he will go through the motions of tapping the ewe's hind legs with the inside of his forelegs in order to prompt her to stand still, although no actual contact may take place. This may go on for some time before the female condescends and the male is able to mate.
the male is able to mate.

pronking

normal action

The bulk of the lambs are born during the rainy season, or just before it. They are hidden by the mothers and remain absolutely still with their long ears pressed flat against the ground even when approached. After a few days they are able to run quite fast if disturbed, and within about three weeks they are able to run strongly with the herd. Springbok often synchronise their births in order to 'saturate the market' with vulnerable lambs which are relatively easily caught by most predators when they are young.
fore the rest are strong enough to out-run them when pursued.

The lambs often form their own nursery groups within the main herd and will lie together under the watchful eye of the grazing females. They eat large amounts of grass by the age of about six weeks. The females remain with the breeding herd but the males leave it to join the bachelor herds at about six months of age.

Klipspringer

Oreotragus oreotragus

Klipspringer

Descriptive notes

This very stoutly built small antelope is more or less yellow speckled with brown in general colour. The hair of the coat is fairly long and spinous, but stiff and brittle, breaking easily, often coming away from the skin in bunches when the animal is struck, but soon growing again. This hair was greatly valued by the old pioneers for stuffing their saddles and the species was greatly persecuted formerly for this purpose. The long hairs are white for the greater part of the body, subterminally dark brown and terminally yellow — the brown showing through. The chin and upper lip are white, with a lighter yellow area above and below the eye. The ears are white inside and whitish for the greater part outside, but with a brownish mark on the upper rim, followed by a white mark; they are shaggily fringed with black at the tips. In front of the eyes are large and very conspicuous black glandular orifices. The tail is short and rather stumpy. The top of the muzzle is brownish, the forehead yellow and the crown blackish. The hooves are set in a peculiar way, being especially adapted for clinging to or balancing upon small projections of rock. They are narrow and cylindrical, and only the tips rest on the ground. The female klipspringers are on average a little heavier and larger than the males, which carry horns.

Distribution and habits

Apart from being found in southern Africa, the klipspringer occurs up the eastern side of the continent as far as Ethiopia wherever there are rocky hillocks or outcropping rock. In areas where they occur, klipspringers may be seen not only on the boulder-clad koppies or krantzes themselves, but also among the bush at the foot of such places, as these sturdy little buck feed principally in such surroundings. When alarmed they usually at once retreat to their rocky abode; nimbly racing up cliff or rockface with the agility of a chamois. One of the most charming sights in nature is that of a klipspringer standing gracefully poised on a projecting boulder or spur; all four feet closely bunched together as, like a ballet dancer, it balances on the tips of its hooves; watching with widespread ears your movement as you pass below. The quaint, charming little figure may easily be overlooked (unless you are specially on the alert for it) because so still does it stand, rigid as a statue, that its small form easily blends with surrounding spurs and jags. Equally easy is it to overlook a klipspringer in the tangled herbage at the foot of such hillocks or outcrops, as the speckled 'pepper and salt' coloured coat is in complete harmony with its surroundings and, as usual with most suspicious or disturbed antelopes, it is probably standing perfectly still. The peculiar spinous and brittle-haired coat is a marvellous provision of nature, forming a springy covering which undoubtedly protects the animal from bruising contact with the sharp edges of the rocks and stones among which it can race about so recklessly.

Klipspringers utter a curious abrupt little squeaking snort, which sounds rather like a child's trumpet. The pair may often call in a duet — the female immediately after the male — this sound notifies the source of danger that it has been seen, and can be heard up to 700 metres away. They are delightful, smug-looking little creatures which, although always very alert, are very inquisitive if the observer remains quiet.

shoulder height: 60 cm
weight ♂: 11 kg
     ♀: 13 kg
horns (average): 10 cm
     (record): 16 cm
gestation: 7 months
number of young: 1 lamb
weaning: 5 months
longevity: 10 years

Order: *Artiodactyla*
Family: *Bovidae*
Subfamily: *Antilopinae*

These animals are usually seen alone, in pairs, or in small family groups of three to four, although sometimes five or six may be seen together temporarily.

The dominant male defends a territory by visual displays, scentmarking and by the use of dung heaps. The dominant female will also mark by rubbing scent from a gland in front of the eye onto a bare twig. The male will often place his tarry, black mark over that of the female and the pair often defecate at these sites as well. There is an interesting relationship with a species of tick which locates marking sites by following the black exudate which gets washed down to the ground by rain. The tick then climbs up the grass stalk or bush and waits for the antelope to visit the plant again to mark, at which time he scrambles aboard for a meal.

The male's displays, which usually take the form of standing on prominent sites or outcrops, normally deter intruders; occasionally, however, fighting does break out and serious wounds can result. Sometimes the female will aggressively defend the territory as well.

These antelope are almost exclusively browsers, eating leaves, berries, fruit, seed pods, flowers and, rarely, grass. They are independent of water and are able to obtain enough water from their food if necessary.

Klipspringer are preyed upon by leopards, spotted hyaenas, caracal, baboons, black eagles and martial eagles.

Breeding

The single young klipspringer may be born at any time of the year in a shelter in the rocks or in thick vegetation. The well-camouflaged young are left hidden by the female and lie flat if approached.

After about two or three months the young start to accompany their mothers and are subsequently chased away at about five months of age. At this time their horns just show through their hair.

After about eighteen months the young animal's horns are the same size as those of the adults.

Descriptive notes

This tiny antelope is dark or speckled yellowish-grey in overall colour. Paler tips to the hairs give its coat a grizzled appearance. The animal has a very elongated and prominent proboscis-like muzzle and a whitish chin. Large black glands in front of the eyes are an obvious feature. The upper throat and eyebrows are also whitish and the insides of the legs and lower parts of the body vary from pure to dirty white. The sides of the crown and round the ears are rusty-yellowish; the hair on the forehead is ginger orange-brown and is long enough to be raised in a distinct crest if the animal is alarmed, or during courtship. There are rubbery pods at the back of the hooves which act as shock absorbers as the dik-dik moves over the rugged and hard terrain in which it lives. Only the males carry horns.

Distribution and habits

Like a number of other species, the dik-dik occurs in two discrete African localities which are about 2 000 km apart. One of these is in Namibia and Angola and the other in East Africa. The development of wetter climatic conditions in the intervening terrain in the past has resulted in the habitat becoming unsuitable for these species which have subsequently been forced apart into two separate populations. A similar pattern can be seen in the case of the gemsbok and, less obviously, in the steenbok.

Dik-dik are typically found in dense thickets and woodland and are frequently associated with broken, rocky terrain. Although they are not found on rocky outcrops themselves, they often live around the fringes of these. They also inhabit riverine bush in places but are only found in arid country, gradually disappearing as one moves into areas of higher rainfall.

They are most often seen alone, in pairs, or in family groups of three and are extremely shy and elusive, tending to keep to the refuge of the very dense bush which they inhabit. Shortridge states that they are 'exceedingly difficult to shoot, as the rough and thorny country in which they hide renders silent pursuit almost impossible. Their pale grey bodies assimilate with the colourless limestone sur-

Damara Dik-Dik

Madoqua kirkii

Damara Dik-Dik

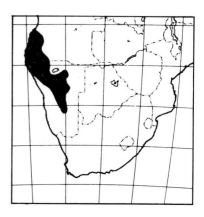

shoulder height: 40 cm
weight: 5 kg
horns (average): 7 cm
      (record): 10 cm
gestation: 6 months
number of young: 1 lamb
longevity: 10 years

Order: *Artiodactyla*
Family: *Bovidae*
Subfamily: *Antilopinae*

roundings, even when running, the shadows cast are more conspicuous than the animals, and they vanish like wisps of smoke...'

The Damara dik-dik may be a territorial species since pairs establish large latrines at which they also frequently scentmark with glands in front of their eyes. By stamping and digging in the dung heap, they transfer scent to their hooves — this scent is then spread along their trails as they walk about. It is interesting to note that most other antelope (particularly the smaller ones) have glands in between their hooves which perform the same function: these are absent in the dik-dik which compensates by behaving in the aforementioned way. They also have the curious habit of depositing their dung (tiny rice-like pellets) on top of rhinoceros or elephant droppings; the reason for this is not certain but it may be to make the droppings more prominent and thus more effective as territorial signposts.

Dik-diks are active in the early morning and late evening and to some extent at night. During the day they lie up in dense thickets. They are almost exclusively browsers, eating stems, leaves, flowers, shoots and fruits. They also sometimes take grass to a small extent when there is no browse available. They will stand on their hind legs and pull branches down in order to reach food and although they are independent of water, they will drink when it is available.

If frightened, Damara dik-dik will utter a single loud whistle and dash into dense cover or will stot off in a stiff-legged fashion, calling as they go. They are preyed upon by leopards and caracal, although other carnivores will also take them if the opportunity arises. They are very susceptible to the snares of poachers as a result of their habit of regularly using clearly defined pathways.

Breeding

The male courts the female by walking stiff-legged up to her with the crest on his forehead erect. The female will crouch before mating takes place. The lamb is normally born from mid to late summer during the rainy season and remains with the mother until the birth of her next offspring.

Oribi

Ourebia ourebi

Oorbietjie

Descriptive notes

The oribi is a small, neatly-built, bright orange-rufous antelope. It resembles the steenbok somewhat but is taller and larger and has proportionately shorter legs and broader ears and a longer, more slender neck. The best way to distinguish the oribi from the steenbok is, however, to look for the strikingly black bushy tip of the oribi's short tail. This feature stands out clearly against its white rump. The oribi's rich golden-fawn colour is more rufous on the back, and gives way to pure white below. There are also characteristic white blazes around the eyes. The hair of the coat is very fine and silky and is occasionally crinkled. The female oribi is slightly larger and taller than the male but does not carry horns as the male does.

Distribution and habits

Oribi are widely distributed across sub-Saharan Africa, with the exception of their sparse distribution in southern and East Africa and their absence from Central Africa They prefer shortish-grassed grassland, flood plains or vleis and avoid woodland; they are thus only found in discrete, localised patches, where these requirements are met.

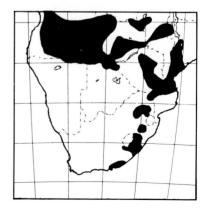

Oribi are usually found singly or in pairs, although family groups of a male and up to five females and their offspring are occasionally seen. These larger groups are

shoulder height: 60 cm
weight: 15 kg
horns (average): 13 cm
    (record): 19 cm
gestation: 7 months
number of young: 1 lamb
longevity: 13 years

Order: *Artiodactyla*
Family: *Bovidae*
Subfamily: *Antilopinae*

temporary. Smaller family groups are more common and remain in specific home ranges until food shortages force them to move on. Males maintain territories which they mark with glands in front of their eyes. If the grass is too long they will nip it off and then rub the black glandular secretion on to it. Males often mark where females have defecated or urinated. Members of a family group use communal dung heaps but these do not appear to have any territorial function.

When alarmed, oribi give a shrill, snorting whistle and start off at a brisk gallop which turns into a curious 'stotting' action: after every few bounds they spring abruptly into the air with all four legs held straight and stiff; this enables them to see above the tall grass in all directions. During this quaint manoeuvre the black-tipped tail is often erected or held stiffly out, and vigorously wagged. When stretched out at full speed oribi can move very fast — galloping with head and neck stretched out in front. They are, however, very curious, and will often stop after a short gallop to look back at the source of their fear, and even walk back to it on occasions — an action which has often led to their downfall at the hands of a hunter.

stotting gait

The oribi is essentially a grazer with a distinct liking for sprouting grass on recently-burnt areas. The grass must be short and oribi are never found far from water although they rarely (if ever) appear to drink.

Cattle ranching, with its frequently associated overgrazing and trampling of long grass, benefits the oribi in the short term. The subsequent bush-encroachment, however, undoubtedly ensures the disappearance of this small antelope. Habitat changes and over-hunting have resulted in a sharp decline in oribi numbers in some areas and their total disappearance in others.

Breeding

Most oribi lambs are born around midsummer. They are hidden in thick grass by their mothers, who frequently return to suckle them. During this period (the first four weeks of its life) the lamb lies dead still if approached, and it joins the family group when about four months old.

ram

Steenbok

Raphicerus campestris

Steenbok

Descriptive notes

The steenbok is one of the most exquisitely beautiful of the small buck, and also one of the most common and widely distributed in our area. Its overall colour is a light rufous-fawn and it is pure white on the abdomen and inside the legs; it also has white eyebrows and a patch of white on the throat. There is usually a small black mark just above the very moist, glistening little black nose and a dark crescent on the crown between the ears, but these features are not always evident. There are conspicuous large black glandular orifices in front of the huge soft, dark brown eyes.

The steenbok's tail is the same colour as its back, and is a mere tuft — hardly visible. This antelope may be confused with the oribi but its longer ears (almost kudu-like in form), shorter neck, absence of black tail tuft and more rufous colour, together with its smaller stature, all distinguish it from this species.

Only the males carry horns and they are lighter and smaller in stature than the females.

Distribution and habits

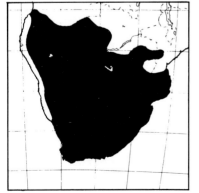

Apart from their distribution in southern Africa, steenbok are also found in parts of Angola and in East Africa. The southern African and East African populations were probably continuous during drier times but are today separated by about 1000 km. They are hardy and adaptable little animals which have managed to hold their own in the face of human encroachment across most of their range and can still be found in highly developed and settled parts of the country today.

The steenbok is essentially a lover of lightly-wooded, or even open, grassy country where it both browses and grazes, whereas the grey duiker prefers denser bush. It is usually seen singly, but two may be seen when a pair is courting or when a mother is with her offspring. A pair will defend its territory by marking with various glands, as well as by establishing latrines on the borders and by displaying to intruders. Although fighting may occur, this is never intense and is always a half-hearted affair.

shoulder height: 52 cm
weight: 11 kg
horns (average): 13 cm
　　(record): 19 cm
sexual maturity ♀: 6 months
gestation: 6 months
number of young: 1 lamb (rarely 2)
birth weight: 1 kg
longevity: 10 years

Order: *Artiodactyla*
Family: *Bovidae*
Subfamily: *Antilopinae*

Steenbok will drink when water is available but can obtain enough moisture from their food when it is not. They are most active in the morning and evening, lying up in bush or dense grass during the heat of the day. They may become semi-nocturnal in areas where they are persecuted or disturbed.

The steenbok's charmingly graceful bright reddish-fawn form is a common sight; often standing gazing, head and neck inclined backwards in curiosity, and large ears widely spread. As it walks quietly from place to place its graceful neck is usually held straight out, but slightly lower than the line of the back. When alarmed or suspicious, a steenbok first of all usually lies down quietly in the grass. If it does not thus escape notice it springs up and rushes away in slightly zigzag fashion, head and neck up but thrust slightly forwards, varying its frisky gallop with a few jumps now and then. It rarely goes far before halting to pause and glance back (an often fatal habit, of course) after which, if the enemy is still in sight, it will retreat further; otherwise it will settle down once more to feeding

ram

or resting. When hunted by dogs, steenbok often seek refuge underground, in old antbear holes, although they will normally rely on their speed to escape. These holes 'serve also as nurseries for the baby animals until they are able to look after themselves' (Stevenson-Hamilton). They will even seek refuge from the strong midday heat in such holes. Like duiker, when caught by dogs or snared, steenbok utter pitiful screams, but normally are silent creatures, occasionally uttering a sniffy little snort. The largest of the savanna eagles — the martial eagle — takes the young, and possibly also adult steenbok. Wild dog and cheetah are probably their worst natural enemies, though jackals, hyaena and lions take the newly-dropped young if discovered, and the former two may trail a pregnant ewe.

Breeding

Steenbok lambs are born at any time of the year with a peak in the midsummer months. They may be born and subsequently hidden in disused antbear holes but more commonly in thick grass or bush. The mother will feed nearby and if disturbed she takes flight while the lamb presses itself flat, ears held sideways, and remains motionless until (if it is fortunate) the danger has passed by.

Descriptive notes

The grysbok (also known as the Cape grysbok) is rather more stoutly built than the steenbok and is a richer shade of deep reddish-brown above, with a much wirier coat in which the numerous white hairs intermingled with the brownish ones impart a grizzled or stippled appearance. This stippling extends onto the forehead and the back of the neck, but is absent from the cheeks, sides of the neck, throat (which is rufous-yellow), chest and the underparts generally, the latter being paler rufous than the back. The ears, which are large and pointed, are brownish-grey externally, and the tail is short. The grysbok differs from the steenbok in that it possesses, usually, very small accessory or lateral hooves. The horns, in the rams only, are much shorter and somewhat stouter than the steenbok's; the sexes are otherwise alike.

Grysbok
(Cape grysbok)

Raphicerus melanotis

Grysbok

Distribution and habits

The exclusively South African grysbok is found only in the areas shown on the distribution map.

Very little is known about this secretive little animal which lives in thick bush in kloofs and coastal forest. It is nocturnal, and found in pairs or in small mixed-sex groups in the mating seasons. It is a predominantly grazing animal but does browse and eat fruits as well. Its habit of nibbling off the tender shoots of vines makes it very unpopular among wine farmers. It may resemble the steenbok, which

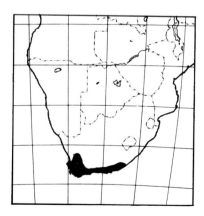

shoulder height: 54 cm
weight: 10 kg
horns (average): 8 cm
         (record): 12 cm
number of young: 1 lamb
longevity: 10 years

Order: *Artiodactyla*
Family: *Bovidae*
Subfamily: *Antilopinae*

false hobves in Grysbok

ram
ewe

often occurs in the same scrub, racing away and dodging through the bushes with its head down until it is soon lost to sight.

Breeding

The single young are usually born in the spring. They are darker than the adults and are kept hidden for the first few months of their lives.

Sharpe's Grysbok

Raphicerus sharpei

Sharpe se Grysbok

Descriptive notes

The Sharpe's grysbok is shorter than the steenbok and has a very wiry coat (in contrast with the sleek fine one of the steenbok) of rich rufous hairs, among which are mingled many white ones, particularly along back and flanks, which impart a grizzled hue at a distance. In some individuals fairly large patches of white hairs occur, in others they may be nearly absent. The false hooves of the grysbok are not present in this species. This antelope has less broad and shorter ears than the steenbok and the black glands in front of its eyes are much smaller than those belonging to the steenbok. The front of the muzzle is umber-brown and the lips and eyebrows are white. There is a dark inverted *V* on the chestnut forehead between the ears. The very short horns are found in the males only.

Distribution and habits

The Sharpe's grysbok is found along the eastern side of Africa as far north as Tanzania but not extending as far as Kenya.

They are normally seen in pairs or singly and are active at night, resting in dense bush during the day. They may, however, be seen in the morning and evening and on overcast days. They occur in areas of scrub and medium height grass. They require quite good ground cover and are often

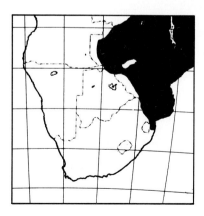

277

shoulder height: 48 cm
weight: 8 kg
horns (record): 10 cm
number of young: 1 lamb

Order: *Artiodactyla*
Family: *Bovidae*
Subfamily: *Antilopinae*

to show lack of false hooves

associated with rocky ground and koppies — normally occurring at the bases of these.

When disturbed, these little grysbok lie close to the ground until the last moment, and then spring up and dart away, twisting and turning among the stones and boulders or bushes, but never pausing to look back — as steenbok do — until they finally squat down in the herbage once more. As it scuttles away, rather like a large rabbit in action, Sharpe's grysbok holds its head straight out in front — not so high as the steenbok — and this very characteristic 'determined, scuttling rush, with no intervening bounds or jumps', head down, easily identifies it.

It is very solitary in disposition; even a ram and a ewe seldom share the same side of a bush when resting, and it is usually seen singly, at most in pairs. It is principally a browser, feeding mainly upon leaves and shoots of various shrubs and bushes, but it sometimes eats young grass. It often returns to the same place to deposit its droppings, and thus heaps of such droppings may be an indication of its presence; the droppings are exceptionally small in size. Its natural enemies are similar to those of the steenbok. Like steenbok, the hornless females average slightly heavier than the males.

Breeding

There is a paucity of information not only on the general habits of this species, as a result of its nocturnal activity pattern and the habitat which it frequents, but also on its breeding habits in particular. The single young may be born at any time of the year with a peak in the early or midsummer months.

young ewe

scuttling action

Suni

Neotragus moschatus

Soenie

Descriptive notes

The suni is a tiny little creature about the size of a blue duiker, but is a rich red-brown colour with the hairs tipped paler, imparting a slightly speckled appearance to the animal. It is more or less whitish below and on the insides of the legs. The ears are moderately long and pointed and the dark brown tail is short with a white tip. The hair on the crown is lengthened, but does not form an actual crest as in the case of the duikers. Only the males carry the relatively long horns.

Distribution and habits

The suni is confined to a strip several hundred kilometres wide, running along the eastern edge of Africa from northern Natal in the south as far as Kenya in the north.

Although several individuals in a family group may sometimes be seen feeding together, suni go about in pairs or are solitary. They are probably territorial, resting in the same places, establishing dung heaps and moving about in small home ranges. In cloudy, cool and wet weather they move about restlessly all day, frequently rising up and lying down again after feeding for about half an hour. This behaviour is a result of their small size, rapid metabolic rate and poor ability to digest cellulose.

During the heat of the day they lie asleep under any shady bush, or even in open ground under the shade of larger trees; but so perfect is their protective colouring, so exactly does it harmonise with the red-brown leaves which strew the ground underfoot, 'that though I have tried over and over again, sweeping the ground ahead with my field glasses, I have never been able to detect one lying down'

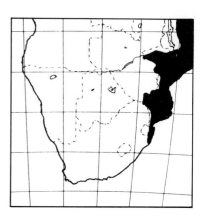

shoulder height: 35 cm
weight: 5 kg
horns (average): 8 cm
      (record): 13 cm
gestation: 4 months
number of young: 1 lamb
longevity: 9 years

Order: *Artiodactyla*
Family: *Bovidae*
Subfamily: *Antilopinae*

ewe

(Vaughan-Kirby). Often, the only sign to give them away is the flicking of their white tails — particularly if they are facing away from the observer. They usually lie very close, jumping up at from 10 to 30 metres when they bound away with wonderful speed, twisting and dodging through the trees. They will also sometimes stand motionless for a long time when danger is seen but are always very wary and shy.

Suni are browsers, almost exclusively eating leaves, and are essentially antelope of dry, forested or densely bushed areas. They never leave dense cover, except in the early morning or evening to feed in the open glades, and are independent of water.

They have three distinct cries, one of which is a very sharp, clear, barking note not unlike that of a bushbuck but less intense, and invariably uttered when they scent or hear anything suspicious at a distance. When startled at close quarters they utter a sharp, whistling snort, and at pairing time the males, when courting the does, utter a low bubbling sound like a goat. Like most of the small antelope which live in dense bush habitats, the suni uses pathways through the underbrush. This makes life much easier for the poacher with his vicious snares and, as a result of this factor, these animals are fast being exterminated in many areas in which they were once abundant. Other factors which may also be endangering these animals are the destruction of their forest habitat at an alarming rate, and the presence of increased numbers of the larger antelope such as bushbuck and nyala which open up and destroy the forest undergrowth in and on which the suni lives.

Their natural enemies include eagles, pythons and most of the medium-sized or large carnivores found within their range.

Breeding

A single suni lamb is normally born around the mid-summer months and is darker than the adults, being a deep reddish-yellow above and cream below, with a faint rufous tinge on the underparts and insides of the limbs.

Impala

Aepyceros melampus

Rooibok

Descriptive notes

The impala is a very graceful antelope, and its warm, rufous colouring, with clear line of demarcation along the upper part of the body, paling to ochre along the flanks, and clear white along the abdomen, renders it easy to identify. There is a small black patch on the flank where the hind leg joins the body; this feature is absent in the springbok. The rump is white below the tail on either side, each white quarter bounded by a conspicuous black mark. The tail is moderately long and narrow, black with a white border and underside and a tuft of white hairs at the tip. Very characteristic features are the blackish brushes or tufts of stiff hair sprouting just above the heels of the hind foot, and these conceal a scent gland. There are white streaks in front of the very large, lustrous dark eyes and a white patch on the throat. Faint indications of gazelle-like darker markings run from the front corner of the eye to the upper lip. The nostrils are somewhat sheep-like and the rather narrow ears are white in front with black tips, rufous-grey behind. The sexes are alike in colour but only the larger and more thick-set males carry horns.

young ram

Distribution and habits

Impala are found along the eastern side of Africa, from northern South Africa as far as Tanzania and Uganda. There is an isolated population of the rare and endangered subspecies, the black-faced impala, in southern Angola and northern Namibia. Impala are very popular animals on game farms and, as a result, have been re-introduced to many parts of their range, where they had been exterminated through over-exploitation or as a result of development.

They usually associate in fairly considerable herds, ranging from ten to one hundred individuals. Such large herds usually form during the winter months. The rut (mating season) is during autumn and has its peak between full moons. During this time, certain males establish territories, and the other males remain apart in bachelor herds. The breeding herds of females and young males of up to a year in age, are herded by the territorial males during the

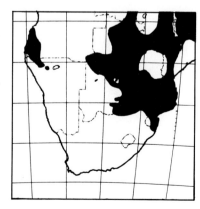

shoulder height: 90 cm
weight ♂: 50 kg
　　　♀: 40 kg
horns (average): 55 cm
　　(record): 81 cm
sexual maturity: 13 months
gestation: 6,5 months
number of young: 1 lamb
birth weight: 5 kg
longevity: 14 years

Order: *Artiodactyla*
Family: *Bovidae*
Subfamily: *Aepycerotinae*

rut. As the amorous rams pursue the dainty ewes, the former fan out their white-margined tails, often curling them impressively over their rumps. Although these males actively maintain their territories during this period, they relinquish them during the rest of the year and join the breeding or bachelor herds.

During the rut, the males chase each other about, uttering loud savage grunting and snorting sounds which would seem more becoming of a large carnivore than an antelope. They also intimidate each other by lowering and thrusting their horns. Sometimes jousting with the horns may take place, and although brief, this intense fighting may result in injury or even death. Territories are demarcated by scent which is rubbed onto vegetation from the rams' faces, and by the latrines at which they regularly defecate.

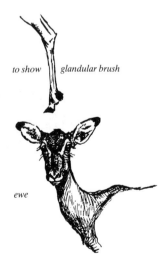

to show glandular brush

ewe

Impala both browse and graze, although they are principally browsers and eat an extremely wide range of plants. They are found in a great variety of country but prefer light woodland or bushveld and require water nearby. Recently a ewe had become well known to visitors to the Kalahari Gemsbok Park over a number of years. She had somehow wandered into the arid sands and was hundreds of kilometres from any others of her kind. She moved about with the springbok herds which seemed to accept her, and the only ill-effect of her life in this apparently unsuitable area was her very long hooves which never wore down on the soft Kalahari sand. Sadly, she met her end in the jaws of a pack of wild dogs while moving still further away from her closest relatives in Namibia. During her time in the area she had wandered several hundred kilometres down the Aoub River and up the Nossob River.

When not rutting, the impala is normally a silent antelope, giving utterance only to a very high-pitched, blast-like alarm snort, not unlike a rather reduced edition of the black rhino's snort. An alarmed or suspicious herd, after uttering a rapid succession of these loud abrupt snorts, will go bounding away, taking the most breathtaking jumps over intervening bushes, roads etc. Indeed, the impala is the finest jumper in Africa, even exceeding the springbok in this respect. They have been known to leap about 3 metres high and about 12 metres in length with effortless ease on occasions.

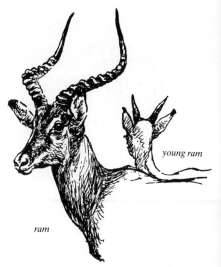

young ram

ram

The usual attitude when walking about is rather hunched, the back drawn in over the tail, which is strongly compressed between the hind legs; on alarm the impala will give a series of quaint, nervous little frisky jumps before beginning to trot away. Impala become astonishingly tame in national parks, and hardly deign to walk out of the way of an oncoming car; they can be studied at extremely close quarters as they group gracefully round shrubs and bushes, ceaselessly nibbling leaves or young grass. They frequently pick up wild fruits or leaves dropped by vervet monkeys or baboons, and are often noticed close to these creatures along riverbanks.

The principal natural enemies of impala are leopard, cheetah, and particularly, wild dog. Spotted hyaenas will pull them down when possible, especially young animals. The vulnerable lambs are also preyed upon by jackals and pythons. Lions also catch impala occasionally, but find them very alert and elusive, and have learnt to take full advantage of the distracting effects of slowly-moving cars in the national parks in order to stalk them successfully.

Breeding

During the rut in autumn the territorial males establish which ewes are receptive by smelling and licking their rears. After a brief and simple courtship, the ram will mount the female a number of times. After mounting he will utter the loud snorts and grunts characteristic of the rams during the rutting season.

The time of year when the lambs drop varies from one area to another but it is normally during the early summer

months. They are born over a very restricted period. This then provides the predators with more prey than they can cope with, and they are unable to take full advantage of the lambs before many of them are strong enough to have a good chance of escaping. The females leave the herd to give birth to their single lambs in thick bush or tall grass. The lambs and their mothers join the herd after about twenty-four hours and remain hidden for about two days. Lambs often remain in a 'crèche' group within the herd and may become temporarily separated from it at times. The females remain in the herd but the yearling males are chased off by the territorial bulls before the time of the rut. They form groups of their own for a period and after joining a bachelor herd they are able to compete for their own territories at about three years of age.

Grey Rhebok

Pelea capreolus

Vaalribbok

Descriptive notes

This antelope is unlike any other species and is very easy to identify. It is a greyish-brown colour above, younger animals being almost pure grey. The face and legs are slightly darker and more rust-coloured than the rest, and the underside is pure white. The bushy tail is also white underneath. The fur is curiously soft and woolly and is rabbit-like in texture; although short, it tends to curl rather than remain straight as is the case with most other antelope. Unlike the reedbuck and mountain reedbuck, the grey rhebok has no bare patches below the ears. The overall build of the rhebok is graceful and slender: it has a long neck and long, pointed, narrow ears. The naked part of the nose is large and swollen and the straight horns are carried by the males only.

Distribution and habits

As a result of the unpalatability of its flesh and the fact that it is found in inhospitable terrain, the grey rhebok's range has not decreased as dramatically as have most other antelopes' in recent times. They are found only in southern Africa and tend to occur on rocky, rugged hills and mountain slopes or plateaux.

Grey rhebok live in family parties which normally number up to twelve but which may, in cases, be as large as thirty when a few family groups have joined up. Adult males hold territories in which they live with a few females and their offspring. Young males leave the family group when they are about a year old and remain on their own until they are about two when they attempt to establish a territory of their own. Only once they have succeeded in this respect, can they attract a female with which to mate. Territorial males defend their areas by displaying, snorting and stamping their feet; fighting between males may break out. The families are relatively stable, although they may change composition over the winter months.

When disturbed, grey rhebok gallop gracefully away over the broken, stony ground on which they live. They are very fast when fleeing and can attain speeds of up to 65 km/h. Their action greatly resembles the 'rocking horse'

ram

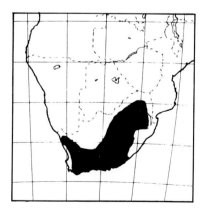

shoulder height: 75 cm
weight: 20 kg
horns (average): 20 cm
　　(record): 29 cm
sexual maturity: 18 months
gestation: 9 months
number of young: 1 lamb
longevity: 9 years

Order: *Artiodactyla*
Family: *Bovidae*
Subfamily: *Peleinae*

motion of the reedbuck and their white tails are also held over their rumps as visual signals to the rest of the group. They are very strong jumpers and usually head directly away from danger towards higher ground and mountain summits where they are impossible to reach. Males and females utter a loud alarm snort and they also hiss and moan at times.

　　Grey rhebok are frequently accused of attacking and killing sheep, goats, and mountain reedbuck, and have been slaughtered on this account. Although this behaviour may occur, it is not commonplace and reports are undoubtedly exaggerated. They are also reputed to be highly aggressive in captivity but any captive antelope may become dangerous and unpredictable.

　　Grey rhebok are exclusively grazers and are active during the day and night, usually resting during the heat of the day, depending on the season. Apart from being found on mountain summits, they also lie up amongst outcropping rocks or patches of bracken on the lower terraces. They are not dependent on drinking water, obtaining the required moisture from their food, if necessary.

　　Their principal predators are caracal, jackals and eagles since the larger carnivores are no longer found in the rhebok's range. They will defend themselves aggressively against such foes if they are attacked.

Breeding

The mating season is around April and at this time the males utter a deep guttural note, particularly during the night. With their forelegs, the territorial males tap the females which are in oestrus on the inside of their backlegs, before copulating.

ewe

Roan

Hippotragus equinus

Bastergemsbok

Descriptive notes

Of all the antelope, the roan is surpassed in size only by the eland. It has a wiry rufous-grey coat, with a ridged mane down the back of the neck and shaggy hair on the neck and throat. The black and white face is the most conspicuous feature at a distance, and the long, narrow and rather donkey-like ears are also prominent. Both sexes have horns, the females' being slightly shorter and lighter than the males'. Although not perhaps so striking in appearance as the closely related black and white sable, with its longer and more sweepingly-curved horns, the roan is none the less a handsome animal and it is one of the most beautifully proportioned of the antelopes. Roan are longer legged, and they carry their heads higher and more in line with their bodies than sable. The roan can be distinguished from the sable by its shorter horns, longer tassled ears, larger size, redder colour and facial 'mask'.

Distribution and habits

The roan is found south of the Sahara in the savanna regions of Central, West and southern Africa. Although it has a reasonably wide range, it is nowhere plentiful and is considered to be an endangered species. The reason for this is probably that the roan has very specific habitat requirements and is very sensitive to changes within its habitat. It needs open stands of long grass within lightly wooded savanna with water nearby. If areas are overgrazed with subsequent bush-encroachment or if the tall grass is trampled or grazed down as a result of overstocking, then the roan is unable to continue to utilise these areas. It is often found in hilly, though not mountainous, country. The roan is also particularly prone to anthrax, a disease which may assume epidemic proportions every so often, and this has certainly also had a lot to do with the roan's precarious situation today.

Roan normally live in small herds of between about five and twelve animals, although these herds may be as large as twenty-five or more. Mature bulls of five or six years old usually dwell alone or may join a herd of wildebeest or zebra. Younger bulls group together in bachelor herds and

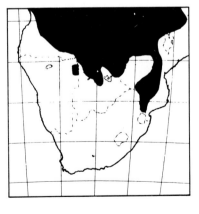

the females and young form breeding herds which are under the control of a dominant bull. These breeding herds may remain in specific areas (which may be as large as 100 square kilometres) for up to thirty years or more. The herd's movements within this area are dictated by food and water availability. Glands in the animals' feet and their habit of horning the vegetation and rubbing their faces on branches advertises their presence (through their scent) to would-be trespassers. The areas of neighbouring groups may overlap and the males are not territorial, but they will react to other bulls which come within about 500 m of the herd by displaying aggressively (which is normally enough to deter intruders), or by actively chasing them off if this does not work. If the trespassing bull tries to overthrow the herd bull, a lengthy and intense fight may ensue; the bulls head butt, clash horns and push and shove each other, often going down on their knees in order to attempt to gain the upper hand. Serious injuries are rare and the vanquished bull may be chased several hundred metres from the herd by the victor.

shoulder height: 140 m
weight: 245 kg
horns (average): 70 cm
  (record): 99 cm
sexual maturity: 2 years
gestation: 9 months
number of young: 1 calf
birth weight: 18 kg
weaning: 6 months
longevity: 18 years

Order: *Artiodactyla*
Family: *Bovidae*
Subfamily: *Hippotraginae*

Whereas the herd bull has the responsibility of keeping other bulls at bay, of breeding and of chasing the young bulls away from the herd when they are about two years old, the dominant cow, or cows, lead the herd's movements from one area to another in search of food, water or shelter.

When feeding, roan keep some distance away from the other group members, thus giving the herd a loose and rather incohesive appearance. They feed mainly in the morning and late afternoon, resting up in the shade during

bull
cow

the heat of the day. They graze predominantly on medium to tall grass although they also browse occasionally, particularly during critical periods of food shortage. When alarmed they will usually run off in single file, unlike sable which tend to gallop in a bunch. Roan are high-spirited and courageous, and a wounded one is apt to charge dangerously. They will defend themselves savagely when at bay. They both kick and bite (chopping with their forehooves) when tackling an assailant, and at such times will utter squeals of rage and hissing sounds, although beyond uttering a horse-like snort when alarmed or suspicious, they are normally silent creatures. Lion are their principal natural enemies (though lions respect both roan and sable antelopes); wild dogs, and probably spotted hyaenas, hunt solitary individuals. Leopard and cheetah will also attack the young when the opportunity presents itself.

Breeding

Female roan may give birth throughout the year, with an interval between calves of about 320 days. The herd male tests the urine of a cow to establish whether she is in oestrus and thus receptive to his advances. Thereafter the two animals go through a ritual courtship in which each animal performs certain steps before mating takes place; should either party not be ready to mate, then the ritual breaks down and the courtship is aborted.

The pregnant female finds a well-concealed spot away from the herd a couple of days before giving birth. For the first few days after the rich-rufous coloured calf is born, the mother remains in the vicinity of its hiding place in order to protect it while it is in such a vulnerable state. For the following six weeks the calf remains hidden, with its mother returning to suckle it in the morning and the evening. After it has finished drinking the mother refrains from following it back to its hiding place in order to avoid laying a scent trail which would give it away to potential predators. In some species the interdigital glands which leave a scent on the ground where the animal has walked, are not functional at an early age and this is presumed to be the case with the roan as well. The calf's only defence at this age is concealment; it lies absolutely still even if one approaches it and it can even be handled. They have been known to mistake horses for their mothers and to jump up and follow when a rider passes close by. At about two months of age the calf is able to run with the rest of the herd and frolics and plays with the other calves.

Sable

Hippotragus niger

Swartwitpens

Descriptive notes

The sable and kudu compete for the title of the most magnificent of the African antelopes; owing to its proud, defiant bearing, the sable usually wins. It stands shorter than the roan and although more robustly and compactly built, the sable is an altogether slighter animal than the roan. It is very horse-like in build. The adult bulls have a satiny, dark brown to almost glossy black coat above on the neck and limbs. The white parts on the belly, inner side of the rump and around the base of the tail are extremely clean and pure in colour. The white and black face is very distinctinve, but does not appear masked as in the case of the roan. The very prominent facial pattern in these two species and in the gemsbok may make them look more fearful when facing a predator. The ears are narrow and horse-like and are not tassled at the tips. Both sexes have horns but in the adult bulls they are stouter and swept backwards in a more beautifully arched curve. The adult cows (particularly younger ones) are very similarly coloured to the males, but are generally more reddish-brown than black above. Small calves are fawn-coloured, with indistinctfacial markings. The winter coat is rougher and less glossy than the summer one, and less rich in hue, and the coat is finer and more silky than that of the roan. The giant or royal sable is a subspecies from Angola which now has a very limited range; it is larger, with more impressive horns and slightly different colouring.

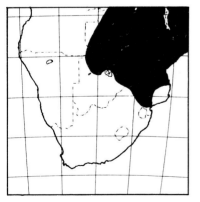

Distribution and habits

The sable is not as widely distributed as the roan is, being found only on the eastern side of Africa and south of the equator. Its distribution has not changed that dramatically in the recent past but its numbers have dwindled and it is restricted to areas of suitable habitat within this region. This species requires open savanna woodland with nearby water and medium to tall grass. As with the roan, sable are adversely affected by bush-encroachment, overgrazing, and the trampling of long grass.

Sable usually live in herds of about twenty animals although they sometimes come together in groups of a couple of hundred for short periods of time. Some of the adult males establish territories whereas the others which are unable to defend a territory join bachelor herds in which they find protection until they are able to challenge a territorial male for his territory or establish a new territory of their own at the age of five or six years. The territorial bulls defend their territories from trespassing bulls by performing intimidating displays in which the neck is held stiffly, while the chin is tucked in and the tail is held out horizontally and twitched. If this display does not succeed in making the challenger lose heart and give up, then a vicious and intense fight may ensue, with the contestants clashing their horns and attempting to spear each other with the lethally sharp tips. This may be accompanied by much snorting and bellowing and not infrequently ends in the serious injury or death of one of the contestants.

The territorial bull attempts to keep the breeding or nursery herds, which consist of cows and juveniles of both sexes, within the bounds of his territory so that he can mate with the females when they come into oestrus. This is the case particularly during the rutting (or mating) season. He rounds them up and keeps them in a small group, sometimes being quite aggressive in his efforts to keep them from straying into his neighbour's clutches. The bull chases the young males out of the breeding herd when they reach the age of about three years. The herd is arranged in a dominance hierarchy, with the bull at the top, the cows arranged in a specific order beneath him, and the younger animals in their order below that. The dominant cows lead the herd in its movements, flight and defence. The often brighter reddish colouring of such parties of cows and juveniles sometimes misleads the inexperienced into mistaking them for roan, but of course the roan are always more greyish-rufous in colour without the sharp line of demarcation between the pure white belly and inner rump of the sable.

Sable principally graze fresh grass of medium height, taking some browse, particularly in the dry season when the grass is not very nutritious. They feed mainly in the morning and late afternoon, resting and lying in the shade of trees during the heat of the day. They normally drink once a day.

The proud bearing of the sable is fully in keeping with

shoulder height: 135 cm
weight: 200 kg
horns (average): 100 cm
    (record): 154 cm
        165 cm (giant sable)
sexual maturity: 2 years
gestation: 9 months
number of young: 1 calf
birth weight: 15 kg
longevity: 18 years

Order: *Artiodactyla*
Family: *Bovidae*
Subfamily: *Hippotraginae*

Giant sable (Angola) note darker face markings

its character. Although it might mingle temporarily with other animals at a drinking place, the sable keeps aloof, and nearly every other antelope at once gives way before that curt, sideways shake of the sabre-horned head as the sable approaches. Having finished their drink, a troop of sable move quickly away from the water, seldom loitering or standing around as do wildebeest, waterbuck and many other species. They rarely associate with other species in the veld. Like roan, sable are courageous, high-spirited, and very dangerous and apt to charge when wounded or bayed. Maberly tells how a tourist stalked a relaxed-looking bull in order to take pictures of it; it suddenly charged and gored the man who was lucky to be rescued by his servant. It turned out that the animal died the next day of wounds it had received in a fight with another bull, prior to its encounter with the unfortunate tourist. Even lions treat a sable bull with respect, and not a few have been fatally impaled by the vicious thrust of the pointed horns as they have attempted to attack the majestic animal which will often reverse into a bush under such conditions. Leopard, cheetah, wild dog and spotted hyaenas occasionally attack females and young.

Breeding

The courtship ritual between a bull and cow sable is an involved procedure which is the same as that of the roan. Part of this ritual involves the testing of the female's urine by the male in order to ascertain whether or not she is in a receptive condition; he also taps her rump and back legs with his forelegs in order to prompt her to stand still so that they may copulate. If the ritual breaks down at any point then mating may not take place.

Calves are born well into the rainy season when the grass is reasonably tall and very nutritious, thus enabling the mothers to maintain a plentiful supply of milk. The sequence of events during a birth is very similar to that which occurs in the roan, with the female leaving the herd a few days before the calf is born. The reddish-brown calf is licked clean and suckled by its mother before being left to hide in the undergrowth. Relying only on its concealment, it lies dead still even if approached.

The mother suckles and cleans it twice a day (cleaning it thoroughly may help reduce give-away odours) and it remains hidden for the first two weeks of its life before it is able to join the nursery herd.

bull

cow

Gemsbok

Oryx gazella

Gemsbok

Descriptive notes

These magnificent antelope rank amongst the most handsome in Africa with their long, rapier-like horns, black and white face patterns and horse-like dark brown tails which contrast with their pale coloured bodies. All this, together with their robust proud bearing, impart an especially impressive appearance to a group of these splendid creatures as they wend their way like a troop of cavalry through the thinly-scattered bush of the dry country they prefer.

Gemsbok are massively-built and thick-necked. Their overall colour is a pale, greyish-fawn with a pure white face and belly. On this ground colour they have a dark brown pattern on the face, legs, flanks, rump and back which appears black at a distance, and when contrasted with their very pale overall colour. This colouration ensures maximum reflection of heat away from their bodies; the white stomach, in particular, absorbs very little of the intense heat which is reflected off the bare sand covering much of the area in which these animals occur.

Distribution and habits

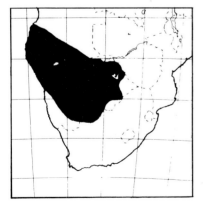

The gemsbok is confined to the arid areas of the African continent. As a result of its habitat being largely unsuitable for agriculture or other use by man, its distribution has not changed as dramatically as that of many other African mammals which occupied land which was colonised, 'civilised' and in some cases ruined by modern man. The gemsbok is also not as easily hunted as many other animals since it is extremely shy and lives in an environment which is very hostile, especially to man. Nevertheless, the gemsbok has been pushed out of the southern reaches of its former range in southern Africa; it no longer occurs in the Karoo, south of the Orange River in Namaqualand, and parts of the northern Cape Province.

Apart from being found in southern Africa, the gemsbok (or oryx) is also found in a separate area in north-eastern Africa; three or four subspecies of the gemsbok (*Oryx gazella*) are found in the northern area. Like a number of other animals with the same distribution pattern, gemsbok used to be found in the intervening area in drier times in the distant past but separated into two populations when the central regions of Africa became too wet for them.

Gemsbok generally form mixed herds of ten to fifteen animals, but frequently as many as twenty or thirty animals may be seen together. The size of the herds is dependent on food availability, which in turn is often dependent on the seasons. Territorial males occupy very large territories and although they are tolerant of other males in the territory, they are always dominant over these males which only rarely have the opportunity to mate with a female. The territorial bull herds the mixed groups of females and subordinate males in order to keep them in his territory. He also displays in an intimidating manner in order to warn other dominant males not to enter his area. If the trespasser persists then the two may become locked in a vicious battle in which the horns are clashed and the two contestants attempt to overcome each other by pushing and shouldering; usually the animal which is defeated will give up and beat a hasty retreat before it is seriously injured by the victor.

The territorial males defecate in a specialised way which differs from other animals of lower social status: they crouch back on their haunches in a most ungainly (and unbecoming!) manner and by doing this they ensure that the faecal pellets fall in a heap, thus remaining moist and retaining their odour for a longer time in the heat and dryness. These piles of faeces then act as 'signposts' for other dominant males who may be contemplating trespassing on already occupied land. The bulls also paw the ground and savage shrubs and bushes with their horns in order to spread their scent and advertise their presence.

The males which live in the mixed herds arrange themselves in a clear-cut 'pecking order' or dominance hierarchy, but are all subordinate to the territorial bull in whose domain they happen to be.

Gemsbok are almost exclusively grazers but will survive by browsing from bushes and eating small herbs if they have to. They are well adapted to going without drinking water indefinitely but will drink regularly if standing water is available. In order to gain as much water as possible from their food, gemsbok will dig out succulent roots and bulbs and also eat fruits, such as the tsama melon, which have a very high water content. Gemsbok are frequently

shoulder height: 120 cm
weight: 210 kg
horns (average): 95 cm
  (record): 122 cm
sexual maturity ♀: 2 years
gestation: 9 months
number of young: 1 calf
longevity: 19 years

Order: *Artiodactyla*
Family: *Bovidae*
Subfamily: *Hippotraginae*

seen digging and eating soil with a high mineral content on pans where there is a high concentration of salts.

The gemsbok is extremely well adapted to life in a very hot, dry environment: it allows its body temperature to rise when the temperature around it gets very high. This

means that it does not have to use precious water by sweating as most other mammals do. In order to shield its brain from the overheated blood which is moving round its body under such conditions, it has a fine network of blood vessels close to the surface of the nose; blood passes through these veins and is cooled by the air flowing in and out of the nose as the gemsbok pants; this cool blood is then used to lower the temperature of the warm blood on its way to the brain in much the same way as water is used to cool a hot mechanical engine. The gemsbok also has an ultra-efficient kidney which allows it to get rid of waste products with a minimal loss of water by concentrating the urine to such an extent that only a few drops of liquid are passed when the animal urinates.

Although they are very shy and quick to move off even when approached at a great distance, these antelope are bold, pugnacious, and very quick with their horns when wounded or cornered. They charge an enemy with determination — human or animal — if it approaches too closely when the animals are in either of the above states. Lions have been frequently impaled on the long pointed horns and it is said that lions which rely to some extent on gemsbok as a source of food will never attack a gemsbok by leaping onto its back as they do with many other antelope species. Instead they grab the animal by the throat from below and thus avoid the lethal horns which would be capable of impaling them if they were clinging to the animal's back.

In the Kalahari spotted hyaenas hunt gemsbok calves and subadults frequently; they are, however, more cautious with an adult animal which will always put up a good fight. The gemsbok often backs into a thornbush in order to protect its rear and then defends itself from the predators with sweeps and thrusts of its longs horns for hours at a time if necessary.

Breeding

Mating in the gemsbok is almost always the privilege of the territorial bull. He will test a female's urine to ascertain whether she is in oestrus and will then court her by tapping her hindquarters with his forelegs; if she is receptive she will then stand and allow him to copulate.

Gemsbok calve throughout the year. The female may stay with, or move away from, the herd in order to give birth to her reddish-brown calf which already shows the characteristic eye-stripe but no other patterning. After cleaning and suckling it, the female may prompt it to find a hiding place, or it may do this of its own accord. It remains hidden here during the day until she returns and calls it out to suckle. The pair may move great distances between one hiding place and another. After three to six weeks the mother and calf rejoin the herd.

Buffalo

Syncerus caffer

Buffel

Descriptive notes

Adult buffalo are large cattle-like animals of dull black or grey colour; the calves and younger animals are decidedly browner. They have a comparatively short muzzle which is well adapted to their grazing lifestyle. A very distinctive feature of buffalo is their large, curved horns which are used in fighting and defence. In adult bulls the horns broaden out over the forehead in a solid helmet-like boss, whereas in cows they are more slender and shorter, with less boss and are more backward directed. In calves the horns first appear as small pointed stubs, which at first grow upwards and slightly backwards; in very aged bulls the tips become almost worn away. The bosses of young bull's horns are covered with hair up to the age of about two or three years.

Distribution and habits

Buffalo used to be found along the entire wet eastern side of southern Africa, but today they have only a very patchy distribution across this area. They are found locally across the whole of Central and West Africa, south of the Sahara. The subspecies which occurs in the forests across most of this area is smaller, redder and has smaller horns than the savanna buffalo in southern Africa.

The rinderpest epidemic of the last century which swept from north-east Africa to the Cape almost exterminated the buffalo but it has recovered well in certain areas. Those in the Addo Elephant National Park are the last remnants of the herds which formerly ranged around Table Mountain, eastwards to Knysna, and northwards to the lower Orange River. Today the major cause of buffalo mortality is still disease or adverse seasonsal effects; their association with foot and mouth disease has resulted in their eradication from many agricultural areas, and this factor has also severely hindered their re-introduction to parts of their former range.

The buffalo is a gregarious species occurring in stable herds of up to several thousand animals. Although the herds may split up temporarily, there do not appear to be any subgroups, such as family groups, within them. The herds migrate in response to environmental conditions and

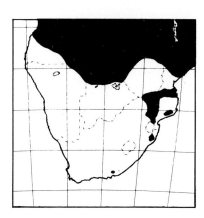

shoulder height: 150 cm
weight ♂: 750 kg
  ♀: 700 kg
horns (average): 91 cm
  (record): 127 cm
running speed: 50 km/h
sexual maturity: 3 years
gestation: 11 months
number of young: 1 calf
birth weight: 40 kg
weaning: 15 months
longevity: 20 years

Order: *Artiodactyla*
Family: *Bovidae*
Subfamily: *Bovinae*

calf

to the availability of water, on which they are dependent. Large herds tend to be a feature of the dry season and they then split up when food and water are plentiful during the wetter months. Old and young bulls may leave the herd to form bachelor groups. Maberly witnessed four such bulls who were drinking at a pan charge a stalking lion and drive him off into the bush. Bulls which remain with the herd are arranged in a 'pecking order' or linear hierarchy which is maintained by threats or by fighting in which the individuals crash the bosses of their horns together with tremendous force.

These animals are amongst the most formidable of African big game, and their only significant natural enemy is the lion, which prefers to pick out a cow or calf if possible. Old solitary bulls are often killed by lions, though frequently the valiant old fellows go down fighting under a combined attack, and it is not rare for a lion to be killed or fatally injured during such an attack. Intelligent and cunning – often schemingly vindictive in attack – African buffalo rank amongst the most dangerous game when wounded. Once a buffalo charges its adversary (which it does with its head held high so that it never loses sight of its opponent – only lowering it to toss at the last moment) it can rarely be halted except by a fatal or disabling bullet. Unmolested, however, the buffalo is not an unduly aggressive animal, and it is by nature placid and peacefully disposed, always preferring to retreat from that which arouses its suspicions rather than to attack. It is inquisitive, and will often stand to stare, nose held high, as it questions the wind, and will often take a few steps forward, accompanied by abrupt snorts and a defiant sweeping and tossing motion of the huge head, before finally retreating – all of which sounds and looks terribly alarming to the inexperienced. Buffalo wandering about and grazing, or lying and chewing the cud, in the protective surroundings of national parks or game reserves are almost as harmless as cattle. Except for cows with small calves at foot, or in the case of a bad-tempered old solitary bull, they are not particularly dangerous in such circumstances. Possibly one of the most dangerous features about a herd of buffalo is its tendency to stampede when alarmed, in a densely-packed mass; if such a confused stampede happens to come in your direction in country in which it is difficult to move fast, the situation can become alarming!

When stampeding, buffalo crash through the bush in a formidable mass, uttering loud snorts of alarm and raising clouds of dust in dry country. A charging bull utters coughing grunts of rage, and a mortally wounded one is said to utter a long-drawn bellow when about to die. Calves bleat like domestic ones in order to locate their mothers. When a herd is threatened, it forms a defensive semicircle, with the bulls on the outer flanks and the cows and small calves in the centre.

Buffalo are grazers, but include in their diet a small percentage of browse as well. They normally drink twice a day, in the early morning and in the early evening, though in very cold weather they may drink only once — just after dark. They graze during the night and for a short while during the early morning, retreating into a shady covert in which to rest during the heat of the day. The bulls will also often wallow in mud-baths at this time in

cow

order to keep cool and to give them some protection from the many parasites which infest them and which their regular companions, the oxpeckers (tickbirds), have overlooked.

In the cool of the afternoon they emerge to graze once more. They prefer lush river valleys with good sweet grass, open grassy plains or lightly-tempered savanna bushveld, but may often be found in quite dense and tall mopane bush. They haunt, also, the vast beds of reeds or papyrus which often border large rivers or swamps, and, well-concealed from view in such surroundings, their presence is often only betrayed by the fluttering white cattle egrets which so often accompany them. In certain localities they often favour mountain forests where there are open glades or surrounding pasture. They avoid overgrazed areas but by trampling old grass they are important in opening up areas for other species to utilise. Sight, hearing and scent are all good; but with increasing age, sight and hearing deteriorate.

The tracks and droppings of buffalo are almost identical to those of domestic cattle.

Breeding

Buffalo calves are normally born during summer with a peak around January and February when the grass is growing fast and is very nutritious. Cows give birth every two years and remain with the herd during the birth. The reddish-brown, newborn calf is unable to walk for the first few hours of life and will often shelter in the undergrowth while the rest of the herd moves on. The mother and calf then catch up when the calf is able to walk. Should the two become separated, the calf bleats and the mother answers with a croaking call.

The calf may remain with the mother for up to two years. About four out of every ten buffalo calves die before they reach maturity.

Kudu

Tragelaphus strepsiceros

Koedoe

Descriptive notes

The kudu bull is a truly magnificent animal of great stature and carries an impressive set of spiralling horns; in rare cases, females have also been known to grow rather stunted horns. The general colour is greyish-fawn (old bulls are always greyer than cows, which are of a warmer, redder fawn hue), becoming tan on the upper legs; below the knees the legs are whitish with a black mark behind the knees. A number of vertical, narrow white stripes adorn the body and rump, and there is a broad white chevron between the eyes and a number of white spots on the cheeks. The chin and sides of the upper lip are white and the front of the face is dark grey but blackish on top of the muzzle. In the bulls only, a heavy brown and white beard or neck fringe adorns the throat, extending as far down as the chest. Both sexes have a narrow mane of upright white hairs down the back of the neck, continuing along the back as far as the tail. These various stripes, spots and patterns help to break the animal's outline in the dappled bush-light in which it spends much of its time. Apart from the males' horns, the two most distinctive features of this species are its exceedingly large and broad ears with fleshy-pink interiors and fringe of white hairs, and the short, bushy, brown tail which is striking white below; when alarmed, the kudu curls its tail over its back thereby flashing a prominent white alarm signal to the other herd members. The massive round ears are indicative of the kudu's highly developed hearing and seem almost to dwarf the cow's faces as they stand and stare at one from the cover of dense bush.

Distribution and habits

Kudu are able to survive in areas even where there is considerable development and hunting pressure. They have, even so, been exterminated in certain parts of their previous range which included the southern districts of the Cape Province eastwards to Natal and northwards through the acacia country. Apart from their wide occurrence in southern Africa, they are found across the continent as far as the equatorial forests of the Congo and up the east-

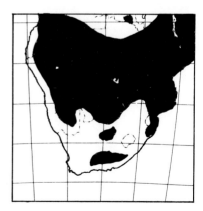

shoulder height ♂: 145 cm
⠀⠀⠀⠀⠀⠀⠀⠀⠀⠀♀: 125 cm
weight ♂: 250 kg
⠀⠀⠀⠀⠀♀: 200 kg
horns (average): 125 cm
⠀⠀⠀⠀⠀*(record):* 182 cm
gestation: 7,5 months
number of young: 1 calf
birth weight: 16 kg
longevity: 18 years

Order: *Artiodactyla*
Family: *Bovidae*
Subfamily: *Bovinae*

ern edge of the continent as far as Ethiopia and the Sahara. They are a savanna woodland species and do not occur in desert, forest or open grassland areas.

bull

These antelope usually associate in small herds of about six to ten animals. In rare cases they may number up to twenty. The herds tend to increase in size during the rut and the period when the calves are born. At other times the males may remain alone or form small bachelor herds. The bulls sometimes fight fiercely during the rut in order to be able to control (and mate with) the cows in the breeding herds. These contests do not normally result in injury or death but numerous cases have been recorded where two large bulls have been found dead after the animals' mighty horns had become inextricably interlocked during a fight over females.

Kudu are almost exclusively browsing animals, but may on rare occasions eat fresh grass. Although they prefer shoots and leaves, they will also eat seed pods, wild fruits and other vegetation. One of the prime reasons for the kudu's success in areas where other species have not been able to survive as a result of the changes brought about by man, is its ability to live off a huge variety of different plants. They eat almost any plant species, including those which are not indigenous, and some which are avoided by other browsers as they are poisonous to them. They may also become a problem in agricultural areas as a result of their wasteful feeding habits and the fact that they are very fond of most crops. They have amazing jumping powers and only a fence over 3 m in height will effectively deter them when there is tasty produce on the other side. Such a jump can be made easily, without even a preliminary canter.

Feeding is normally done in the early morning and late afternoon; the animals lie up in the shade of a thicket during the midday heat. They seem to prefer broken, hilly but well-bushed country and are fairly independent of water, but drink regularly when it is available.

The call in both sexes is reputed to be the loudest vocalisation made by any antelope and is a hoarse, harsh bark: *'Bogh';* that of the bull is deeper and harsher than that of the cow. They call most frequently at night or when disturbed, and will thus signal the presence of lion, leopard or any other predators. During the mating season the bark of the bull develops almost into a short roar.

When alarmed and cantering away, kudu curl their bushy tails over their rumps, fanning out the under-surface into a conspicuous 'white flag'. This serves to maintain visual contact, to act as an alarm signal, and to confuse the predator as it comes and goes through the bush in much the same way that a flashing torch may confuse one in the twilight. When dashing through thick bush, the bulls lay their great horns back almost along their shoulders, tilting their chins upwards as they break through the dense thickets.

cow

In spite of their great size and enormous horns, kudu are relatively gentle and inoffensive by nature in the wild state, rarely charging even in self-defence, unlike the other large well-armed African antelope. There are rare records of bulls putting up a fight and in captivity, like any antelope, they are unpredictable and can be very dangerous. The adult bull is seldom attacked by predators other than lions, or occasionally wild dogs, but the cows, and particularly the calves, fall prey to all the larger carnivores.

Breeding

Although kudu calves are normally born from January to the end of summer, they may be born at any time of the year. The mating season is around midwinter. The calves are hidden in the long midsummer grass after their mothers have cleaned and suckled them. The mothers return to feed the calves until they are strong enough to join the herd.

Young bulls can be aged by the appearance of their horns since the spirals develop with age. Horn growth begins at about five months; the first curve starts to show as an inward curve at just over a year of age and this curve is completed by about twenty-one months. The second outward curve develops by about thirty months and the horns continue to grow in three beautiful full curves throughout the animal's life.

Sitatunga

Tragelaphus spekei

Waterkoedoe

Descriptive notes

This is a rather long-haired, brownish grey antelope somewhat resembling a bushbuck but larger, with curiously long, narrow and pointed hooves. The horns of the males are longer and more twisted than those of bushbuck. The males are grey-brown in body colour, and the females more rufous-tinted. There are some indistinct white spots on the cheeks, white patches on the throat, and a white chevron between the eyes, and rather faint white spots or marks along the flanks and quarters, but in adults these are all less conspicuous than in bushbuck or nyala. Young animals are dull grey or rufous, and striped with pale yellow. The tail is not bushy but rather thin-haired basally with a tuft at the tip. There is no dorsal mane, but the hair on the throat is shaggy. The hair of the coat in both sexes is very long and only the males carry horns.

Distribution and habits

Sitatunga are found in the aquatic areas of Central and West Africa; their marginal occurrence in our area in northern Botswana represents the southern limits of their range.

They are semi-aquatic, inhabiting dense reeds or papyrus swamps, and their range is entirely restricted to such habitats. They are wary, shy creatures which rarely issue from the dense swamp vegetation and little has been recorded of their habits. They are confined to dense vegetation during the day where they may remain active feeding except during the hottest part of the day when they may rest on partially submerged papyrus or reed platforms. At night they may move onto the more open grass areas bordering the swamps or rivers to browse or graze grass shoots. They appear to favour shorter grass and are particularly fond of the fresh green shoots which sprout after an area has been burnt.

They usually crash and splash away through the reeds and water when alarmed but they are strong swimmers and may submerge their bodies entirely, exposing only the nostrils above water. The bark, which is uttered by both sexes, has been described as rather muffled, not unlike the grunt of a pig. Sitatunga go about in pairs or

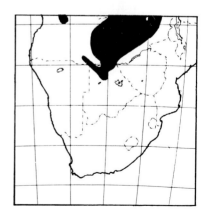

shoulder height: 90 cm
weight: 90 kg
horns (average): 64 cm
      (record): 92 cm
gestation: 7 months
longevity: 19 years

Order: *Artiodactyla*
Family: *Bovidae*
Subfamily: *Bovinae*

ewe

small parties of four or five, an adult ram accompanied by several females. On hard ground, its elongated hooves (designed for a swampy surface) render its movements awkward and clumsy and they leave an easily recognisable large elongated *V*-shaped track in softer ground.

Sitatunga often use regular paths through the reedbeds when moving about leisurely but avoid these when fleeing. Leopard, lion and possibly crocodile are their chief natural enemies, and pythons no doubt take females or young inside papyrus swamps.

ram

Breeding

Most calves are born in June and July. They are very unsteady on their legs for some time and tumble about when disturbed, usually falling into the water and then attempting to escape by swimming away for a few metres below the surface. They are concealed by the mother in tall grass or on platforms of reeds in amongst the papyrus and make little effort to flee when approached.

Nyala

Tragelaphus angasii

Njala

Descriptive notes

The nyala is somewhere in between the kudu and the bushbuck, both in size and looks, and is a decidedly 'large', medium-sized antelope. The ram is much larger than the ewe and is dark slaty-grey or brown, inclining to chocolate-brown on neck, face and above knees and hocks. There is a white chevron between the eyes and several white spots on the cheeks. The chin, front of the upper lip and the lower throat are white and the ears are reddish with black tips. The neck is covered with long dark hair, which extends along the belly and haunches to the knees. There is a white tuft on the dewlap (arranged in the shape of a whorl or crown), another under the belly and one on the flanks and the thighs. Along the back of the neck to the shoulders is a dark brown crest of longer hairs; from the shoulders to the rump the dorsal fringe is white with dark tips. There are twelve to fourteen narrow, rather faint white stripes down the body and a number of white spots on the haunches. The tail is bushy and reaches to the hocks. It is dark brown above and white below. The nyala ram, owing to his shaggy coat and chest fringe, looks considerably heavier and more massive than he is in reality. The smaller female is a bright reddish-chestnut – almost orange – with a distinct black dorsal line from the crown of the head to the root of the tail. The narrow white stripes down her flanks and rump are more numerous and more vividly white than in the male. She has no white chevron between the eyes but a dark line down the centre of her face. There are white spots on the cheeks and haunches and sometimes a few, forming a broken line, down the lower sides of the flanks. Her tail is also bushy and is chestnut-brown above, with a darker tip, and white below. The female nyala is a most graceful and beautiful antelope.

A good many inexperienced visitors to game reserves are apt to confuse young kudu bulls, with their horns in the first spiral, with nyala rams. In fact, the colouration of the two species is very different: the kudu being a warmer, more fawn grey; and of course he stands high on the leg, has a more definitely humped shoulder, and quite lacks the heavy chest and haunch fringes of the nyala and also the pale tips to the lyrate horns.

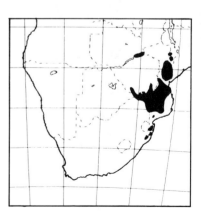

shoulder height ♂: 112 cm
♀: 97 cm
weight ♂: 108 kg
♀: 62 kg
horns (average): 64 cm
(record): 84 cm
gestation: 8 months
number of young: 1 calf
birth weight: 5 kg
longevity: 14 years

Order: *Artiodactyla*
Family: *Bovidae*
Subfamily: *Bovinae*

Distribution and habits

Nyala are found only in southern Africa and appear to be increasing in number and actually extending their range in response to the protective measures which they are afforded. They have also been introduced to certain reserves where they have established themselves well. Nyala are more gregarious than bushbuck, the females and their young, and the young males often associating in small herds of three to eight, occasionally up to thirty in preferred feeding areas. The older rams are often seen in pairs or are solitary – though solitary rams sometimes attach themselves to herds of other antelope, notably impala in the Kruger Park. The nyala groups vary in composition and may comprise any mix of animals of different age and sex. The groups (especially when males are involved) are extremely unstable and literally change hour by hour as individuals leave and join them. The most stable unit is the family group which consists of one or more females and their offspring. Family groups may join up for certain periods and may be accompanied by males for a time, especially when a female is in oestrus. This highly flexible and transient social system is obviously not compatible with any form of territoriality.

Male nyala do, however, have hierarchies which are enforced by various displays and rituals; these include pawing or horning of the ground or bushes and raising the white crest on the back while lowering the head and lifting the legs up slowly and much higher than usual as they move forward in a stiff, mincing gait. Although intense fighting between males is rare, it may take place over an oestrus female and the contestants run the risk of death. In displays, the largest-looking (often longest-haired) males tend to emerge victorious. Females lead the family groups and are never aggressive towards each other.

Where persecuted, nyala become exceedingly shy and secretive, dwelling in the densest bush from which they emerge only at dusk to feed, returning to cover at the first signs of dawn. For many years, therefore, according to the observations of Selous and other hunters, they were regarded as entirely nocturnal. Likewise, it was many years before it was discovered that nyala existed in the dense, tropical riverside bush along the Pafuri River in northern

Kruger Park. Under complete preservation, however, it has been found that nyala quickly lose their former shyness; much more quickly, in fact, than the decidedly nocturnal bushbuck, and they tend to move about freely by day and can easily be seen by tourists in the park.

young ram

One of the more locally distributed of the African antelopes, this very handsome species is well worth seeking out. The older rams look massive and very impressive as they move about, browsing in the thickets, richly marked and 'gowned' with mantles of long dark hair. Their long (about 30 cm) bushy tails are briskly waved from side to side — revealing a flash of the white underside — and their pale-tipped lyrate horns are carried nobly. Their fine appearance is often set off at Pafuri by the most magnificent scenery in the Kruger Park — the lush, green and very tropical river surroundings in which the enormous, widely-spreading and densely-crowned 'nyala' trees dominate the scene, and whose small dropped fruits are greatly relished by nyala and other animals. Nyala will often take advantage of the presence of baboons feeding overhead in the trees by eating the fruit on the ground which they have dislodged. The small parties of richly-striped and spotted chestnut females and their babies quite often feed among impala groups, and may thus be overlooked by the unobservant, as the two female antelope are similar in size and, at a very casual glance, general tone.

Nyala browse mainly off a great variety of shoots, wild fruit and the pods of the acacia and other trees, but they also eat young good grasses. They are not as dependent on drinking water as bushbuck are, but will drink regularly where water is in plentiful supply. The call is a deep harsh bark, similar to that of kudu and louder than that of bushbuck. The principal enemies of nyala are leopards which as a rule abound in their favourite habitats. Lions and spotted hyaenas undoubtedly kill a few and wild dogs will hunt them if the opportunity arises. The ram is courageous and will charge furiously if wounded or cornered.

ram · ewe

Breeding

Nyala calves are born throughout the year with a peak in early summer. Courtship is an involved procedure, with the male first sniffing the female's genitals and exhibiting 'flehmen' in order to gauge her reproductive state. If she is in oestrus, the male stands behind her, touching her with his forequarters; she keeps moving away and then the male begins to push his head between her legs violently, sometimes lifting her off the ground. This activity may continue for up to twenty-four hours and more dominant males may take over from their inferiors. Eventually the male forces the female's head downwards with his own — into the submissive 'head-down' posture and then manoeuvres himself to her rear in order to copulate.

The calf is usually born in dense bush and the female hides it for two to three weeks, frequently returning to suckle and clean it.

Mobile calves which are separated from their mothers utter a loud bleat. When tending the calf, the female makes a soft clicking sound.

Bushbuck

Tragelaphus scriptus

Bosbok

ram

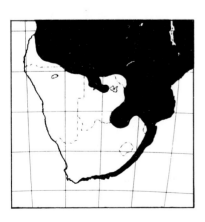

Descriptive notes

Bushbuck are dark brown, with a rufous tinge becoming darker below except on the abdomen which is white. They are also darker on the haunches, chest and forequarters. An erectile crest of long, coarse hairs, dark brown on the shoulders and on the back of the neck, becomes white along the ridge of the back in the rams, but is shorter and darker in ewes. Sometimes a few white spots in the form of a longitudinal bar are present along the flanks, and a few white flecks on the haunches on which the hair is wiry and long. Two white spots occur on the dull rufous cheeks merging into the white of the chin, and an indistinct white mark can be seen in front of each eye. There is a white patch on the throat and a very pronounced white bar across the upper chest — rather reminiscent of a clergyman's collar! In older rams the body markings (apart from the cheek spots and chest gorget) become indistinct. The inner sides of the lower parts of the legs are white. The outer sides of the legs, continued in a patch around the knees and hocks, are dark brown to black. The ears are of medium length but broad and white-fringed in front. The neck in rams is exceedingly thick and muscular, the lower part with a curious 'collar' of very short hairs. The tail is bushy, dark brown above, and white below. Females and young rams are more rufous in tone. The ewes are considerably smaller than the rams and do not carry horns.

Three subspecies of bushbuck occur in southern Africa: the Cape bushbuck in the south and along the east coast, the Chobe bushbuck in the northern regions and the Limpopo bushbuck, which occupies the zone between these two. The Chobe bushbuck is the most colourful of the three and is also lightest and more rufous in general colouration. It has a very distinctive pattern of white spots on the shoulders, hindquarters and flanks and a series of as many as eight white stripes running vertically down the flanks and back. It also has attractive white markings on the neck. The Cape subspecies is much plainer than the Chobe bushbuck; it does not have the white stripes of the latter and only has a few spots — it is also much darker and less rufous in colour. The Limpopo bushbuck — which occurs geographically between the other two subspecies, seems to fall between the two in its colour and markings.

Distribution and habits

As their name suggests, bushbuck need thick cover and dense vegetation. They also need a plentiful supply of water. These requirements have restricted them to the very eastern side of southern Africa (especially in the south) but to the north of our region they are found throughout sub-Saharan Africa, with the exception of most of Ethiopia and the Somali Republic.

Being more or less nocturnal, bushbuck are seldom seen, even where fairly plentiful, except in the early mornings or late afternoons when they emerge from the dense covert, in which they lie up during the day, to feed. They feed all night. They prefer thickly-wooded ravines or gullies, well-timbered kloofs, or patches of forest, and in the more open country usually haunt the neighbourhood of rivers or streams which are usually bordered by 'marginal' forest, or at least denser growth of reeds, trees, or shrubs. They are solitary creatures, dwelling either singly or in pairs, perhaps occasionally in family groups. The older rams tend to lead a quite solitary existence, and where undisturbed, they will live in the same relatively small area for years, provided there is always water within reach.

Bushbuck mainly browse a large variety of leaves, shoots, seedpods and wild fruits, but they like young sweet grass, and graze the fresh young grass sprouting from recently burnt areas. Unfortunately they are very destructive to all kinds of garden flowers (particularly roses, hydrangeas, and the succulent leaves of some geraniums), granadilla vines, and a variety of agricultural produce when accessible; and, like kudu, they are good jumpers and can clear any fence under 2,5 m. Like blue duiker, bushbuck often take advantage of the presence of samango monkeys feeding in the trees above them by picking up the fruits that are dislodged or dropped, and they also eat the monkeys' droppings which are often full of undigested seeds.

Bushbuck tend to remain in localised areas but they do increase their home ranges and move more widely during the wet season when they are less dependent on the permanent water supplies. They are very shy and alert animals and as a result of this and the fact that they inhabit impenetrable thickets, they often manage to survive close to

shoulder height ♂: 80 cm
　　　　　　　♀: 70 cm
weight ♂: 40 kg
　　　　♀: 30 kg
horns (average): 40 cm
　　　(record): 52 cm
sexual maturity ♂: 11 months
　　　　　　　　♀: 14 months
gestation: 6 months
number of young: 1 lamb
birth weight: 4 kg
longevity: 12 years

Order: *Artiodactyla*
Family: *Bovidae*
Subfamily: *Bovinae*

ewe

highly populated or well-developed areas, even when they are persecuted by humans.

Where bushbuck occur, the loud hoarse bark uttered by both sexes (an abrupt, hollow *'bogh'*, similar to, but of lesser volume than, that of a kudu and nyala) is a common nocturnal sound and a delightful one. This bark is used as a challenge in the rutting season; a communication call; and an alarm signal when danger, in the form of man, marauding dogs, or leopard has been perceived. Maberly used to listen to the local bushbuck signalling the movements of a leopard after dark so efficiently that he could follow the carnivore's whole route by ear – assisted occasionally by its sullen rasping grunts. Although Roberts states that 'bushbuck females always utter a louder bark than the males', in Maberly's experience the ram has a much harsher and deeper note, and in a rocky valley where the echo is tossed from place to place, it can be very impressive.

The rams fight savagely during the rut, and are apparently frequently killed as a result. The bushbuck is a most courageous antelope, charging dangerously when wounded or bayed, and many dogs and not a few hunters have been badly mauled by rams in such circumstances, as the short stout horns, dagger-sharp in young animals, manipulated by the powerful muscular neck, can be used with deadly effect. In captivity, too, the rams often become treacherous and dangerous.

When alarmed in thick bush or undergrowth, bushbuck plunge through the herbage in great jumps, their motions signalled by a steady crash! crash! crash! their bushy tails bobbing up and down or else curled over their rumps like kudu. They rely greatly on dense covert, however, as they are not particularly fast in the open — when they are easily run down by dogs. They are very strong swimmers and will readily take refuge in shallow water when pursued, or in order to hide. Their principal natural enemies are leopards and wild dogs when the latter can catch them in the open. Lions and spotted hyaenas also prey on them and the lambs may fall victim to pythons and caracals as well.

Breeding

The young may be born at any time of the year, but there are seasonal peaks which probably differ from one area to another. In northern Botswana these peaks are in autumn and spring. The lamb is hidden by the female until it is strong enough to move about competently. During this time she frequently returns to suckle and clean her offspring.

Eland

Taurotragus oryx

Eland

Descriptive notes

The eland is the largest and tallest of the African antelope and is rather cattle-like in build. Both sexes have distinctive spiralled horns but these are much heavier and more stout in the case of the male. Cows' horns are often curiously malformed: some absent altogether, whereas others are either twisted or stick out at strange angles. The colour of the coat is rufous-fawn but old adults are tinged with a smoky blue-grey colour on account of the sparsity of their coat hair. Further north and east of Botswana, whitish stripes running vertically over the rib-cage become more prominent and numerous; they are completely lacking in the eland from southern Botswana whereas the eland in Zambia show six or seven distinct white stripes. These antelope have a very distinct dewlap and on the forehead there is a long tuft of dark hair which often takes on a strong smell from the exudate of the glands at its base.

Distribution and habits

Eland used to be distributed across most of southern Africa as far south as the Cape where they were common at Hout Bay and the Liesbeek and Salt rivers. Like buffalo, eland suffer very badly from rinderpest and they were very nearly wiped out of many areas of their range during the bad epidemic which swept down Africa from the Somali Republic at the end of the last century. Today they occur only in the far northern Cape and in parts of the Transvaal but have been introduced onto many farms across their former range as a result of their great potential as meat-producing animals in marginal beef areas. They are well-adapted to drier conditions but avoid forests and are thus absent from Central Africa but are found in East Africa.

These antelope generally live in small herds but occasionally, especially when migrating, they aggregate into herds of well over a thousand animals. Although their social organisation has not been studied in any great detail, it appears that the females join the immature animals to form nursery herds during the spring; at this time the calves are born and the bulls group together into separate

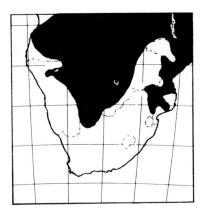

herds. During the summer months the adult bulls associate with the nursery herds and mate with the females. As the winter draws nearer the adults start spending more and more time away from the nursery herds. These young animals are eventually left on their own over winter, and are joined again by the adult females in the spring in time for calving.

shoulder height ♂: 170 cm
♀: 150 cm
weight ♂: 700 kg
♀: 460 kg
horns (average): 71 cm
(record): 102 cm
sexual maturity: 4 years
gestation: 9 months
number of young: 1 calf (very rarely 2)
birth weight: 34 kg
longevity: 15 years

bull / cow

Order: *Artiodactyla*
Family: *Bovidae*
Subfamily: *Bovinae*

Dominance is asserted between individual eland by displays and gestures which normally prevent fights from breaking out. Occasionally, bulls fight violently, locking their horns together and attempting to push each other over. These fights can result in death or fatal injury to the animals if one manages to spear the other with its very sharp, heavy horns. In spite of its great size and strength, the eland is, however, one of the gentlest natured of the antelopes, seldom making any attempt to charge even when wounded or at bay.

Eland are great wanderers: they either move about locally, or are nomadic (continually on the move), or seasonally migratory. Food availability usually dictates these movements and large-scale migrations in search of food still take place in south-western Botswana. The herds grow in size as the animals move southwards, and a recent large-scale migration ended unhappily for the eland when they found their route blocked by the farm and game fences in Namibia and South Africa. The great milling and

confusion which then took place resulted in many of the young calves being separated from their mothers; nature conservation authorities and farmers caught these animals in their hundreds to be released later onto private game farms.

Eland are primarily browsers of almost all vegetation, depending on the time of the year, but will also eat small amounts of grass, especially the new shoots which emerge after a fire. They are also partial to roots, melons and tubers from which they obtain a great deal of water. They are very quick feeders, grasping the foliage with their lips and then nipping it off with their teeth. Using their horns, the animals sometimes break off fairly thick branches in order to reach foliage that is too high for them. They need never drink, and are able to obtain enough water from their food if none is available for drinking. Eland are well adapted to the dry environment in which they live. They do not sweat in order to keep cool (thereby saving precious water) but allow their body temperature to increase by several degrees during the heat of the day and then lose this heat over the course of the cold desert night.

Although eland are such heavy, robust animals, they are able to move at a very fast, comfortable walk and are very shy of humans, often breaking into a brisk trot when one is still a couple of hundred metres away. They are also capable of galloping at great speed for short distances and are able to jump extremely well. A 2 m fence poses no problem to even the heaviest eland bull which will walk slowly up to it, crouch back onto his hindquarters and then jump clear over the top of it with apparent ease and absolute grace.

Eland are normally silent but are capable of uttering belching grunts, moos, barks and bellows, and the calves bleat for their mothers. When they walk or trot they make a loud clicking noise which apparently comes from their knees, but was for a long time thought to come from their hooves.

Although very shy in the wild, these gentle-natured animals become extremely tame and tractable when in captivity. This, and other factors have lead to the eland being used extensively for its meat on a semi-domestic, sustained yield basis on game farms. They utilise a great number of plant species and browse rather than graze; they do not need water, they are not susceptible to many cattle-diseases and their meat and milk is very good. A problem with these animals, which may be related to their nomadic nature, is that they tend to lose condition under semi-captive conditions when their movement is restricted. This may be tied in with their food requirements and at present eland are generally used to supplement, rather than to replace cattle in most areas.

The lion is the principal enemy of the eland, though spotted hyaenas and wild dogs occasionally hunt them, and leopard and cheetah may pull down young calves. The females defend their calves very aggressively and may drive off wild dogs, hyaenas and even a lioness on occasions.

old bull

Breeding

Eland calves are born throughout the year with a peak in the early summer months before the rains. The dominant bull in a herd will stay close to a cow in oestrus and will aggressively chase any younger bulls which approach. He also courts the female by rubbing his head along her flanks, horning her gently and pawing the ground. The cow lies down on her side to have the calf which is able to run after about three or four hours. The calves are able to recognise their mother's particular call and vice versa. The cows will hide their very young offspring in the undergrowth or under a bush while they are off feeding and once the calves have been weaned they will join others in the nursery herds. The bonds between the calves in these herds are often stronger than the mother-calf bond and may be fairly long-lasting as well.

more product prominent stripe in NE Transvaal type

Reedbuck

Redunca arundinum

Rietbok

Descriptive notes

These medium-sized antelope are gracefully built and have a pale tawny or reddish-buff general colouration. Their coats are rather dull and wiry and the tail, which is very bushy and white below, bobs up and down conspicuously as the animal canters away in a very typical 'rocking horse' fashion. These animals are pale whitish below and have pale patches on the sides of the face and around the eyes, as well as a distinct white patch on the throat. There is a rounded swelling on the nose and in some areas a small circular bare patch below the ear. The front of the legs is very dark, more conspicuously so in the fore than the hind legs. The eyes are very large and dark, and the ears are also large, but narrow. Only the males carry horns and they are slightly larger and heavier than the females.

Distribution and habits

Reedbuck require tall grass or reeds and water. As a result of these specialised habitat requirements, they have always been confined to specific areas and have had a patchy distribution. They have, however, had their numbers seriously reduced in many parts of their range and are not common anywhere. It has been estimated that reedbuck have disappeared from eighty per cent of their range in recent times. They have been exterminated in parts of the Cape Province where they were previously found and are now confined to a small area in the east. To the north of southern Africa the species is found across the continent, almost as far north as the equator.

Reedbuck are not gregarious and usually occur in small family parties of from three to six, frequently in pairs, and are sometimes quite solitary. Territories are occupied by pairs, who keep in contact using various whistling calls and other signals. The male defends the territory by chasing off trespassing males and advertises his presence by standing in a particular way, with head held high and legs stretched out backwards. He also warns interlopers off by uttering a curious whistling cry and by bounding about with a peculiar stiff-legged gait. Fighting does sometimes break out between males, and, during such conflicts, the horns are

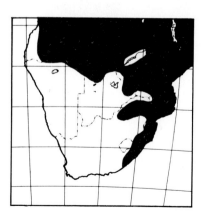

shoulder height ♂: 90 cm
　　　　　　　♀: 80 cm
weight ♂: 80 kg
　　　　♀: 70 kg
horns (average): 38 cm
　　　(record): 46 cm
gestation: 8 months
number of young: 1 lamb
longevity: 14 years

Order: *Artiodactyla*
Family: *Bovidae*
Subfamily: *Reduncinae*

ram

crashed together. The fights may last for a long time, with the contestants occasionally stopping to rest or graze, but are of such low intensity that injuries do not occur.

When alarmed, or when calling to one another, reedbuck utter their curious whistling cries (a characteristic sound at night in reedbuck country) and a series of short whistling squeaks sometimes accompanies each jump as they bound away through the grass. The stotting action of a reedbuck moving thus is most characteristic. Though graceful, it is rather stiff, with fore and hind legs kicked out stiffly with each jump — producing the previously mentioned 'rocking' horse' like motion. The bushy tail is fanned out over the rump (kudu-like), or else bobbed conspicuously up and down, the white under-surface gleaming weirdly when viewed in the dusk. When closely pursued they tend to break into a fast gallop.

Where undisturbed, reedbuck tend to become very tame and confiding, and they will often attempt to avoid observation by lying very flat, neck extended along the ground. Their buff-coloured coats harmonise perfectly with the long rank veld herbage, and even when they are standing upright perfectly still they are very hard to notice. They depend very much upon good grass or reedy covert, and when this is ravaged by drought or human interference, and particularly when the countryside has been devastated by violent grass fires, reedbuck suffer terribly, as in the open they are easily run down by dogs and fall an easy prey to wild predators. Their natural enemies are leopard, cheetah and wild dogs, and caracal probably prey on females and young. They graze mostly during the very early mornings and evenings, and during moonlight nights, spending the hotter hours of the day resting in the shade. This pattern is affected by food availability; they prefer a nocturnal lifestyle when food is abundant.

Vaughan-Kirby has observed them taking refuge by submerging themselves in water when pursued by dogs, although they normally avoid entering water and are very cautious when approaching it to drink. When resting they lie apart and all face in different directions in order to keep a look-out for approaching danger. Although primarily grazers, reedbuck will eat herbs and browse when grass is not available or very dry.

Breeding

Courtship in the reedbuck is very simple, with the male simply approaching the female with nose up and head forward before sniffing her rear. The female lowers her head if she is receptive and copulation takes place.

The lambs are born throughout the year, with a peak during the summer months. The female finds a secluded spot in which to give birth and returns to suckle and clean the lamb once a day. The lamb hides itself in a new place each time its mother leaves, to reduce the chance of its being found by predators. When it is about two months old the two begin to move about together. After approximately another two months, the pair join the male to form a family unit.

ewe

Mountain Reedbuck

Redunca fulvorufula

Rooiribbok

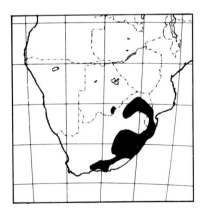

Descriptive notes

This species is smaller than the previous one, the males have much shorter horns and the coat is soft and woolly. Mountain reedbuck also lack the black stripes found on the forelegs of the previous species and are pure white down the throat and on the underparts. Their overall colour is greyish-rufous. The tail is bushy and, as in the reedbuck, is also pure white on the underside. Females are smaller and lighter than the males and do not have horns.

Distribution and habits

Mountain reedbuck are found in the hills and mountains of southern Africa and a population also exists in a similar terrain in East Africa. They are found, too, in a small area in Central Africa. As a result of their preference for areas which are not usually sought after for development by man, they are still widely spread across their original range. Nevertheless, their numbers have certainly declined in the face of hunting pressure. Mountain reedbuck are more gregarious than reedbuck — the breeding herds numbering from about five or six to a couple of dozen individuals. Some of the males have territories through which the female herds pass; the other males either remain solitary or form small groups.

Unlike grey rhebok which are usually found high up on exposed mountain tops, mountain reedbuck are usually found lower down on the sunny mountain slopes and in shallow gullies. Although one can get to such places more easily than to the mountain peaks, mountain reedbuck are not easily approached except when they are lying down and think themselves to be unseen. If disturbed, they are quite as agile and active as grey rhebok as they bound away through the rocks with a very similar motion to that of the reedbuck and with their tails also always fanned out. Mountain reedbuck invariably run either round or obliquely down a hill, seldom running upwards towards the summit as the grey rhebok does.

These antelope are strictly grazers and they require water on a regular basis. After dark they move down towards the nearest water, feeding as they go. They graze near the water during the night, moving up to their more rugged mountain haunts before dawn.

Breeding

The mountain reedbuck has the same breeding habits as the reedbuck, but has a peak in births in autumn, as opposed to summer. The lambs of both species suffer heavy predation while they are still too young to join the herd and are spending most of their time lying hidden. The territorial males chase the young males out of the breeding herds when they are about a year old whereas the female lambs remain with the herds, moving from one to another throughout their lives.

shoulder height: 75 cm
weight: 30 kg
horns (average): 15 cm
       (record): 25 cm
gestation: 8 months
number of young: 1 lamb
birth weight: 3 kg
longevity: 14 years

Order: *Artiodactyla*
Family: *Bovidae*
Subfamily: *Reduncinae*

Waterbuck

Kobus ellipsiprymnus

Waterbok

bull

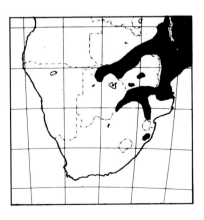

Descriptive notes

Waterbuck are robust, heavily-built antelope with coarse and long coats, heavily-maned necks, rather short though broad ears, and moderately long tails with only slightly tufted extremities. Both sexes are coloured greyish or greyish-brown and are paler on the flanks with a darker abdomen and limbs. The muzzle is darker and there are conspicuous white markings around the eyes, nostrils and chin. The dark brown legs usually have a white band round the hooves and there is a white throat fringe which is especially prominent in the bulls. There is a very characteristic white 'ring' round the tail which makes the animal unmistakable in the field. Waterbuck have large watery and rather appealing eyes and placid-looking faces; the males carry an impressive pair of horns and are larger and heavier than the cows.

Distribution and habits

The common waterbuck (which occurs in southern Africa) is found up the east side of the continent as far as Kenya. In East, Central and West Africa as well as Zambia and Angola, a very closely-related species, the defassa waterbuck is found; this animal has a solid white patch on the rump rather than the circle which is found on our local species. These two types are now generally considered to be one and same species.

Waterbuck are among the most handsome of the large African antelope and the bulls, in particular, are magnificent creatures, which, both in bearing and in habits, much recall the European red deer stag. The cows, with shaggy necks and no horns, rough wiry coats and rather clumsy aspect, appear almost donkey-like at a distance, but the fuzzy babies are delightful.

They are gregarious, associating in herds of up to twenty-five or thirty, though the herds usually number a dozen or less. During times of food shortage the herds break up and fewer waterbuck are seen together. At the age of about five or six the males may be capable of defending a territory which will give them the chance to mate. They defend their territories by displaying to other males, but fights (sometimes to the death) are not uncommon in this species. The bulls are very aggressive towards other territorial males which trespass but may tolerate the younger bulls which have been pushed out of the breeding herds and have formed bachelor herds. The territorial bulls go to some lengths to keep the females in their own specific areas in order to have the chance to mate with them when they come into oestrus.

shoulder height: 130 cm
weight: 250 kg
horns (average): 75 cm
     (record): 100 cm
gestation: 9 months
number of young: 1 calf (occasionally twins)
weaning: 9 months
longevity: 14 years

Order: *Artiodactyla*
Family: *Bovidae*
Subfamily: *Reduncinae*

Defassa waterbuck   *Common waterbuck*

Although most of their food consists of grass, waterbuck do browse certain bush leaves. They will also eat the fruit of certain trees such as the marula. Nyala compete directly with waterbuck and they may be forced to move out of prime areas where there are large numbers of nyala.

As their name suggests, waterbuck are often found near water of some kind, and they may immediately make for the water when pursued by wild or domestic dogs or other predators, completely submerging their bodies with only their nostrils protruding. A bull, thus at bay, defends himself with sweeping thrusts of his great horns. It is a strange fact that waterbuck betray less fear of crocodiles than almost any other antelope, frequently wading into the water right up to their shoulders when drinking. Although most partial to the neighbourhood of rivers, swamps, etc., waterbuck are quite often found in quite rocky, hilly country

cow

not too far from a large river, and they are among the few antelope which graze the coarse, reedy growth covering vleis where the soil is highly mineralised.

Although an adult bull is not often attacked by anything lesser than lions (which appear to be very partial to their flesh), young bulls, calves, and cows are frequently killed by cheetah, leopards, spotted hyaenas and wild dogs. A wounded bull will not hesitate to charge and it can be a dangerous opponent. Waterbuck flesh has a somewhat musty flavour and if not properly skinned can be almost inedible as a result of contamination by the glands under the skin. They exude a turpentine-like scent which is so strong that it is often very perceptible if you are close to a herd.

Breeding

Bull waterbuck go through a behaviour called 'flehmen' in order to see whether the females are in a condition to be mated. This behaviour is exhibited by many other species of antelope and involves the smelling of the female's rear and the 'tasting' of her urine to test her hormone levels. The male's head is held high, his lips are curled back and his nose is wrinkled and twitched in a very characteristic manner which may be seen quite frequently in both wild and captive animals. The male may prompt the female to copulate by nudging her rump with his head and horns and will tap her back legs with the inside of his front legs.

The calves may be born at any time of the year although calving peaks occur in the summer in some areas. The calf is left by the female to hide once she has cleaned and suckled it and eaten the afterbirth in order to lessen the chance of it being discovered by a predator. The calves lie hidden until they are about three or four weeks old. They are at great risk during this time and the mother keeps them as clean as possible to reduce their smell. When the males are just under a year old, they are ejected from the breeding herd by the bull, whereas the females may stay with their mothers for a long while.

Red Lechwe

Kobus leche

Rooi-lechwe

Descriptive notes

These are robust, yellowish-red antelopes with fairly coarse-haired coats, though these are less wiry than those of waterbuck, to which they are related. Only the rams carry horns and they are larger and more robust than the ewes. The underparts, chin, throat and fore-part of the neck are white and there are white markings around the eyes and around the nostrils. The fronts of the forelegs and the hind legs from the hocks downwards (with the exception of a broad white hoofband) are black or dark brown. The tail is of medium length with a black terminal tuft reaching as far as the hocks. Lechwe are similar in some ways to puku; for differences between the two species the reader is referred to the descriptive notes on the puku.

Distribution and habits

Apart from their occurrence in northern Botswana, red lechwe are found in small isolated areas where there is permanent water in Zimbabwe, Zambia and southern Angola.
Lechwe are water-loving antelope which usually occur in herds of about twenty, but at certain times large aggregations numbering thousands of these creatures can be seen. The herds are dynamic and change regularly in composition and size. They tend to prefer very open, grassy floodplains and shallow water, but are also quite at home in much deeper water. They are most active early and late in the day and lie up on dry ground during the heat of the day. When disturbed or chased they may snort, then break up into smaller groups and head for wetter areas over which they can travel fast. Their hooves splay widely, giving them good purchase on swampy ground and they plunge and leap through the water or reedbeds with their heads held flat and low in order to push through the vegetation. The males lift their chins up and their long horns are pressed back against their necks. They may also take to deep water when chased, and are capable swimmers. These animals almost exclusively graze on semi-aquatic grasses and the shoots of reeds. They fall prey to most of the larger predators.

ram

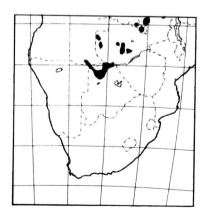

shoulder height: 100 cm
weight ♂: 103 kg
   ♀: 80 kg
horns (average): 71 cm
    (record): 94 cm
sexual maturity ♂: 15 months
         ♀: 12 months
gestation: 7,5 months
number of young: 1 calf
birth weight: 5 kg

Order: *Artiodactyla*
Family: *Bovidae*
Subfamily: *Reduncinae*

ewe

Breeding

The mating system of lechwe is interesting. During the rutting season the males move to a specific area (or lek) which is a few hundred by a few hundred metres square. Within this area they fight and compete for the most centrally positioned areas, to which the female herds move in order to mate. In this way the strongest males are able to do the most mating. Although serious injury is not common when establishing these territories in the lek, fighting may become intense. It is not prolonged, however, and many rituals and threat displays are used to keep the risk of injury to a minimum.

Territorial males sniff at the females' rear in order to ascertain whether or not they are in oestrus. They then raise their forelegs, following closely behind the female before mounting her frequently and eventually copulating successfully.

The calves are born at any time of the year; the females move away from the main herd to dry ground with tall grass or reeds in which to give birth. The calves remain hidden here for the first two weeks, with their mothers grazing nearby and returning to suckle them twice a day. During this period of their lives the calves are at high risk from predators and once they are able to move about they become independent of their mothers relatively quickly.

Puku

Kobus vardonii

Poekoe

Descriptive notes

Puku are somewhat like lechwe but are slightly smaller, with rather thicker necks and shorter, less sweepingly curved horns. The hair of the coat is fairly long, especially on the back and loins where it displays a marked tendency to curl. The general colour of the puku is reddish or brownish orange-yellow ('foxy'), and it is paler below. There is a whitish mark above the eye and the ears are fringed with black as opposed to the white fringes on the ears of the lechwe. The legs are also uniform rufous in the puku whereas those of the lechwe show black markings. The tail is short, narrow and fringed and has a darker tip.

Distribution and habits

Puku are widely distributed in the wetter areas of Central Africa but their occurrence in our area is limited to one small area on the south bank of the Chobe River (the Pookoo Flats) in northern Botswana.

These antelope tend to keep to the drier, narrow grassy banks of rivers and swamps rather than the wet open floodplains which are generally preferred by the lechwe. The two species may, however, be seen together along the Chobe River at times.

ram

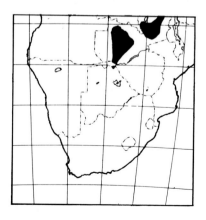

shoulder height: 80 cm
weight ♂: 74 kg
   ♀: 61 kg
horns (average): 45 cm
   (record): 53 cm
gestation: 8 months
number of young: 1 calf

Order: *Artiodactyla*
Family: *Bovidae*
Subfamily: *Reduncinae*

ewe

Puku live in small herds of four or five to a dozen or more animals; on rare occasions they will congregate in masses numbering several hundred. Males occupy territories which are maintained more by threat than by direct aggression. The female groups are herded within these areas and although other males may be chased off, bachelor herds may be tolerated if they are sexually inactive.

They are most active around sunrise and sunset; when disturbed they utter a repeated whistle and may stot off in a typical stiff-legged fashion, with the head held high up rather than down low as in the case of the lechwe. Puku and impala are often seen grazing together and they share common natural enemies in most of the larger predators.

Breeding

The territorial males test the females' reproductive status by sniffing their genitals with their horns held back and chins high. They will prompt the females to stand still and copulate by placing their forelegs between the females' hind legs and then tapping them on the abdomen.

The calves are born in winter and are left by their mothers to hide themselves. As in the lechwe, the mother-offspring bond is not very strong and the calf becomes independent soon after gaining its mobility.

Glossary

Antelope: for the purposes of this book, the more gracefully built horned ruminants.

Arboreal: living in or being adapted to living in the trees.

Browse: to eat woody tissue, bark, leaves and shoots other than grass.

Crepuscular. active around sunset or sunrise.

Display: a behaviour or sequence of behaviours usually following a ritualised or set pattern in which information is communicated by the animal performing the display to those to which it is displaying.

Diurnal animal: one active by day.

Dominant: Term referring to an animal which has prior access to food, place or a mate, usually relative to other members of the same species.

Ecosystem: a community of organisms and their inorganic environment.

Environment: the living and non-living (e.g. climate, soil, topography) features of an animal's surroundings.

Flehmen: a behaviour performed by many adult male mammals in which he sniffs the urine and vulva of the female to test whether she is in oestrus. The male points his wrinkled nose upwards while holding his head up, and pulling his lips back. This action opens a special duct to the animal's Jacobsens organ, where the scent molecules are analysed.

Fulvous: reddish-yellow or tawny.

Graze: to eat grass.

Gregarious: living together in colonies, herds or other types of groups.

Home range: the area in which an animal or group of animals habitually moves, feeds, and rests.

Insectivorous: subsisting mainly or entirely on insects.

Midden: a specific site, usually with social implications, at which defecation and sometimes other behaviour such as scentmarking, digging etc. may take place.

Nocturnal animal: one active by night.

Oestrus: the intensification of behaviours in female mammals associated with mating and characterised by changes in sexual organs.

Pronk: a high prancing action in certain antelope (particularly associated with springbok) in which the animal bounds high into the air with legs stiff, hooves bunched, back arched and the dorsal crest raised. This is frequently repeated, the animal thus moves more dramatically vertically than horizontally.

Ruminant: mammal, often with bone-cored horns, making use of a rumen (storage compartment) in the digestion of its food.

Rut: the discrete time period over which mating is most prevalent. Usually accompanied by specific associated behaviour in most members of the population.

Stot: a stiff-legged, prancing gait in certain antelope (particulary gazelles). Similar to, but not as exaggerated as pronking.

Terrestrial: living in or being adapted to living on the ground.

Territory: an area which an individual or social group uses exclusively and defends.

Select Bibliography

Principal Reference

Smithers, R.H.N. *The Mammals of the Southern African Subregion.* Pretoria: University of Pretoria, 1983.

Other Key References

De Graaf, G. *The Rodents of Southern Africa.* Durban: Butterworths, 1981.
Dorst, J. and Dandelot, P. *A Field Guide to the Larger Mammals of Africa.* London: Collins, 1970.
Grobler, H., Hall-Martin, A. and Walker, C. *A Guide to the Carnivores.* Johannesburg: Macmillan, 1984.
Haltenorth, T. and Diller, H. *A Field Guide to the Mammals of Africa including Madagascar.* London: Collins, 1980.
Nicol M. *Mammals of Southern Africa.* Cape Town: Struik, 1984.
Rowland Ward's Records of Big Game, XVII Edition (Africa). Sussex: Rowland Ward, 1977.
Smith, S.J. *The Atlas of Africa's Principal Mammals.* Fourways: Natural History Books, 1985.
Zaloumis, E. and Cross, R. *A Field Guide to the Antelope of Southern Africa.* Johannesburg: Wildlife Society, 1984.

Index of English Names

Aardvark 177
Aardwolf 58
African civet 140
African wild cat 105
Antbear 177

Baboon, chacma 20
Badger, honey 130
Banded mongoose 170
Bat-eared fox 108
Black-backed jackal 119
Black-footed cat 102
Black rhinoceros 198
Black wildebeest 230
Blesbok 247
Blue duiker 252
Blue wildebeest 233
Bontebok 244
Brown hyaena 68
Buffalo 301
Burchell's zebra 207
Bushbaby, lesser 13
    thick-tailed 17
Bushbuck 316
Bushpig 211
Bush squirrel 52
Bushy-tailed mongoose 155

Canerat, greater 55
    lesser 55
Cape clawless otter 125
Cape fox 117
Cape grey mongoose 162
Cape grysbok 275
Cape hare 35
Cape mountain zebra 204
Caracal 99
Cat, black-footed 102
    small spotted 102
    wild, African 105
Chacma baboon 20
Cheetah 73
Civet, African 140
    palm 138
    tree 138
Clawless otter, Cape 125
Common duiker 256

Damara dik-dik 267
Dassie, rock 188
    tree 192
    yellow-spotted rock 188

Dassie rat 57
Dik-dik, Damara 267
Dog, hunting 110
    wild 110
Duiker, blue 252
    common 256
    grey 256
    red 254
Dwarf mongoose 174

Egyptian mongoose 158
Eland 320
Elephant 180

Fox, bat-eared 108
    Cape 117

Galago, greater 17
    lesser 13
Gemsbok 296
Genet, large-spotted 147
    rusty-spotted 147
    small-spotted 143
Giraffe 225
Greater canerat 55
Greater galago 17
Grey duiker 256
Grey rhebok 285
Grey squirrel 210
Ground squirrel, 46
    mountain 46
Grysbok 275
    Cape 275
    Sharpe's 277

Hare, Cape 35
    scrub 33
Hartebeest, Lichtenstein's 238
    red 240
Hartmann's mountain zebra 206
Hedgehog, South African 11
Hippopotamus 219
Honey badger 130
Hook-lipped rhinoceros 198
Hunting dog 110
Hyaena, brown 68
    spotted 60
Hyrax, rock 188
    tree 192

Impala 281

Jackal, black-backed 119
    side-striped 123
Jameson's red rock rabbit 38

Klipspringer 264
Kudu 305

Large grey mongoose 158
Large-spotted genet 147
Lechwe, red 333
Leopard 79
Lesser bushbaby 13
Lesser canerat 55
Lesser galago 13
Lichtenstein's hartebeest 238
Lion 86

Meerkat 149
Meller's mongoose 164
Mongoose, banded 170
    bushy-tailed 155
    Cape grey 162
    dwarf 174
    Egyptian 158
    large grey 158
    Meller's 164
    Selous' 154
    slender 160
    small grey 162
    water 167
    white-tailed 165
    yellow 156
Monkey, samango 28
    vervet 24
Mountain reedbuck 328
Mountain zebra, Cape 204
    Hartmann's 206

Natal red rock rabbit 37
Nyala 311

Oribi 269
Otter, clawless, Cape 125
    spotted-necked 128

Palm civet 138
Pangolin 31
Polecat, striped 135
Porcupine 40
Puku 335

Rabbit
    red rock, Jameson's 38
        Natal 37
        Smith's 37
    riverine 39
Rat, dassie 57
Ratel 130
Red duiker 254
Red hartebeest 240
Red lechwe 333
Red rock rabbit, Jameson's 38
    Natal 37
    Smith's 37
Red squirrel 51
Reedbuck 325
    mountain 328
Rhebok, grey 285
Rhinoceros, black 198
    hook-lipped 198
    square-lipped 193
    white 193
Riverine rabbit 39
Roan 288
Rock dassie, 188
    tree 192
    yellow-spotted 188
Rock hyrax 188
Rusty-spotted genet 147

Sable 292
Samango monkey 28
Scrub hare 33
Selous' mongoose 154
Serval 106
Sharpe's grysbok 277
Side-striped jackal 123
Sitatunga 309
Slender mongoose 160
Small grey mongoose 162
Small spotted cat 102
Small-spotted genet 143
Smith's red rock rabbit 37
South African hedgehog 11
Spotted hyaena 60
Spotted-necked otter 128
Springbok 259
Springhare 44
Square-lipped rhinoceros 193
Squirrel, bush 52
    grey 210
    ground 46
    ground, mountain 46
    red 51

    striped tree 50
    sun 49
    tree 52
    yellow-footed 52
Steenbok 272
Striped polecat 135
Striped tree squirrel 50
Striped weasel 133
Sun squirrel 49
Suni 279
Suricate 149

Thick-tailed bushbaby 17
Tree civet 138
Tree dassie 192
Tree hyrax 192
Tree squirrel 52
    striped 50
Tsessebe 249

Vervet monkey 24

Warthog 215
Waterbuck 330
Water mongoose 167
Weasel, striped 133
White rhinoceros 193
White-tailed mongoose 165
Wild cat, African 105
Wild dog 110
Wildebeest, black 230
    blue 233

Yellow-footed squirrel 52
Yellow mongoose 156
Yellow-spotted rock dassie 188

Zebra, Burchell's 207
    mountain, Cape 204
        Hartmann's 206
Zorilla 135

Index of Scientific Names

Acinonyx jubatus 73
Aepyceros melampus 281
Alcelaphus buselaphus 240
Alcelaphus lichtensteinii 238
Antidorcas marsupialis 259
Aonyx capensis 125
Atilax paludinosus 167

Bdeogale crassicauda 155
Bunolagus monticularis 39

Canis adustus 123
Canis mesomelas 119
Cephalophus monticola 252
Cephalophus natalensis 254
Ceratotherium simum 193
Cercopithecus albogularis 28
Cercopithecus pygerythrus 24
Civettictis civetta 140
Connochaetes gnou 230
Connochaetes taurinus 233
Crocuta crocuta 60
Cynictis penicillata 156

Damaliscus dorcas 244
Damaliscus dorcas phillipsi 247
Damaliscus lunatus 249
Dendrohyrax arboreus 192
Diceros bicornis 198

Equus burchelli 207
Equus zebra hartmannae 206
Equus zebra zebra 204
Erinaceus frontalis 11

Felis caracal 99
Felis lybica 105
Felis nigripes 102
Felis serval 106
Funisciurus congicus 50

Galago crassicaudatus 17
Galago senegalensis 13
Galerella pulverulenta 162
Galerella sanguinea 160
Genetta genetta 143
Genetta tigrina 147
Giraffa camelopardalis 225

Heliosciurus rufobrachium 49
Helogale parvula 174
Herpestes ichneumon 158

Hippopotamus amphibius 219
Hippotragus equinus 288
Hippotragus niger 292
Hyaena brunnea 68
Hystrix africaeaustralis 40

Ichneumia albicauda 165
Ictonyx striatus 135

Kobus ellipsiprymnus 330
Kobus leche 333
Kobus vardonii 335

Lepus capensis 35
Lepus saxatilis 33
Loxodonta africana 180
Lutra maculicollis 128
Lycaon pictus 110

Madoqua kirkii 267
Manis temminckii 31
Mellivora capensis 130
Mungos mungo 170

Nandinia binotata 138
Neotragus moschatus 279

Oreotragus oreotragus 264
Orycteropus afer 177
Oryx gazella 296
Otocyon megalotis 108
Ourebia ourebi 269

Panthera leo 86
Panthera pardus 79
Papio cynocephalus 20
Papio ursinus 20
Paracynictis selousi 154
Paraxerus cepapi 52
Paraxerus palliatus 51
Pedetes capensis 44
Pelea capreolus 285
Petromus typicus 57
Phacochoerus aethiopicus 215
Poecilogale albinucha 133
Potamochoerus porcus 211
Procavia capensis 188
Pronolagus crassicaudatus 37
Pronolagus randensis 38
Pronolagus rupestris 37
Proteles cristatus 58

Raphicerus campestris 272
Raphicerus melanotis 275
Raphicerus sharpei 277
Redunca arundinum 325
Redunca fulvorufula 328
Rhynchogale melleri 164

Suricata suricatta 149
Sylvicapra grimmia 256
Syncerus caffer 301

Taurotragus oryx 320
Thryonomys gregorianus 55
Thryonomys swinderianus 55
Tragelaphus angasii 311
Tragelaphus scriptus 316
Tragelaphus spekei 309
Tragelaphus strepsiceros 305

Vulpes chama 117

Xerus inauris 46
Xerus princeps 46

Index of Afrikaans Names

aap, Blou 24
    Samango 28
Aardwolf 58
Afrikaanse siwet 140

Bakoorvos 108
Bastergemsbok 288
bergsebra, Kaapse 204
    Hartmann se 206
Bergwaaierstertgrondeekhoring 46
Blesbok 247
Blouaap 24
Blouduiker 252
Blouwildebees 233
bobbejaan, Kaapse 20
Bontsebra 207
Bontebok 244
Boomdas 192
Boomeekhoring 52
boomeekhoring, Gestreepte 50
Boomsiwet 138
Borselstertmuishond 155
Bosbok 316
Bosnagaap 17
Bosvark 211
Bruin hiëna 68
Buffel 301

Damara dik-dik 267
das, Boom= 192
    Klip= 188
Dassierot 57
dik-dik, Damara 267
duiker, Blou= 252
    Gewone 256
    Rooi= 254
Dwergmuishond 174

eekhoring, Bergwaaierstert
    grond= 46
    Boom= 52
    Geelpoot= 52
    Gestreepte boom= 50
    Grys= 210
    Rooi= 51
    Son= 49
    Waaierstertgrond= 197
Eland 320
Erdvark 177

Gebande muishond 170

Geelpooteekhoring 52
Gemsbok 296
gemsbok, Baster= 288
Gestreepte boomeekhoring 50
Gevlekte hiëna 60
Gewone duiker 256
grondeekhoring, Berg-
    waaierstert= 46
    Waaierstert= 46
Groot grysmuishond 158
Groot otter 125
Groot rietrot 55
Grysbok 275
grysbok, Sharpe se 277

haas, Kol= 33
    Spring= 44
    Vlak= 35
hartbees, Lichtenstein se 238
    Rooi= 240
Hartmann se bergsebra 206
hiëna, Bruin 68
    Gevlekte 60

Ietermagog 31

Jagluiperd 73
jakkals, Rooi= 119
    Witkwas= 123
Jameson se rooiklipkonyn 38

Kaapse bergsebra 204
Kaapse bobbejaan 20
Kameelperd 225
kat, Klein gekolde 102
    Rooi= 99
    Tierbos= 106
    Vaalbos= 105
Klein gekolde kat 102
Klein grysmuishond 162
Kleinkolmuskejaatkat 143
Klein otter 128
Klein rietrot 55
Klein witstertmuishond 154
Klipdas 188
klipkonyn, Jameson se rooi= 38
    Natalse rooi= 37
    Smith se rooi= 37
Klipspringer 264
Koedoe 305
Kolhaas 33

Kommetjiegatmuishond 167
konyn, Jameson se rooi-
    klip= 38
    Natalse rooiklip= 37
    Rivier= 39
    Smith se rooiklip= 37
krimpvarkie, Suid-Afrikaanse 11

lechwe, Rooi 333
Leeu 86
Lichtenstein se hartbees 238
Luiperd 79

meerkat, Stokstert= 149
Meller se muishond 164
muishond, Borselstert= 155
    Dwerg= 174
    Gebande 170
    Groot grys= 158
    Klein grys= 162
    Klein witstert= 154
    Kommetjiegat= 167
    Meller se 164
    Slang= 133
    Stink= 135
    Swartkwas= 160
    Witkwas= 156
    Witstert= 165
muskejaatkat, Kleinkol= 143
    Rooikol= 147

nagaap, Bos= 17
Nagapie 13
Natalse rooiklipkonyn 37
Njala 311

Olifant 180
Oorbietjie 269
otter, Groot 125
    Klein 128

Poekoe 335

Ratel 130
renoster, Swart= 198
    Wit= 193
ribbok, Vaal= 285
    Rooi= 328
Rietbok 325
rietrot, Groot 55
    Klein 55

Rivierkonyn 39
Rooibok 281
Rooiduiker 254
Rooi eekhoring 51
Rooihartbees 240
Rooijakkals 119
Rooikat 99
Rooikolmuskejaatkat 147
Rooi-lechwe 333
Rooiribbok 328
Rot, dassie= 57

Samango-aap 28
sebra, Bont= 207
    Hartmann se berg= 206
    Kaapse berg= 204
Seekoei 219
Sharpe se grysbok 277
Silwervos 117
siwet, Afrikaanse 140
    Boom= 138
Slangmuishond 133
Smith se rooiklipkonyn 37
Soenie 279
Soneekhoring 49
Springbok 259
Springhaas 44
Steenbok 272
Stinkmuishond 135
Stokstertmeerkat 149
Suid-Afrikaanse krimpvarkie 11
Swartkwasmuishond 160
Swartrenoster 198
Swartwildebees 230
Swartwitpens 292

Tierboskat 106
Tsessebe 249

Vaalboskat 105
Vaalribbok 285
vark, Bos= 211
    Vlak= 215
Vlakhaas 35
Vlakvark 215
vos, Bakoor= 108
    Silwer= 117

Waaierstertgrondeekhoring 46
Waterbok 330
Waterkoedoe 309

wildebees, Blou= 223
    Swart= 230
Wildehond 110
Witkwasmuishond 156
Witkwasjakkals 123
Witrenoster 193
Witstertmuishond 165
    Klein 154

Ystervark 40

Photographic Acknowledgements

Our sincere thanks for the help and co-operation of the following photographers who permitted their work to be published in this edition:

Duncan Butchart
Dr Peter Christie
Lex Hes
Johannesburg Zoological Gardens
James Marshall
National Parks Board
Professor J D Skinner
Chris and Tilde Stuart
Dr Rudi van Aarde
Gus van Dyk
Wildlife Society of South Africa

Front cover

D Butchart
Suricates

Johannesburg Zoological Gardens
Leopard
Wild dog

Rudi van Aarde
White rhinoceros
Vervet monkey
Ground squirrel
Cape fox

Back cover

Johannesburg Zoological Gardens
Eland

National Parks Board
Grey rhebok
Lesser bushbaby

Rudi van Aarde
Yellow mongoose
Chacma baboon
Gemsbok

Colour section

Duncan Butchart
Tree squirrel
Bat-eared fox
Lion
Small-spotted genet
Yellow mongoose
Water mongoose
Hippopotamus
Giraffe
Blue wildebeest
Springbok
Red duiker
Damara dik-dik
Sitatunga
Nyala
Bushbuck
Waterbuck
Reedbuck
Red lechwe
Puku

Dr Peter Christie
Thick-tailed bushbaby

Lex Hes
African civet

Johannesburg Zoological Gardens
Aardwolf
Wild dog
Cheetah
Leopard
Suricate
Black rhinoceros
Red hartebeest
Kudu
Mountain reedbuck

James Marshall
Large-spotted genet
Steenbok

National Parks Board
Lesser bushbaby
Greater canerat
Cape hare
Caracal
Side-striped jackal
Small spotted cat
Cape clawless otter
Striped polecat
Slender mongoose
Meller's mongoose
White-tailed mongoose
Dwarf mongoose
Antbear
Grey rhebok
Klipspringer
Sharpe's grysbok
Suni
Grysbok
Bontebok
Blesbok

Professor J D Skinner
Red squirrel
Black wildebeest
Lichtenstein's hartebeest

Chris and Tilde Stuart
Dassie rat
Smith's red rock rabbit
Springhare
Scrub hare
Striped weasel
Small grey mongoose
Large grey mongoose
Blue duiker

Rudi van Aarde
Vervet monkey
Chacma baboon
Porcupine
Ground squirrel
Rock dassie
Riverine rabbit
Spotted hyaena
Brown hyaena
Cape fox
Black-backed jackal
African wild cat
Honey badger
Banded mongoose
Pangolin
White rhinoceros
Cape mountain zebra
Burchell's zebra
Bushpig
Warthog
Grey duiker
Gemsbok
Buffalo

Gus van Dyk
Hedgehog
Serval

Wildlife Society of
South Africa
Elephant
Impala
Tsessebe
Oribi
Roan
Sable
Eland